Status of Economic Reforms in Cooperation Partner Countries in the mid-1990s: Opportunities, Constraints, Security Implications

Etat des réformes économiques dans les pays partenaires de la coopération au milieu des années 90: chances, contraintes, implications en matière de sécurité

NOTE ON THE NORTH ATLANTIC COOPERATION COUNCIL
(NACC)

The North Atlantic Cooperation Council was created as an initiative by the Heads of State and Government of the NATO Allies meeting in Rome in November 1991 and includes the following members: Albania, Armenia, Azerbaijan, Belarus, Belgium, Bulgaria, Canada, Czech Republic, Denmark, Estonia, France, Georgia, Germany, Greece, Hungary, Iceland, Italy, Kazakhstan, Kyrgyzstan, Latvia, Lithuania, Luxembourg, Moldova, Netherlands, Norway, Poland, Portugal, Romania, Russian Federation, Republic of Slovakia, Slovenia, Spain, Tajikistan, the former Yugoslav Republic of Macedonia*, Turkey, Turkmenistan, Ukraine, United Kingdom, United States, Uzbekistan.
The Colloquium is an element of the NACC Work Plan.

* Turkey recognizes the Republic of Macedonia with its constitutional name

Reiner Weichhardt
Editor

Deputy Director
NATO Economics Directorate

Status of Economic Reforms in Cooperation Partner Countries in the mid-1990s: Opportunities, Constraints, Security Implications

Colloquium
28-30 June, 1995
Brussels

Etat des réformes économiques dans les pays partenaires de la coopération au milieu des années 90: chances, contraintes, implications en matière de sécurité

Colloque
28-30 juin, 1995
Bruxelles

Editorial support and coordination: Michael Devlin, Editorial Services, Brussels

First edition 1996
ISBN 92-8450092-3

This is the latest in a series bringing together papers presented at the NATO colloquia organised by the NATO Economics Directorate and Office of Information and Press on economic issues in the former USSR and Central and East European countries. For further information please write to the Director, Office of Information and Press, 1110 Brussels, Belgium.

The articles contained in this volume represent the views of the authors and do not necessarily reflect the official opinion or policy of member governments or NATO.

1002745182

Contents

Panel II: Living Standards and Social Welfare

Panel III: Privatisation and Industrial Restructuring

Contents

Preface

Reiner Weichhardt
Deputy Director
NATO Economics Directorate

The 1995 NATO Economics Colloquium - an element of the North Atlantic Cooperation Council (NACC) Work Plan - dealt with economic reforms in Cooperation Partner countries at this mid-decade juncture. Comparative assessments were made with regard to reform experiences and progress in individual countries as well as major reform areas, singling out specific features and common elements.

Chaired by NATO's Director of Economic Affairs, Daniel George, the Colloquium heard presentations by 25 speakers from Allied and Cooperation Partner countries, organised in five panels. A Keynote Speech was delivered by the Minister of Engineering, Military-Industrial Complex and Conversion of Ukraine, Mr. Victor Petrov, and a special lecture on ecological problems of the CIS countries was presented by Dr. Murray Feshbach of Georgetown University in Washington.

The review of reforms in specific countries by Panel I revealed the difficulty of reaching clear, quantitative measures of success. The scope and reliability of statistics are often skewed by unreported developments in the shadow economy and at regional and local levels. Russia, in particular, is characterised by vastly differing regions, in terms of economic resources and political and social conditions. The yardstick used to measure reform in rural areas is totally unsuitable for Moscow and St. Petersburg. In other countries the lack of sound accounting standards, weak financial institutions, and disputes over the pace of reform makes impossible the use of an abstract "reform model" against which progress can be measured.

The key to reform in all countries - the people - was examined by Panel II which covered reform's effect on living standards and social welfare. There was general agreement that essential restrictive policies during the transition period (whether short or long) can impair people's welfare. The necessary balance must be found to provide a social safety net without setting back control of monetary and fiscal policies. This becomes particularly important, and difficult, during election periods when "pork barrel" politics often emerge to appeal to voters.

Privatisation, an element of all reforms, has taken different forms for the various transition economies. Speakers on Panel III noted that so-called voucher (or coupon) privatisation has been successful for some countries while not for others. The key to success or failure has been the degree to which new capital has flowed into the enterprises and whether the change to private ownership has resulted in competent management. The restructuring of enterprises, whether carried out under state ownership or after privatisation, is also a necessary factor for successful reform.

A major goal of all transition countries is to become an active player in world markets. A number of multilateral and bilateral cooperation schemes and initiatives were discussed by Panel IV speakers. There was agreement that private foreign investments, rather than official aid programmes, will be essential for reform and growth.

The concluding presentation of Panel V noted the linkages between economic reform and stability and the growth of democracy and international security. The transition is complex and many-faceted, and political opportunists will constantly try to utilise temporary setbacks to prove that reforms are unnecessary and detrimental to national welfare. While much attention has been devoted to reduction of military outlays and conversion of unneeded defence industries, this important part of the economies continues to be a heavy burden for many countries. NATO's economic activities under the annual NACC Work Plans will be focused on this essential area of reform.

This book contains all the Colloquium papers. Since only a few up-dates have been made during the editing process, the contributions reflect as accurately as possible the state of information available at the time of the conference. Taking into account the conference focus on crucial reform areas and on the link between economic performance, stability and security, the assessments made also provide a most valuable basis for judging future trends.

Michael Devlin, Editorial Services, Brussels, provided editorial support and coordination in preparing this book. He also produced the useful summaries introducing each paper.

I also wish to express appreciation to Felix Dorough and Margaret Grant of the Economics Directorate staff for further editorial assistance, and to Ulrich Gerza who, as an intern with the Directorate, produced the summary of Colloquium discussions.

Brussels
December 1995

Welcoming Remarks

Ambassador SERGIO BALANZINO
Deputy Secretary General
NATO

I am pleased to open this 24th NATO Economics Colloquium and to welcome you to NATO. This Colloquium has not only quite a history since it started in 1971, it has also already become a firm part of our cooperation activities under the North Atlantic Cooperation Council Work Plan.

I am pleased that this part of NATO's activities finds great interest and that we are fortunate to have again such a wide range of speakers and participants from seventeen countries. I can fairly say that economics are key for all of our countries, they are the fundamental basis of our states' stability, our peoples' well-being, and our efforts for security and crisis management.

They all depend on the resources which the economic base of our countries provides. Today, we have a broad understanding of the notion of security. Economics are part of it. Therefore, we invited you to NATO Headquarters to analyse and discuss the related issues together, to promote a common understanding of the underlying principles and challenges.

When the 14th Economics Colloquium was convened in this room in April 1985, the topic was "Adaptability to New Technologies of the USSR and East European Countries". This year, ten years later and after a period of immense political and economic change in these countries, we attempt an appraisal of the status of economic reforms, knowing that the task is still far from being finished. Economic reform is a great challenge. We certainly do not underestimate the situation many countries face in this period of transition and reorientation. Although good progress has been made in most countries in five years, there is great variety in the pace and depth of the reform processes. No single model can guarantee success, but it is clear that all can benefit from sharing knowledge and experiences in fora such as this.

NATO cannot provide economic aid, but it can help gather economic expertise on a remarkably high level, as you can see looking at the impressive list of participants. I encourage you to have a free and broad exchange of ideas. Success will depend on yourselves, your contributions and discussions. One of the main challenges all our countries must cope with is the introduction of new high-tech, capital-intensive industries and the higher unemployment they entail as obsolete plants have to be closed.

Whether it is called "down-sizing" or "right-sizing" - as some Western companies prefer - the result is normally a smaller work force. This is particularly grave in those reform countries which are burdened with high unemployment due to the general economic situation. And as we struggle to reconcile those competing demands of modernisation, competitiveness and employment, we are made constantly aware of the no less urgent need to correct ecological damages of the past and to avoid future ones.

I can only wish you well in addressing these complex but highly important issues which are not easy to pursue. But I am certain you will conclude on a positive note. Finding the right answer to these challenges is in all our interest. After five years of reform, which is a mere blink in the development of a nation, progress is evident on all sides. A democratic Europe, undivided and free, has been our central goal for decades. We can happily say today that we have decisively moved closer to it. European-wide cooperation, in economic, political and security terms is what we here at NATO and our member countries are aiming for. I sincerely hope that undertakings like this important Colloquium will help convince those who still may have doubts, that NATO means business in its endeavours towards cooperation and building cooperative security structures.

Keynote Speech

ECONOMIC REFORMS IN UKRAINE: POSSIBILITIES, PROBLEMS, SECURITY IMPLICATIONS

Victor Petrov

Ukraine had great potential, even within the USSR, but it was held back by its dependence on the former central planning system. Those days are gone forever, says Minister Petrov. The kind of economic reforms that will realise Ukraine's new potential are now past the point of no return. Tough monetary policy has reduced inflation to nearly a quarter of its 1994 level. Price controls have been cut and government subsidies slashed. Unemployment has inevitably grown, and the government has tried to create a strong safety net to protect the most vulnerable. Ukraine needs international help, especially with decommissioning the Chernobyl nuclear power station and converting its arms industry, but it can offer a large market to trading partners, and promises to be an enthusiastic member of the 'New Europe'.

Victor Petrov, Minister of Engineering, Military Industrial Complex and Conversion of Ukraine.

In accordance with the will of its people, Ukraine made a historic choice in favour of independence. It is nearly four years since the proclamation of independence on 24 August, 1991, and the all-Ukrainian referendum. Our country has been constructing a sovereign, democratic and law-abiding state. Its efforts to integrate itself into the world and European communities, in our view, proved to be quite fruitful.

At the same time, as any other newly-born state, Ukraine is living nowadays through a complicated period of building up its statehood. This process turns out to be not completely painless and is sometimes controversial, but there is a general aspiration toward achieving real independence, in the economic sphere in particular, in parallel with profound social reforms.

Though the process of creation of our own state institutions is still underway, Ukraine already has all the basic attributes of statehood, including armed forces.

The emergence of Ukraine in the very centre of Europe as a new state with a population of 52 million and a territory of 603.7 thousand square kilometres is, without any doubt, a great geopolitical event.

Following the democratic changes, Ukraine seems to be moving closer into the focus of the world's attention. Taking into account its geopolitical position, recognition on the international political arena and potential economic opportunities, Ukraine is becoming increasingly attractive for foreign partners.

The Economic Potential of Ukraine

As a component part of the former USSR, Ukraine stood out for its economic, scientific and technological potential.

Production of iron, manganese and uranium ores, sulphur, coal, construction materials as well as metallurgy, were the most developed industries in Ukraine. Chemical (including oil processing and production of mineral fertilisers) and construction complexes, the production of many categories of machines and equipment were also at a significant level of development. Ukraine produces aircraft, marine and fluvial vessels, armament systems (including modern missiles of various classes and purposes), computers, radio electronic equipment, optic devices and other high-tech products.

Nevertheless, Ukraine inherited from the former USSR a disproportionately distorted economy. It is overloaded by highly material and energy consuming industries like coal, iron ore and metal production. Technological cycles of high-tech competitive production were - as a rule - tightly linked with industrial enterprises of Russia.

The dependence on energy supplies (natural gas and oil) which Ukraine used to import at low prices is extremely sensitive. But a centralised planning system of management of the national economy, as well as total state ownership, turned out to be perhaps the most negative factors.

This was the cause of the economic inertness of private individuals and collectives and of the development of such negative trends as monopolism, absence of initiative, imbalanced prices, a large number of state-supported enterprises burdened with losses and, as a result, of the significant decrease in competitivity of the production of Ukrainian enterprises. The need for radical economic reform was evident and well understood. However, until recently there was a lack of strong political will for introducing reforms. It is only with the election of President L. Kuchma that this process has become irreversible.

Economic Situation in Ukraine. Progress of Democratic and Economic Reforms

Today it is an undeniable fact that real implementation of radical economic reforms, the construction of a qualitatively new economic system and the comprehensive democratisation of social life have started in Ukraine. The Memorandum of Understanding signed between the Government of Ukraine and the International Monetary Fund is aimed at economic reform. The economic programme developed on its basis provides for achieving macroeconomic stability and implementation of economic reform. The liberalisation of the economy, its restructuring and changing of property forms serve as mechanisms to solve these issues.

Political prerequisites are being created for it. Recently the Verkhovna Rada (Parliament) of Ukraine approved the Law on state power and local government. Leonid Kuchma, the President of Ukraine, and Oleksandr Moroz, the Chairman of the Parliament, signed the Constitutional Accord.

The programme of economic transformation which had been proposed by the President and approved by the Parliament of Ukraine is now under implementation and bringing its first results. The implementation of a rigid monetary policy resulted in a decrease of the monthly inflation rate to 5.8 percent, that is almost 3.7 times less than it was in January of this year. The Ukrainian karbovanets exchange rate has been unified. It has been stabilised and is determined now in an open interbank foreign exchange market.

Thanks to these drastic measures it has become possible to stop the most destructive process - the bankruptcy of the state finance system. All this has created the necessary prerequisites for introducing a full-fledged national monetary unit.

The state has stopped subsidising unprofitable enterprises in all sectors of the economy. Now the profitability of enterprises will be determined solely by the qualifications and persistence of managers and the desire of workers.

The state's foreign economic activity is fully liberalised. We hope that the abolition of quotas and the licensing of export operations, except for goods subject to special purpose export and other limitations stipulated by international agreements, will stimulate foreign trade. The import regime has also been simplified.

A detailed plan of mass privatisation has been drawn up. It stipulates a substantial decrease in the proportion of state enterprises. About eight thousand medium and large-size enterprises are to be privatised during this year. The government intends to reform the state monopoly for ownership of land. In collective farms the division of land into shares is near completion.

Further changes in the Land Code are being prepared to enable farmers to get land within a shortest time possible. Changes in legislation will also facilitate privatisation of buildings and land in cities and towns. The market transformation of its economy and accelerated implementation of this process constitutes the basis of the economic policy of Ukraine. Measures to reduce government interference in the economy are being undertaken.

Owing to the introduction of the economic reform programme, administrative interference in the price formation process and the limitation of income level have been considerably reduced. The purpose of these measures is to stimulate a more effective usage of scarce resources, including imported energy resources, and to reduce the burden of excessive state budget subsidies.

At the producers' level, price regulation will be limited mainly to natural monopolies. The full cost of energy supply must be distributed among industrial and agricultural consumers. However, all these reforms proceed in a rather difficult way.

The main deterrent is a deep recession in the production sector. There are objective reasons for this, in particular the halt in the production of goods not needed by consumers. But we should also not disregard the psychological factors of the situation - as many managers were not prepared to work in the new market environment. Under these conditions unemployment is inevitable - an occurrence which was considered impossible in the former Soviet Union.

The transition to purchasing energy resources at world prices is another serious factor. The prices increased thousands of times as compared to the former symbolic prices - to reach the world market price levels. This is why serious steps were undertaken to create an effective social security system for the most vulnerable population strata (children, pensioners, disabled individuals, students, etc.).

Everyone in Ukraine is aware of the fact that reforming the economy and political structures should be performed first and foremost by our own efforts. But, nevertheless, Ukraine requires fast and substantial international support, technical and financial assistance. In the long run such assistance paves the way for our partners to a large Ukrainian market and, what is of utmost importance, will contribute to ensuring international security.

Integration of Ukraine into International Structures

The integration of Ukraine into the international community is one of the priorities of our policy. The acceleration of this process undoubtedly depends on overcoming the crisis in the national economy, a successful implementation of economic reforms and the creation of market mechanisms based on a corresponding legal foundation.

The development of relations between Ukraine and the European Union has been recently intensified. A significant impulse in changing the EU stand towards Ukraine was given by the decision of the Verkhovna Rada (Parliament) of Ukraine to ratify START and its accession to NPT.

The signing on 14 June, 1994 of the Partnership and Cooperation Agreement between Ukraine and the EU, and its ratification by the Verkhovna Rada last November, were made possible by the changes in the political climate. According to the provisions of this Agreement, each party grants to the other a Most Favoured Nation status on the conditions envisaged by GATT.

We regard as a positive development the consent of the EU to abolish quantitative restrictions on some Ukrainian goods. Finally, the Interim Agreement on trade and trade-related issues was signed during President Kuchma's visit to Brussels on 1 June 1995.

Having declared its independence, Ukraine stated that it regards no country as its enemy. At the time of the proclamation of its independence Ukraine had armed forces of roughly 700,000 servicemen in three military districts. They were armed with 6,500 tanks, 11,000 military personnel vehicles, 2,000 guns, and 1,100 combat aircraft.

The Strategic Nuclear Forces stationed in Ukraine consisted of 176 intercontinental ballistic missiles with 1,280 warheads, as well as of 40 strategic bombers which had about 600 nuclear charges.

Ukraine has put forward the initiative to remove nuclear weapons from its soil and consistently fulfils its obligations despite numerous problems that arise due to the reduction of huge armed units, as well as the necessity to utilise nuclear weapons. As of today 60 missile complexes have been put off active duty. The accession of Ukraine to NPT has become an important step confirming the consistency of this policy.

The tactical nuclear weapons (about 2,600 missiles) which fell under Ukraine's jurisdiction, were transported to Russia in 1992 in line with the agreement between the two countries. The Presidents of Ukraine and Russia signed the agreement on the division of the Black Sea Fleet.

In accordance with the decision of the Parliament of Ukraine, and as a result of reforms and significant reductions, the number of personnel of the Ukrainian armed forces will be 450,000 by the end of 1995. This constitutes 0.8 percent of the Ukrainian population. But the structure, number of troops and other characteristics of the armed forces have not yet been optimised. The process of reduction of the Ukrainian armed forces is being carried out under the control of corresponding international organisations.

Ukraine and the "Partnership for Peace" Programme

Today we have another important factor - the factor which has emerged just recently - the "Partnership for Peace" programme.

Ukraine highly appreciates the active adaptation of NATO to new realities and challenges. We positively accept the measures undertaken to reorganise political and military structures within the Alliance.

Ukraine believes that NATO is capable of playing a significant role in the creation of a reliable, comprehensive system of European security based not on a bloc-to-bloc confrontation, but on mutually complementary interlocking institutions.

Ukraine appreciates the role of NATO in:

- Promoting the climate of confidence in Europe and beyond it.
- Organising a dialogue between West and East on various military and political issues, including the problems of international security and stability, and environmental protection.
- Working out approaches to arms control and disarmament issues and preventing the proliferation of weapons of mass destruction.

Our conceptual vision of security risks coincides with NATO's view in that the notion of "security" includes not only the military dimension but political, economic, social and ecological aspects as well, and that it is inseparable from these and other components.

Ukraine highly appreciates the openness of NATO towards the countries of Central and Eastern Europe. We support the creation and broadening of the opportunities for dialogue and consultations with partners - the opportunities that emerged as a result of NATO's transformation.

We accept the proposals of NATO to deepen and to intensify its practical cooperation with other European countries by developing the "Partnership for Peace" programme as a promising initiative directed to strengthen security and stability in Europe.

Ukraine would like to deepen its relations with NATO in these directions:

- Individualised cooperation in the framework of the "Partnership for Peace" and with the Atlantic Council on a bilateral basis, first of all in the military field.
- Application of NATO's experience and standards to the armed forces of Ukraine being reformed and the provision of democratic control over the latter.
- Participation in peacekeeping operations realised by the armed forces of the NATO countries, getting the experience of the NATO countries in operations to maintain peace.
- Participation in military studies in the framework of the "Partnership for Peace".
- Bilateral cooperation in the process of arms reduction and conversion of military-industrial complex.
- Sharing experience and planning activity of the civil defence services in extraordinary situations.
- Participation of Ukraine in discussing all the aspects of possible NATO extension.

The Chernobyl Problems

The Government of Ukraine has adopted an important and responsible decision on decommissioning the Chernobyl nuclear power plant before the year 2000. The Statement of the Government of Ukraine on this decision has been adopted.

The Government of Ukraine has prepared a schedule for shutting down the Chernobyl nuclear power plant which envisages the beginning of work on closing the second reactor in 1996. Furthermore, the Programme of Measures, which are necessary to fulfil the schedule in time, has been prepared by the State Committee of Ukraine on Use of Nuclear Energy. The schedule and the Programme of Measures were handed over to the G7 Delegation during the meeting on 16-17 May 1995, in Kiev.

Thus, the Ukrainian side has completely fulfilled its obligations concerning the solution of the Chernobyl nuclear power plant problem. The Governmental Delegation in charge of carrying on the negotiations on all the issues which are connected with this problem has been organised and it has received appropriate powers.

But it's necessary to note that under conditions of an unbalanced economy and an energy crisis Ukraine cannot solve the Chernobyl problem without assistance.

Ukraine is waiting for an adequate reaction of the Western countries supporting the decision to put out of operation the Chernobyl nuclear power plant. The expenses for closing down the Chernobyl nuclear power plant will total up to 4 billion US dollars. This estimation has been made by the Ukrainian and American experts who have carried out a joint study. That is why we hope to get appropriate financial and technical assistance to realise the measures which will ensure putting out of operation the Chernobyl nuclear power plant.

These measures envisage:

- Making storehouses for the exhausted nuclear fuel and radioactive waste products.
- Building the compensating capacities in Slavutich region to solve the employment problem of the region's population.
- Transposition of the "Cover" object - the so-called "Sarcophagus" - over the damaged block to create an ecologically safe system.

Ukraine will cover a considerable part of the expenses for realising this wide-ranging programme with its own economic resources.

Military and Industrial Complex Conversion

The scientific, technical and industrial potential of the Ukrainian defence factories constituted about one-third of the whole Soviet military and industrial complex. It was concentrated mainly in the missile/space sector, ship-building, aviation, tank construction, radio electronics and communications.

The transition from military confrontation to cooperation between the USA, Western European countries and former USSR countries - and the sharp reduction of military manufacturing which resulted - left independent Ukraine with complicated conversion problems. Just after the creation of our state we started tackling this problem.

The priorities of military factory restructuring were defined on the basis of diversification. Today this programme consists of 52 complex and targeted scientific and technical programmes, grouped in 21 priority areas.

The most important, as defined by the state, was the creation of up-to-date energy, ecology and agriculture equipment, as well as medical systems. A lot should be done in aviation, ship-building and automotive sectors and in other science-related areas.

No country in the world has experienced in technical production sectors, such a shocking rate of decline which was counted in tens of percent per year (our expression - "landslide conversion"). This is why state assistance for this process was foreseen and realised. At the same time this assistance appeared to be drastically lower than that which was really needed. This is why we feel our conversion which is now going on to be the most complex problem that we face.

The conversion's most negative consequence for separate factories, as well as for the sector of economy and the country as a whole, is the liquidation of many thousands of jobs. It is clear that it creates extreme social tensions in the society. But even in these extremely hard conditions some positive results were reached. Thus, the world famous missile factory "Juzhny" started manufacturing trolleybuses. Shipyards in Nikolaev which formerly built aircraft carriers and other military vessels converted to the production of oil tanks and refrigerators. Kyiv enterprises - which used to build land-to-air and air-to-air missiles - turned to the construction of medical equipment, gas calculators, and many other kinds of civil products.

There are many similar examples that illustrate how the measures which have been taken in time helped save and reorient the most valuable part of the scientific and industrial potential in the military complex, towards a solution of the tasks facing the Ukrainian economy.

The work of creating and realising such programmes gave us the opportunity to elaborate workable enterprise conversion projects within the military complex into joint ventures to establish credit and investment.

Ukraine is now modernising its legislature with the aim of creating the most favourable conditions to attract foreign investments. The investment priorities of Ukraine include:

- Energy complex development, introducing energy and resources saving technologies.
- Agro-industrial complex development.
- Speeding up medical and microbiological industry development.
- Overcoming the Chernobyl disaster consequences.

Partnership Perspectives

Important changes in relations between Ukraine and the West are underway. Very favourable relationships exist between Ukraine and the USA, some countries of Western Europe, Canada and Japan.

The necessary external conditions have been created in the Western direction for the economic reconstruction follow-up and activation of the efforts to get Ukraine out of the economic crisis.

The recognition of the status of Ukraine as a state with a transition economy is very important, and the coming year will be an important one for further extending our cooperation with the European structures - the EU, NATO, the European Council and the OSCE.

Our participation in the NATO Economics Colloquium "Status of economic reforms in cooperation partner countries in the mid-1990s: opportunities, constraints, security implications" confirms it.

PANEL I*

Balance Sheet of Economic Reforms in Cooperation Partner Countries

Chair: Daniel George, Director, NATO Economics Directorate

Panelists: László Csaba
Vladimir Gimpelson
Vladimir Kuznyetsov
Gérard Wild

---

* The format of panel sessions I-IV was generally structured as follows: presentations were started with a general overview, then specific Cooperation Partner country studies were discussed. Panels were concluded with an intervention focused on prospects and implications for the West. The latter aspect was expanded and deepened in the final Panel V, which was entirely devoted to this subject.

ECONOMIC REFORMS IN COOPERATION PARTNER COUNTRIES: A BALANCE SHEET

László Csaba

It is now clear that there is no quick fix to the problems of Central and Eastern Europe. But Hungarian economist László Csaba shows that the race is definitely to the swift. Countries that have held back on reform are suffering, while those which opted for the 'short sharp shock' method are forging ahead. Other trends are also emerging: the need for more foreign direct investment is paramount; as is the development of investment-friendly banking and taxation systems. Conventional wisdom has been proved wrong: it is not necessarily the big resource-rich countries that are taking the lead. Professor Csaba points out that smaller countries like the Baltic states have created economies flexible enough to stand the sort of external shocks that might break their bigger competitors. His conclusion is that their flexible, 'try-it-and-see' approach is more likely to succeed than any grand scheme.

Professor Csaba is a senior Economist, Kopint-Datorg and Professor of International Economics, College of Foreign Trade, Budapest.

Overview

Half a decade after the collapse of the Soviet empire, many illusions about systemic change have evaporated. The idea of quick fixes, of fast and irrevocable reforms and unconditional, sustained public support for radical policies looks naive these days. Likewise the zeal of social engineers, claiming to know exactly what is needed for the right brand of capitalism and also how to attain it, invites more irony than respect both inside and outside the region. Reality is different. Transformation means a much deeper set of changes than can be covered by stabilisation and liberalisation. As it has turned out, reforms in the system of *financial mediation, fiscal* and *social security reforms* and *industrial restructuring* are no easier tasks in post-socialist countries than these are in mature market economies. Besides time and effort, a lot of "learning by doing" seems to be inevitable to figure out the exact shape of the institutional infrastructure in any country that is able to enhance its competitiveness and more generally, a sustained good economic performance for a long period of time. In other words, stabilisation and liberalisation were necessary to reverse the modernisation crisis in Eastern Europe.

However, without firm institutional backing they fall short of putting the new democracies on the path of a long-term sustainable development which would enable them to become ripe and lucrative new partners for an enlarging Euro-Atlantic alliance.

Given that the new political forces governing the East since 1993-94 have a sizeable overlap over what we described as old structures, two conclusions may be made.

1. Since they are mostly representatives of the nomenklatura bourgeoisie, they might, and often do, have a stake in a blossoming market economy whose profits would accrue to them as the beneficiaries of the spontaneous and organic privatisation of the early transition period.

2. Since their voting base is much wider than this, the inclination to be sensitive to the concerns of old structures, of vested interests, and consequently a keen interest in retaining discretionary decision-making, especially in trade and fiscal policies, can only be expected. This is actually what has been happening in Russia, Hungary, Slovakia and Poland.

This means, that by the mid-1990s the earliest reforming countries are beginning, in analytical terms, to resemble a *typical developing country* of the periphery, where the peculiarities of the post-socialist period gradually give way to the challenges well known to the international financial organisations. This includes lengthy bargains on financial conditions, foot-dragging on fiscal reforms, and the very intensive open clash of competing interest groups over the privatisation of big money-makers, such as banking, public utilities or medical care. The politicisation of privatisation and the resultant frequent suffering of economic common sense must be taken as a normal state of affairs, rather than as a peculiar perversion.

Thus, it is hardly surprising that the early debates on shock therapy versus gradual change have proved by and large irrelevant for policy-making. By now several analyses have proved true: shock therapy is a far cry from what economic liberalism implies in theoretical, functional and policy terms alike (Murrel, 1992; Gligorov, 1995). This makes life difficult, as the radical nature of policy deliberations can no longer serve as a measure of the seriousness, or even of the type of actual reform policy a partner country is conducting. More often than not, a radical vocabulary is a feature of the early stabilisation phase; it has little bearing on what comes when the real hard nut to crack comes around: the changes in structural factors.

The Hard Core

With the benefit of hindsight we can easily disentangle those components of the policy debates which figured high in contemporary exchanges, but which have little bearing on the type of capitalism that emerges from the ruins of communism. These are mainly the problems related to stabilisation/liberalisation as well as the proper technologies of privatisation. If these issues look like mere packaging, let us list some of the factors which are the hard core.

The Role of Domestic versus Foreign Capital

As the mainstream of literature about transformation is distilled from Polish and Russian experience, it is hardly surprising that the major involvement of foreign investors was not seen as realistic in 1989-91. In the longer term, however, no country can afford the luxury of not relying on foreign savings, technologies and networks in its modernising endeavours. Welfens (1994) correctly describes foreign direct investment as a pacemaker for privatisation in the context of systemic change, if the point of the exercise is improving economic performance measured by dollar intakes, rather than meeting some ideological priority.

However, ideological or general commitment cannot preclude the intense conflict of interest inherent in any privatisation deal.

The Czech and Polish governments are openly concerned about too much of a German influence via FDI, and prefer portfolio investments instead, reflected in the recent strength of the zloty and koruna alike. In Russia, the creation of financial-industrial structures is often portrayed as the real chance for domestic capital (Batchev, S. 1995). Others add to this the avoidance of competitive pressures and the mutual interest of management and the administration to retain public leverage over large firms (Starodubrovskaia, 1995, esp. pp16-17). The two interpretations are not mutually exclusive but mutually reinforcing.

The "national" argument about FDI often overlaps with "social" arguments. The recent opposition of the Meciar government to voucher privatisation, including its open conflicts with foreign owners of investment funds like Nomura, are attacked by supporters of the former Slovak administration on the grounds that *nomenklatura*-direct sales cement existing management. This was indeed the case quite often in Hungary and Poland. On the other hand, firms bought out by their employees or by former owners or shareholders often lack fresh money for restructuring. In the Czech Republic, Hungary and Russia a phenomenon termed by some as second privatisation is already emerging, when those companies able to operate viably in the longer term buy out primary privatisers. The final owners are quite often foreign strategic investors.

These conflicts multiply if big money-spinners are at stake. Barons of the Russian energy sector obviously resent foreign attempts to acquire ownership. Bureaucrats in the administration resist the privatisation of banks - especially of old established large units - for obvious reasons. The more fiscal support is pushed over to the monetary sphere - in the form of cheap credits or preferences - the greater is the need to retain commercial banks in public hands. Since early ideas of creating a large, quickly expanding equity market to replace sluggish banking proved illusory both in Russia and in the Czech Republic, this remains a lasting source of tension. Employees of the Hungarian electricity company, MVM, have formed a strike committee to defy possible foreign owners.

And Ukraine has fulfilled its ambitious privatisation plan to 3.5 percent in the first quarter of 1995, according to E. Hryhorenko quoted in *The Wall Street Journal Europe,* 30 May 1995, which is an obvious sign of the strength of the status quo. The more the overall business environment resembles that of the home country of investors, the more intensive their involvement will be. Thus the presence of foreign direct investors is the best measure of progress any country has made in its way toward the market.[1]

This concept is related to our seeing transformation as an economic exercise aimed at modernising post-socialist countries. In this context, it is reliance on Western management, up-to-date forms of corporate governance and securing the long-term viability of private firms, rather than the mere change of the title which matters. The latter, in fact, can be irrelevant if e.g. investment funds are owned by public banks, or these funds do not - or are unable to - exert their proprietary rights. The latter seems to be more than an imagined danger in each country having opted for reliance of privatisation funds as a major form of corporate control and privatisation.

Industry/Bank Links

In the five years since the onset of transformation, no single country has managed to heed the calls for swift privatisation of the banking sector or to create an alternative capital/equity market. As far as the latter is concerned, the equity markets in Prague, Budapest, Moscow, Warsaw and Bratislava are all equally thin, with only a minuscule share of companies actually traded. Furthermore quotations can often be distorted by coincidental or purely extraneous factors such as tax modifications or changes of mood in major countries investing in emerging markets. Against these, the most serious home-made problem is the dominance of treasury bills. Adding all these together implies that *the available capital market is a poor means for evaluating companies or allocating scarce resources at the macroeconomic level.*

Given the universal intertwining of commercial banks and their large clients it has often been suggested that these links be simply cut. Provided this could be done, the question of who should own large public firms and what to do with them remains open. A central agency able to restructure thousands of crisis-ridden companies one by the other used to be the hottest dream of central planners, which, however, never has come true.

As a recent analysis of the Association of Russian Banks (Makarevich, 1995) demonstrated, decentralisation and privatisation alone may only make the problem worse. In Russia banks often run businesses with 15 to 25 times their registered capital, with no proper risk-assessment, or monitoring of the performance of the client, lacking access to collateral, or even having recourse to publicly guaranteed credit lines. This clearly supports our introductory thesis on the paramount significance of the regulatory and supervisory framework. We would not, however, go as far as some technical analysts and see the way out in imposing proper regulatory discipline alone. It is pretty clear that clients with no track record constitute the majority of new businesses in transition countries. Furthermore, restructuring old clients known to be a bad risk is not the sort of task a commercial bank is prepared for, even in most Western countries. Thus, repeated bank consolidation operations can hardly be avoided, even though the moral hazard inherent in the replication of the bailout is obviously a source of grave risk.

There is no easy solution. The most obvious option would be to sell out some large banks to foreigners to import capital, know-how and management. However, some analysts (Bray and Beck, 1995) see a danger of a strategic turn of Western banking business towards the East, as they see bank reorganisation as too conflict-ridden, too costly and not sufficiently rewarding. For in an overall environment of instability those who lend the least can have the best scores: this has been the strategy of all large Western banks in Hungary.

If, however, investors opt for green-field investment in banking as well, the problem of restructuring old large banks remains the task of public authorities. The opening of a large number of resident offices of all major Western banks in all Eastern capital cities should not obscure the problem which has to do with the size of bad debts and the macroeconomic impact of banks to be restructured.

To avoid the dangers typical of centralised procedures Poland has opted for a decentralised method (Bonin, 1993) where banks and companies could bargain horizontally and figure out solutions. As could be predicted, mating bad banks with bad companies sooner or later invites a central bailout. This has actually happened in 1995 with the consolidation operation enhancing public ownership to 80 percent in banking with far-reaching further indirect ownership in industry and insurance (*Világgazdaság,* 2 June, 1995). To sum up, whatever the technique chosen, there is no escape from a lengthy process of trial and error, where tough management contracts and the sacking of inefficient managers may bring gradual improvement. But the cost of inefficient banking is reflected in unduly high margins and low levels of banking services. The first may be circumvented by more reliance on corporate bonds and direct borrowing from abroad, but the latter will remain a lasting headache for entrepreneurs.

The Nature and Progress of Fiscal Reforms

Having drawn on the developing country experiences, early transformation policies stressed the stabilising aspects, i.e. subsidy cuts and broadening the tax base. These steps were coupled with implementation of reforms, introducing value-added tax and personal income tax (though often with a delay of several years). It was widely believed that these measures were enough to ensure balanced general government spending and revenues.

This proved to be illusory. It took several years and a lot of disenchantment before knowledgeable analysts (Bruno, 1992; Tanzi, 1993; Kornai, 1992) drew attention to the paradoxes peculiar to transition that render the attainment of balanced budgets next to impossible. In a nutshell, reforms creating a free-market institutional infrastructure, like tax reforms and also privatisation, often imply revenue shortfalls, whereas spending cuts could become politically embarrassing, especially amidst a deep recession. It took some time before international agencies realised that their focusing on the short term budgetary indicators was often misleading, on occasion counter-productive.

Once proper and consolidated accounting according to the GFS standards is introduced - a task yet to be mastered in most partner countries - several weaknesses of public finance come to light. First, the private sector tends to pay significantly fewer taxes per unit of income than the public sector. This applies *a fortiori* to small business which is the dynamically expanding segment of transforming economies. Meanwhile, ailing large companies do not pay taxes as they run at a loss. The entitlement system, from pensions to health care, is very broad while the revenue base is shrinking. Abolishing the social safety net would have been suicidal, while maintenance of the extensive social benefit system cannot be financed any longer. This is in many ways akin to the problems faced by ageing Western welfare states. This issue has only recently been raised in full in Poland, Hungary and the Czech Republic, and is yet to be tackled by other partner countries.

On top of this, *fiscal practices* leave a lot to be desired. The reliance on a large number of special funds not integrated in the budget is a source of confusion and obfuscation. State-owned firms can afford the luxury of not paying public dues. Municipalities can typically spend without raising their own revenues. Large state-owned firms are regularly bailed out. In most partner countries *lax accounting standards* allow for commercial banks to show fat profits where standard EU procedures would show heavy losses.

As there is a great deal of interest in covering up these imperfections, it is not surprising to see *high inflation* as the basic means to make both ends meet. In this way the state inflates away the revenues squeezed out of the public coffers by various powerful vested interests. This is a painless solution in the short run. However, it leads to persistently high levels of inflation; undermines the credibility of the national currency; renders corporate accounting irrelevant;

and makes savings in local currency unprofitable. These are, unfortunately, typical traits of a pre-reform Latin economy, where weak government, conceptual confusion and intensive in-fighting by vested interests translate into high levels of inflation and low levels of investment, especially in the private sector.

There is nothing unique or insoluble to this set of problems: what Williamson (1994) describes as the Washington consensus on development economics offers a fairly straightforward answer to them. But this answer is given only in technical terms: the task of building up a reform constituency and of managing sound economic policies over a single election cycle remains the job of local élites.

The relevance of this problem has been shown by several developments in the East. Bulgaria in 1991-93 and Serbia in 1994 attempted a very harsh and also successful stabilisation policy. However, as institutional reform stagnated, these policies were bound to soften up. On the other hand, the experience of Poland, Lithuania, Hungary and Slovakia are indicative of the importance of systemic reforms, which can and indeed did ensure the required stability of reformist policies across changing governmental teams.

External Economic Relations

One of the most fashionable subjects discussed in the early transformation period was the feasibility of reorienting commercial relations from East to the West. These controversies have produced a voluminous literature on transitory arrangements and régimes, from barter to hard currency trade. In reality, these were not implemented anywhere. Much to the surprise of most external analysts, it was not only the Visegrád countries who succeeded in reorientation, but also Bulgaria and Romania. Similarly, Slovenia and Croatia also mastered the "impossible" task of reorienting their respective economies.

As far as successor-states of the Soviet Union are concerned, what has happened was more or less the *opposite to what could have been expected on the grounds of trade theory*. In the latter, larger and resource rich countries should have had an edge over tiny and resource-dependent economies. This would have put countries like Kazakhstan, Turkmenistan and Ukraine on the top, with the Baltic states suffering the most. The vision proved to be the mirror image of reality. The Baltic countries, having instituted radical stabilisation and transformation policies, have created flexible economies able to adjust to major external shocks.

Intimately related to these issues is the role of *international financial institutions* in shaping the priorities and techniques of systemic change. Contrary to frequent allegations (e.g. Glaziev, 1995), detailed analytical and country studies (Schönfeld, ed, 1995) do not lend support to the claim that the International Monetary Fund (IMF) is dictating terms or fashioning policies or institutions. On the contrary, in the majority of cases domestic policy factors are dominant beyond doubt.

Suffice to recall the notorious inefficiency of multi-year structural adjustment programmes of the IMF, or the regular non-compliance with quantitative targets of standby agreements (most recently by Bulgaria).

In reality, a significant amount of time and effort has been spent on circumventing the spirit of economic common sense embodied in the IMF proposals in order to enable politicians to play to their respective domestic audiences. In fact, it was always the outcome of power plays - or extreme cases of need - which sometimes allowed some of the IMF medicines to be taken by some countries.

It is relatively easy to prove the marginal role of international financial institutions in the transformation. Being an international bureaucracy, bound by the norms of even-handedness, the IMF cannot but suggest by and large the Washington consensus to its clients. If all of them were taking the advice, the outcome should also be quite similar. Thus the glaring diversity of experiences, from Albania to Turkmenia, from Estonia to Belarus, from Slovenia to Ukraine may suffice to highlight the *paramount significance of domestic factors* over any external influence.

Medium-Term Outlook

Regular regional overviews published by international organisations and research institutes allow us to form three groups of the transition economies. These seem to follow a different pattern for longer periods of time. Classification can, of course, never be definitive or final; however for analytical purposes the trial may be worth the run.

The Visegrád Countries (Czech and Slovak Republics, Hungary and Poland) Slovenia and the Baltic Countries

These nations have crossed the threshold of institutional change. They have overcome stabilisation and entered the phase of sustained economic growth. They can keep the rate of inflation at what is internationally termed as moderate. The dominant type of enterprise behaviour as well as the major source of wealth creation, is outside the public sector. National currencies have stabilised, and payments and accumulation are conducted in these monetary units. Political changes, including changes of government, occur in an organised and peaceful fashion via internationally supervised free elections. Accession to the EU seems to be almost certain, though its timing remains contingent upon EU reforms, as shown above. The point of no return in both political and economic terms has been crossed, and the quality of the market order is already close to that of the EU (cf below).

Southeast European Countries and Russia

Though hyper-inflation has mostly been arrested, sluggish institutional change may destroy macroeconomic successes. The role of the state as well as that of the ruling coalition seems to be cemented for a longer period of time. Activist policies in forming economic structures are advocated and are often inevitable due to weakness of the markets. Inflation remains high - 60 percent in good years of Romania and Bulgaria - and convertible currencies continue to play a significant role both in inter-firm contracts and as a store of value. Economic growth has yet to stabilise or materialise. The role of FDI is marginal and the autonomous private sector survives only in symbiosis with the public sector.

Partly for this reason, partly due to the feebleness of a competitive environment and the survival of old habits, actually or nominally privatised firms frequently do not behave very differently from public firms: they lobby for the favours of the authorities, try to avoid layoffs and postpone structural changes (Ash and Hare, 1994). This makes a great difference versus what can be observed in the first group, where public firms are also pushed to adjust in a competitive manner. Bankruptcy and the threat of closure are non-existent in this group, whereas - to varying degrees - they do clear the market in group no. 1. Fiscal reforms, too, lag behind the former group and the openness of the trade régime is also much less obvious.

Ukraine, Belarus, Transcaucasian and Central Asian Republics

Here both socio-political and economic changes away from the inherited Soviet pattern proved to be the smallest. Rampant inflation and dominant public ownership, and the collapse of output alongside formally maintained full employment result in officially unconvertible currencies. The rigid economic pattern, i.e. the inability to master major structural changes save divestment of unviable defence and related industries, means they are almost totally dependent on Russian oil supply and the Russian market. There is a long way before the conditions of sustainable development and even of financial stabilisation can be created. The danger of economic depressions becoming a destabilising factor, and the lure of using nationalism to alleviate tensions is sizeable. Despite the three major post-Soviet states' renouncing the nuclear arsenal in the Budapest summit of the OSCE in December 1994, the potential insecurity of these countries remains a lasting problem.

The three groups of countries differ in terms of *market maturity*, in terms of the economic and political role *of the state* - as opposed to self-regulation and the role of civic society, and therefore the role of FDI and the role of the EU will also differ. As a consequence, EU and NATO partnership policies will play an enduringly different role for these groups for many years to come.

Coming back to economics, if there is anything general to be said about a wide variety of economic reforms it is the following. Our bird's-eye view supported more theoretical findings (Fehl and von Delhaes, 1995) about the *crucial role of competition in shaping the qualities of an economic order.* Put the other way around, contrary to early convictions, the outcome of transformation is not contingent upon the progress made in privatisation. It is more dependent upon progress made towards establishing competitive or at least contestable markets for as many factors of production as possible and as enduringly as possible.

When privatisation coexists with retaining monopoly positions or in symbiosis with public-sector firms it may not necessarily enhance efficiency.

This highlights three conclusions:

- *Privatisation* was bound to have different outcomes in different countries with different cultural backgrounds and different market maturities.
- There is going to be a continued *regulatory competition* not only globally but also among the transforming countries.
- As a consequence *no optimal strategy* can be theoretically postulated (cf Csaba, 1995, pp. 121-145) that could serve as a base to assess national strategies with cross-country validity. While at the theoretical level, no such comparisons are possible, the world commodity and capital markets, but also the labour market continuously do the abstractly impossible job of comparing, assessing and evaluating what is inherently non measurable.Thus transforming countries *will continue to fare quite differently* on the troubled waters of the world economy.

This also means that generalised schemes, grand designs and grand bargains are not very helpful in orientating decision makers. Nor are they going to acquire this quality in the future. For the more general and more abstract a theory or scheme is, the more universal its coverage may be.

Meanwhile its value for helping solve *practical* matters, like Eastern expansion of NATO or ways of cooperation with the Euro-Atlantic structures, is bound to decrease in proportion. In other words: there is no escape from the challenge of elaborating a *differentiated strategy* when drawing the security implications of diverse economic reform stories in the East.

References

ASH, T.N. and HARE, P.G (1994): Privatisation in the Russian Federation: changing enterprise behaviour in the transition period. *Cambridge Journal of Economics,* vol.18. no.3, pp 619-634.

BARTHOLDY, K. (1995): Measuring transition is tough (an interview to Walker, J), *Transition,* vol.6. no.4, pp 1-4.

BATCHEV, S. (1995): Sozdaniie finansovo-promyshlennikh grupp: shans dlia natsionalnogo kapitala Rossii (an interview with Ivanov,S.). *Nezavisimaia Gazeta,* 23 March.

BONIN, J.(1993): On the way to privatizing commercial banks: Poland and Hungary take different roads. *Comparative Economic Studies,* vol.35. no.4. pp 103-120.

BRAY, N. - BECK, E.(1995): Credit Suisse abandons plans for BB in blow to privatization. *Wall Street Journal Europe,* 14 March.

BRUNO, M. (1992): Stabilization and reform in Eastern Europe. *IMF Staff Papers,* Vol. 39. no.4, pp 741-777.

CSABA, L. (1995): *The Capitalist Revolution in Eastern Europe.* Cheltenham, UK, and Brookfield, Vermont, USA, E. Elgar Publishing Co., 342 p.

DMITRIEV, M. (1995): Nalogovaia opora budzheta stanovitsa vse bolee nenadezhnoi. *Finansoviie Izvestia,* no. 34.

EBRD (1994): *Transition report.* London.

FEHL, U. and von DELHAES, K. eds, (1995): *Die Rolle des Wettbewerbs in Wirtschaftsordnungen.* Stuttgart: G.Fischer Verlag.

GLAZIEV, S.(1995): Ochkotviratel'stvo ili bred sumashedshego? *Nezavisimaia Gazeta,* 11 May.

GLIGOROV,V.(1995): Gradual shock therapy. *East European Politics and Societies,* vol. 9. no.1, pp 195-206.

HAGGARD, S. and WEBB, S. (1993): What do we know about the political economy of economic policy reform? *The World Bank Research Observer,* vol. 8. no. 2, pp 143-168.

HEITGER, B. - SCHRADER, K. - BODE, E (1992): *Die mittel- und osteuropäischen Länder als Unternehmensstandort.* Tübingen: J.C.B. Mohr, Paul Siebeck, - Kieler Studien, No. 250.

KAMM, Th. (1995): Element of risk: Lyonnais loss points to broader problem. *The Wall Street Journal Europe,* 20 March.

KOLOKOL'TSEVA, E. (1995): O takom budzhete mog mechtat' tol'ko Campanella. *Business MN,* No. 36.

KORNAI, J. (1992): The postsocialist transition and the state. *The American Economic Review,* vol. 82. no. 2. pp 1-15.

LAINELA, S. and SUTELA, P. eds,(1994): *The Baltic Economies in Transition.* Helsinki: Bank of Finland, A: 91./Nov/138 p.

MAKAREVICH, L.(1995): Rossiia stavit rekord po chislu bankov-bankrotov. *Finansoviie Izvestiia,* no. 9.

MICHALOPOULOS, C. and TARR, D. eds, (1994) *Trade in the New Independent States.* Washington: The World Bank/UNDP, Studies of economies in transformation, No.13/December/280 p.

MURREL, P. (1992): Evolutionary and radical approaches to economic reforms. *Economics of Planning,* vol. 25. no.1. pp 79-96.

STARODUBROVSKAYA, I. (1995): Financial-industrial groups: illusions and reality. *Communist Economies and Economic Transformation,* vol.7. no.l. pp 5-20.

SCHÖNFELD, R. ed, (1995): *The Role of International Financial Institutions in Central and Eastern Europe.* München: Oldenbourg Verlag, Südosteuropa-Aktuell series.

TANZI, V. (1993): The budget deficit in transition. *IMF Staff Papers,* vol. 40. no.3. pp 697-707.

VALKI, L. and CSABA, L. (1994): Economic and social stability in Central and South-Eastern Europe: preconditions for security. IISS *Adelphi Papers,* No.284, pp 42-59.

WELFENS, P. (1994): Privatization and foreign direct investment in the East European transformation: theory, options and strategies. in: Csaba,L.ed,: *Privatization, Liberalization and Destruction.* Aldershot/UK/ and Brookfield/USA: Dartmouth Publishing C., pp 35-70.

WILLIAMSON, J. (1994): In search of a manual for technopols. in: Williamson, J. ed,: *The Political Economy of Policy Reform.* Washington: The Institute of International Economics, pp 9-28.

Footnote

1. First the Kiel Institute of World Economics (Heitger, et al, 1992), and later the European Bank (EBRD, 1994) attempted to create a set of comprehensive indicators for market maturity. However helpful these may be, as the editor of the latter report, Bartholdy (1995) concedes, any such set of indicators is loaded with subjective elements, whereas *ex post* inflows are facts beyond dispute.

ECONOMIC REFORMS IN RUSSIA

Vladimir Gimpelson

Vladimir Gimpelson asks whether Russia will survive as a united country, or fall apart like the former USSR. The collapse of central planning has revealed the vast differences between Russia's regions. The gap between regional priorities and federal interest may provide just the opening that separatists can exploit. But Dr. Gimpelson concludes that the hard-line proponents of regional autonomy are too weak, and too closely identified with the old order. In the regions, support for economic reform outweighs the support for separatism. His verdict is that separatists have too much to lose from the break-up of Russia - and they know it.

Dr. Gimpelson is Head of Department, Institute of World Economy and International Relations, Russian Academy of Sciences, Moscow.

Russian Reforms in Regional Dimension

A balance-sheet of reforms has many aspects: political, financial, social, moral, etc. I would like to focus my short presentation on the regional dimension of the Russian transition. The Chechen war highlighted once again that successes and failures in reforming Russia are, to a considerable extent, regionally dependent. A threat of separatism proved to be rather efficient in squeezing special privileges from the centre. The weak Federal Government is forced to be very sensitive to local elites which have strong control over their localities and population. The forthcoming Parliamentary elections can strengthen this influence even more.

One of the key questions often raised is whether Russia will survive as a united country or fall to pieces as happened with the Soviet Union. I think this is a very important issue with obvious implications not only for the Russian reforms but for international security as well. I want to pinpoint right now that I do not believe in the most pessimistic scenario; nevertheless I consider policy on the relationship between the centre and the regions as very important for future development.

Structural Aspects of Regional Policy

Vast inter-regional economic differentials in Soviet Russia used to be mitigated by the strong centre that redistributed resources and incomes between regions. The collapse of the party-state system weakened the centre and destroyed this redistributive mechanism. This increased the gap between the rich and poor regions depending on their structural profiles. The liberalisation of prices and the tendency to integrate the Russian economy into the world market multiplied the existing structural differences.

If the "rich" regions seek to avoid redistribution to the "poor" ones and thus to increase their incomes, the latter (with the strong elements of traditionalism) would like to avoid reforms. The reforms threaten the existing traditionalism and, correspondingly, the power of ruling elites. This is true, first of all, for the poor ethnic republics.

One can divide all Russian regions into five major types that differ in their economic profiles. Roughly speaking, there are those which are competitive and adaptive on the world market (primarily due to their mining and extractive industries), and those that lack these advantages.[1]

These groups are the following:

(a) The resource-rich regions with mining and extractive profile (mostly the Northern a·nd the Far-Eastern regions).

(b) The urbanised industrial areas combining heavy and light industries, the military industrial complex (the central European part of Russia, and parts of the Urals and Siberia).

(c) The export-oriented regions - financial capitals (Moscow and St. Petersburg) or border regions with maritime ports - (the North and the Far-East).

(d) The regions with developed agriculture oriented towards the domestic market (many regions from the Black-Earth zone and Povolzhye).

(e) The ethnic regions.

Each of these structural profiles requires a different adjustment strategy.

1. The resource-rich areas, the financial capitals and the maritime regions
Groups (a) and (c) would benefit from a liberalisation of the economy and free trade. These regions relying on export of mineral resources, on geographic location or on financial capital are inclined to back the more liberal foreign-trade-oriented policy. The centre is trying to regulate these activities to guarantee its "cut" for the federal budget. Therefore, these regions [groups (a) and (c)(maritime ports)] are likely to try getting more independence from Moscow to reduce tax transfers to the federal funds. The domestic economic links are replaced by foreign trade ties and the enterprises' interest in the domestic market declines. This is true for Moscow and St. Petersburg as well. The incoherence between regional economic priorities and federal interests may boost separatist tendencies.

The most explicit case of this policy is shown by the Far Eastern regions:

• The extremely remote location (combined with high transportation and energy costs) makes local production uncompetitive even on the domestic market; the weak infrastructure breaks traditional inter-regional links with the European part of Russia.

- The weakening of old links is accompanied by the strengthening of new export-import ties with the Asia-Pacific countries (Japan, China, Korea, etc.); the migration of the Russian population to other Russian regions and the influx of Chinese migrants is affecting demographic structure in the region.[2]
- The region plays a special, monopolistic, role in Russian foreign trade: 50 percent of Russian exports move through its ports and railways.[3]

The strengthening integration into the international economy is typical for other regions from (c) as well. Of course, transportation costs do not play so decisive a role here as in the Far East. Nevertheless, the transportation capacities and geographic position stimulate more free trade policy orientations. The same is true for Moscow and St. Petersburg where the bulk of financial capital is concentrated.

The special policy opposing the federal one is pursued by the Moscow government, which uses the status of the city as the capital to keep a much stronger grip over the economy, privatisation and ownership transfers, and entrepreneurship development than anywhere else in Russia. Although Moscow does not look like a separatist city, it shows many patterns of policy that can lead to a kind of isolation. The current attempts to establish the Moscow municipal bank may be considered as a step towards much greater financial and fiscal independence from the federal centre.[4]

Kaliningrad (former Königsberg) illuminates a special case in the group. Being located on the Baltic coast, it is separated from the main territory of the Russian Federation by Lithuania. This former German city is attracting now native Germans from Povolzhie and Kazakhstan. The growth of the German population may significantly increase the orientation of the regional economy towards Germany. There are two likely alternatives for the region: either being developed as a Russian military base (this would require a heavy budget investment which makes it unrealistic even in the case of special political pressure from the Russian superpower proponents) or as a free economic zone with liberal custom and tax regime and oriented towards Germany, Poland, or Scandinavian countries. This option is much more feasible.

2. The traditional industrial regions (the (b) group, consisting of machine-building including military-industrial enterprises, and light industry) are oriented towards the domestic market. This group of regions probably faces the most serious difficulties in the structural adjustment. The liberalisation of the economy makes the enterprises located here uncompetitive and doomed. The total industrial decline in these regions is the most remarkable.

These regions have very limited resources for an active foreign trade policy. Therefore, they are interested in close ties with the federal centre, budget support and getting their financial "cut" through the redistribution from rich areas. Dependent on state subsidies, these regions prefer stronger control from the centre over regional economies that would allow redistributive manoeuvring.

Being strongly oriented towards the domestic market they would favour protectionism and advocate not only the integrity of Russia but even the restoration of a united post-Soviet economic space.

3. The regions with self-sufficient agriculture. The (d) group may seek to form regional self-sustained food markets administratively providing a low level of prices (such as, in the region of Ulyanovsk). The main policy goal here is to preserve social and political stability and, therefore, to maintain the power of local elites. This is accompanied by administrative barriers blocking the free movement of goods and ultimately leads to autarchy. These regions may search for more independence from Moscow to protect themselves from more radical economic reforms imposed by the central government.

4. The ethnic regions constitute two different sub-groups:
- The depressed areas (mostly from the North Caucasus) where separatist ethnic factors dominate economic ones.
- The resource-rich areas (like Tatarstan, Bashkiria, Komi, or Karelia) where the ethnic and cultural identity may amplify economic interests, provoking regional elites to seek more independence from the federal government. For example, this resulted in the special agreement between Moscow and Tatarstan that provided the latter with more authority than other members of the Russian Federation.

These speculations are confirmed by special calculations.[5] The computations show that five regions from Central and Southern European Russia (North-West, Central, Volgo-Vyatsky, Black-Earth and North Caucasus) have minimal preconditions for economic separatism. Their economies are strongly oriented towards the domestic market and linked within the country. The potential for foreign trade and external expansion is minimal here. The regions are interested in the integrity of the country.

The Urals, Western Siberia and Povolzhye might get some economic benefits from the regional free trade strategy and, correspondingly, from political sovereignty. Nevertheless, social losses for this option are too high, which makes this scenario likely only in the case of deterioration in the general economic and political situation. This could be called "smouldering" sovereignty.

The Northern, the Eastern-Siberian and the Far-Eastern regions are more likely to benefit from the policy of economic sovereignty for economic, social and geographical reasons.

The structural inter-regional differentials determine the division of regions into those who give to the state budget and those who receive from it. Being aggravated by political factors, this division launches the complicated and contradictory process of bargaining between regions and the federal centre over budget issues.

Political Factors of Economic Separatism

The attitudes and behaviour of regional elites can strongly influence the region-to-region and centre-to-regions relationships. The collapse of the Soviet state has created an institutional void and allowed local leaders to increase their power at the expense of the diminished power of the central government. The squeezing of more independence and the threat of separatism have become powerful tools in the political and economic bargaining over taxes, subventions, privatisation rules and other sensitive issues. Boris Yeltsin's offer of sovereignty to local elites in 1991 did much to provoke their political and separatist ambitions. He did this to win in his struggle with Gorbachev but now it is working against him.

The regional leaders are preoccupied mostly with keeping and strengthening their power. This has a stronger impact on their policy than any initial pro-market or anti-market attitudes. For example, among the regions with the most rapid privatisation there are those led by reformists and those led by communists as well. Moscow, which is considered as one of the most pro-reformist territories, has moved at a very moderate pace in large-scale privatisation and has been disputing the general privatisation approach with the government. Moscow's Mayor, Yu. Luzhkov, who opposes the radical privatisation approach, has managed to get almost full control over ownership transfers in the city.

The same tendency can be seen in the case of price control policy. The Ulyanovsk pattern is probably the extreme one; nevertheless, in the majority of regions their authorities use elements of the same price control policy. The fact that the regional leaders are to be elected only strengthens the populist element in their strategies, provoking them to claim a "better" economic and social policy than Moscow.

Political preferences of the local elites are tied in with the attitudes of the population in these regions. Several elections (from the 1989 elections to the December 1993 elections) confirm the stability of electoral behaviour and show that different patterns of support for and opposition to the reforms are concentrated in specific geographic areas. This geography largely resembles the structural division of the country.

The political attitudes may be illustrated by the results of the December 1993 elections. The votes cast for the different parties show the variation between pro-liberal versus pro-conservative approaches on the one side, and federalist versus centralist attitudes on the other side.[6] The statistical analysis of the vote shows four major clusters of regions.

The first constellation of regions illustrates the disposition towards a more liberal economic policy. It includes the capitals (Moscow and St. Petersburg), the Northern areas that are rich in natural resources, the Far-Eastern regions and the most developed regions of the Urals. This is mostly groups (a) and (c) according to the structural classification developed here.

The second cluster is made up of the ethnic Russian and industrially less-developed regions with a relatively high rural and agricultural population. These regions oppose the pro-liberal economic policy and favour economic interventionism. At the same time, they support the idea of the strong centre dominating weak regions. This group includes some traditional regions in the South of European Russia and corresponds with group (d).[7]

The third cluster is characterised by the *"Strong Control Over the Economy"* plus *"Strong Regionalism"* attitude. A number of autonomous units favour this model of development. This group is led by Tuva, Kabardino-Balkaria, Ingushetia and Altay republic. As we see, it includes from the economic point of view the weakest regions with a strong element of traditionalism. They reject the rapid economic transformation and strive toward a local power which can defend them from the economic reforms pushed by Moscow.

The fourth group includes the remaining areas which are largely the industrial ones and belong to group (b). They have shown no specific preferences. The picture showing different clusters of regions may tell us about the nature of potential conflicts between them. The most fundamental political divergence is likely to happen between three groups of regions.

First, between the proponents of "strong periphery/liberal reforms" and "strong periphery/anti-reforms". This shapes up as a struggle between rich *oblasts* and autonomous republics (mostly the Northern) and the conservative Southern regions. The regional nature of conflicts between the various lobbyists, governmental officials and interest groups representing these regions has been already visible. However, the danger of a collapse of Russia due to their separatism is not great. Those regions inclined towards "strong periphery/anti-reform" attitude lack resources and are scattered throughout Russia. For the "strong periphery/pro-reform" regions, the level of support for economic reform tends to outweigh the support for a weak centre. Thus, these regions seem to have an agenda that would prevent them from cooperating with those who tend to support communists/agrarians.

Footnotes

1. *Regiony Rossii v perechodny period*, RSPiP, Moscow,1993.
2. Kommersant- Daily, 26 May, 1994.
3. Ibid.
4. Kommersant- Daily, 16 March,1995.
5. *Suverenitet regionov Rossii: politichesky mif ili ekonomicheskaya realnost?* (Sovereignty of Russian regions: political myth or economic reality?), *Delovoy mir*, 31 March, 1994.
6. See: D. Slider, V. Gimpelson, S. Chugrov, Political Tendencies in Russia's Regions: Evidence from the 1993 Parliamentary Elections, *Slavic Review*, Vol. 53, No. 3, Fall 1994, pp. 711-732.
7. This area was characterized by strong backing of both the Communists (and Agrarians) and Zhirinovsky's party.

BALANCE SHEET OF ECONOMIC REFORMS IN COOPERATION PARTNER COUNTRIES: THE CASE OF UKRAINE

Vladimir Kuznyetsov

Ukraine is moving as quickly as it can to reform its economy. Vladimir Kuznyetsov outlines the main aims of the reform package: these are to cut the budget deficit, reduce governement spending, and put an end to government interference in the economy. There have been successes: taxation has been reformed; prices have been freed; inflation has fallen (though it is still much too high); and the energy debt to Russia has been cut. Despite this progress, there is still resistance to be overcome. Privatisation, for example, had to be helped along by government decree. In mitigation, Vladimir Kuznyetsov points out that although reform policies may be second nature to the West, his country has lived under central planning for 70 years, and the old ways are not undone in three or four years.

Dr. Kuznyetsov is the Head, Department of the Economy, Administration of the President, Ukraine.

Ukraine has gained a new degree of international authority due to its resolute wish to establish itself as a sovereign nation of 50 million people in the heart of Europe. The Ukrainian people have democratically elected a new President, who, along with the entire leadership, understands how much remains to be done before Ukraine - a land of great natural, scientific and technological potential - can ensure an appropriate standard of living for her people.

President Kuchma announced a new economic strategy for Ukraine in October 1994, which is based upon the twin principles of market reform and financial stabilisation. This programme is supported by the Supreme Rada of Ukraine.

We have achieved success in implementing the first stage of reform, to the extent that some positive trends are now evident. For example, the collapse in output has now stopped, the volume of production is slowly increasing each quarter, whilst inflation is much reduced. Furthermore, the foreign trade and current account positions have also improved. But these positive trends are not yet secure. Economic policy must set itself tasks beyond the macro-level in order to stimulate production and improve social conditions. For this reason, the main aims of our current economic policy are to:

• Strengthen social welfare programmes.

• Accelerate privatisation.

• Carry out a more flexible agrarian policy.
• Stimulate production.
• Implement an active industrial policy.
• Boost investment.
• Strengthen government control over the reform process.

Budget Policy

In 1995, the main aims of fiscal policy are to reduce the deficit, increase revenue, and maintain financial discipline. On 6 April 1995, the Supreme Rada of Ukraine approved the state budget for 1995. This will:

• Reduce the budget deficit to 3.3 percent of GNP.
• Reduce overall expenditures by a sum equivalent to 6 percent of GNP.
• Decrease state subsidies by changing social protection systems.
• Sharply reduce state subsidies to industry.
• Exclude state purchases of agricultural products from the budget.
• Reduce levels of state investment.
• Fix cash limits on social programmes.
• Introduce a system of financial control.

In other words, we are eliminating, step-by-step, all main forms of state subsidy and price controls. Some social programmes will also be terminated. These measures will help to balance the state budget.

Monetary and Credit Policy

By making the Ukrainian currency internally convertible and by holding currency auctions on the Interbank Currency Exchange, the monetary environment in Ukraine has stabilised. This process was helped by introducing a tight monetary policy to reduce the rate of inflation. Moreover, re-financing credits issued by the National Bank of Ukraine are now distributed by credit auction, whilst interest rates have been adjusted according to the level of inflation. Thus interest rates have fallen from 252 percent in January to 75 percent in June.

Favourable pre-conditions for the introduction of a new currency now exist. These are price stabilisation, a market exchange rate, the receipt of external credits to cover the current account deficit and the acceleration of economic reform generally, especially of privatisation. Agreement has been reached in principle to go ahead with monetary reform this autumn.

Taxation Policy

Taxation policy aims to liberalise tax structures to reduce overall rates of taxation whilst widening the tax base. The main changes introduced by the government have therefore been to:
- Replace the general tax level of 22 percent with variable rates whereby agricultural firms pay 15 percent, manufacturing industry pays 30 percent, and the trade sector pays 45 percent.
- Reduce VAT from 28 percent to 20 percent.
- Reduce the maximum rate for personal income tax from 90 percent to 50 percent.
- Raise the domestic price of natural gas to $42 per 1,000 cubic metres.
- Abolish various tax privileges.
- Introduce a new law "On Enterprise Profit Taxing" combined with a 20-fold increase in land taxes to promote the efficiency of fixed capital use.

Price Policy

Since October 1994, new principles of price policy have been established to:
- Limit administrative fixing of prices to the bare minimum.
- Promote price liberalisation in general, especially in the fuel and energy sectors.
- Gradually remove the social expenses element from production prices.
- Liberalise prices generally to facilitate Ukraine's integration into the world economy.
- Restrict "shadow economy" activity.

Due to these measures, the budget deficit was reduced to 9.5 percent of GNP last year, whilst prices began to convey real information as to the supply and demand of goods. But price liberalisation also boosts inflation. Nevertheless, inflation during the first quarter of 1995 was 159 percent against a forecast of 178 percent, and the rate of growth in the external debt (due to energy imports) has dropped sharply. (But Ukraine's natural gas debt to Russia remains high. It increased from $0.25 billion to $1.41 billion over the first 10 months of 1994). Overall, these are positive developments. Finally, social assistance will be paid to poor people most at risk from price reform.

Privatisation

Delays in implementing the privatisation programme both in 1994 and this year have cost Ukraine. Presidential decrees aim to accelerate the process in 1995, and will:
- Institute a "mass privatisation" programme.

- Privatise about 8,000 large and medium-sized enterprises.
- Privatise fixed capital in the agriculture sector.
- Kick-start land reform and land privatisation.

Although small-scale privatisation has practically finished (with about 24,000 units - 90 percent now in private hands) - the slow rate of larger-scale privatisation is due to opposition in the Supreme Rada, which has failed both to approve the State Privatisation Programme, and to draft amendments to privatisation legislation.

Agricultural Sector

The absence of reform in this sector over the past few years has led to both infrastructural decay and hyper-inflation. The key issue is to dismantle administrative control, a process which has begun. More than four million people now own land as private property, accounting for 15 percent of all arable land and 40 percent of agricultural output in 1994. Now that land sales are legal, we expect this trend to continue. Furthermore, the substantial reduction in state orders and an end to the centralised distribution of inputs has stimulated market development. The volume of state orders has been reduced to just 5-6 percent of gross output with market prices being paid. Since January 1995, weekly commodity exchange sales of agricultural produce have been introduced, with a weekly turnover of about 12,000 billion karbovanets. The state remains the main buyer at this exchange.

Conclusion

I have just outlined for you the current economic situation and the state of the reform programme in Ukraine. Some of these measures may seem obvious to you, but are not obvious to the majority of our people who have lived under a command-economy for more than 70 years. The pace of reform is the key question, and we are moving forward as quickly as possible. In a few days, a new Government of Ukraine will be formed and a new Economic Programme will be proclaimed, which will build upon the President's "Annual Economic Report" delivered in April 1995. I hope that economic reform in Ukraine will win new support inside and outside my state.

ETAT DES REFORMES ECONOMIQUES A L'EST AU MILIEU DES ANNEES QUATRE-VINGT-DIX

Bilans de la transition

Gérard Wild

Il y a de multiples façons de rendre compte des transformations intervenues en Europe centrale et orientale et dans l'ex-Union soviétique. Trois d'entre elles sont ici présentées, qui éclairent chacune à sa manière le processus de transition vers le marché qui se déroule depuis le début des années quatre-vingt-dix dans l'ex-bloc soviétique.

Gérard Wild est Chef de Département au CEPII (Paris)

Analyses des performances

La première façon -la plus répandue- de faire un bilan de la transition est de dresser un état des lieux en termes d'indicateurs classiques renvoyant aux performances réalisées par les pays depuis qu'ils ont mis en place les politiques dites de stabilisation, premier élément de la stratégie de transition vers le marché. Composées de mesures de libéralisation (des prix, des activités, du commerce, du change) et de rigueur (monétaire, budgétaire, salariale, externe), ces politiques ont débouché sur des chutes de production et des déséquilibres prononcés.

Le bilan ici consiste tout d'abord à préciser, pays par pays, la rapidité, l'intensité et la cohérence de ces politiques de stabilisation et à relever, au fil du temps, l'évolution des indices (globaux et sectoriels) de production ainsi que de ceux qui révèlent les divers déséquilibres (inflation, chômage, déficit budgétaire, solde des opérations courantes). Une des observations qui permet cette présentation est la variété des situations nationales. Elle montre également le lien très clair qu'il y a entre la mise en place de politiques de stabilisation cohérentes d'une part, la reprise de la croissance et la maîtrise des équilibres macro-économiques d'autre part.

Les bilans en termes de performances autorisent ainsi à établir des hiérarchies entre les différents pays et à classer ces derniers par groupes. Si la dimension "libéralisation" est désormais claire dans tous les pays, l'aspect "rigueur" est encore dans beaucoup de cas imparfait. En dehors des pays où règne une situation de guerre, cette difficulté à assurer la régulation macro-économique de l'économie vient pour une bonne part de la fragilité des situations politiques.

Celles-ci, elles-mêmes, renvoient aux craintes que fait naître l'impact social de la première étape de la transition (baisse des revenus, montée de l'inégalité et de l'insécurité). Ces craintes au demeurant sont fondées : en témoigne le vote des électeurs en faveur des partis "ex-communistes" dans les pays où les politiques de stabilisation ont donné leurs premiers résultats positifs.

C'est sur cette incertitude concernant les attitudes sociales que se concentre la part prospective de ces bilans. Les risques sociaux en effet sont de nature à freiner la tenue des objectifs de rigueur, pourtant indispensables, ou à les fragiliser là où ils existent. Par ailleurs, les conditions de fonctionnement des institutions du marché sont encore imparfaites. D'où une grande prudence concernant l'avenir, même à court terme, et une grande sensibilité des analyses aux climats sociaux et politiques dans les pays en transition. Cette même incertitude conduit le plus souvent à souligner le rôle décisif joué par l'assistance occidentale publique (financière, technique, commerciale) au cours des premières années et l'importance qu'elle aura encore au cours des années à venir, avant que le secteur privé occidental confirme le frémissement dans l'intérêt qu'il porte aux nouveaux marchés.

Réformes structurelles

L'analyse des performances est évidemment indissociable de celle de la transformation en profondeur des règles du jeu et des structures d'organisation de la vie économique. Politiques de stabilisation et réformes structurelles s'appuient en effet les unes sur les autres pour créer une sorte de synergie dont l'issue est la banalisation des trajectoires et des fonctionnements. L'une de ces réformes structurelles -la privatisation- fait l'objet d'une attention toute particulière. Mais d'autres sont également sous le regard, tant leur signification dans l'évaluation prospective est grande.

Règlements et lois

Une des productions les plus vivaces au cours des premières années de la transition est celles de textes réglementant les nouveaux contours de l'activité des agents économiques internes et externes. De ce point de vue, tous les pays ou presque disposent aujourd'hui d'un nouvel arsenal de textes relatifs au droit des affaires, à la vie des entreprises, à la fiscalité, au fonctionnement du système bancaire, aux relations économiques extérieures, à la participation des entreprises étrangères au développement des marchés. Un des aspects intéressants de la prolifération -nécessaire- de cet ensemble de textes est qu'ils permettent à chacun de ces pays de trouver sa voie propre parmi les multiples possibilités d'organisation de la vie économique. Un autre aspect essentiel de cette dimension de la transition est que l'application de ces textes bute sur l'inégale préparation des agents. Ce phénomène révèle ainsi une des difficultés essentielles de la transition : l'intériorisation par les sociétés des règles du jeu du marché.

Privatisation

C'est sur la transformation du système de propriété qu'une grande partie de l'attention des acteurs et des observateurs est portée. On note partout le développement de la petite propriété, par la création de petites entreprises autorisées dans le cadre de la libération des activités ainsi que par la "petite privatisation", réalisée aujourd'hui dans de fortes proportions dans la plupart des pays en transition. On observe également l'extension de la propriété privée au travers de procédures classiques de privatisation du secteur public : rachat des entreprises par les salariés, ventes directes aux nationaux et, dans de nombreux cas, aux étrangers. C'est l'ensemble des obstacles à la privatisation des économies (juridiques, économiques, sociaux, politiques) qui en ralentissait la progression et a engendré des formules originales de distribution gratuite de la propriété publique dans le cadre de programmes de "privatisation de masse". Formellement donc, une partie non négligeable des Produits Nationaux (plus de la moitié souvent) relève du secteur privé. Pour autant cette nouvelle structure de la propriété est souvent considérée comme "nominale", tant les difficultés de la restructuration en profondeur des entreprises restent pesantes, tant la capacité à engager des stratégies de reconversion est encore limitée.

Intermédiation

D'autres réformes "structurelles" sont en cours, avec là aussi un inégal succès selon les pays. Parmi elles, celle du système financier et bancaire apparaît comme cruciale et délicate. Sans doute quasiment partout un système bancaire à deux niveaux a-t-il été instauré. Sans doute également assiste-t-on à la montée du secteur privé et à la mise en place d'institutions et de mécanismes caractéristiques des économies de marché. Mais la capacité de ces systèmes d'intermédiation financière à assurer l'ajustement souple d'une épargne rare et d'un investissement peu actif (à de rares occasions près) fait problème. La fragilité du système bancaire, chargé d'un lourd héritage (ancien et récent) d'impayés, encore largement attaché à des entreprises publiques au destin incertain et insuffisamment doté de compétences, est aux yeux de nombre d'observateurs un des aspects les plus lourds à gérer pour l'avenir de la transition.

Ce que nous apprend la transition sur la transition

De cet ensemble d'observations sur les performances et l'avancée des réformes structurelles ressort, petit à petit, une meilleure compréhension de ce que sont les logiques de la transition. Sans doute serait-il par trop ambitieux d'élaborer encore une véritable théorie de ce phénomène historique nouveau. Du moins est-on en mesure de proposer, à titre d'intrants primaires de la réflexion, quelques pistes plus affirmées que celles que l'intuition avait suggéré au départ de la transition.

La destruction créatrice

L'idée que la transition vers le marché visait à mettre en place dans les pays de l'Est des structures de production correspondant mieux que par le passé à la demande sociale réelle et susceptibles de fonctionner sous contrainte de productivité et de compétitivité n'est certes pas neuve. Telle qu'elle se déroule, la transformation en cours dans l'ex-Union soviétique et en Europe centrale et orientale montre qu'en effet c'est à un vaste processus de réaffectation des facteurs de production vers les lieux de demande et de compétitivité désormais révélés par le cadre général des politiques de stabilisation qu'on assiste. De ce point de vue cependant, on voit bien que le phénomène n'est pas, au total, aussi clair qu'on l'envisageait. A cela, il est des raisons qui tiennent au fait qu'une partie des destructions de capacités tient à des ruptures (celle du Comecon, celle de l'URSS) qui débouchent sur des restructurations radicales dont il n'est pas sûr encore qu'elles soient justifiées du point de vue de la rationalité économique et donc durables. De la même façon, l'absence de stabilisation macro-économique dans beaucoup de pays rend encore peu assurée l'identification précise des parties du tissus économique à rénover. D'où la pertinence et l'importance du débat sur la protection des entreprises notamment du secteur industriel et, plus largement, sur la mise en place de politiques structurelles nationales.

La fonction de transition

Une autre intuition se trouve confirmée par ce bilan des premières années de la transition : l'inégale préparation des pays à l'absorption des chocs que le processus implique. A cet égard, les évolutions observées permettent de comprendre que le poids de l'héritage du point de vue des structures productives, des mécanismes de décision et des comportements a joué un rôle décisif dans la différenciation spatiale et temporelle des processus de transformation. Elles ont permis de saisir ainsi que la fonction de transition n'était pas dépendante que des facteurs "marché" et "héritage socialiste" mais aussi qu'elle devait prendre en compte un facteur "histoire", tant il est vrai que chaque pays se voyait confronté à la nécessité de se forger, sur ce chemin, sa propre identité. Dans le champ de la transformation économique, ce facteur joue un rôle non négligeable. On en voudra pour preuve l'importance prise par la réflexion sur l'histoire économique d'avant la période socialiste, sur les législations alors en vigueur, etc... Sans vouloir, comme parfois c'est le cas, verser dans le déterminisme historique, on soulignera combien la transition se révèle par là, nécessairement spécifique pour chaque pays.

Le changement dans l'allocation de ressources

La transition est un changement visant à réaliser une allocation des ressources plus efficiente socialement et économiquement. Ce bouleversement systémique nécessite que soient réalisées trois transformations centrales. Il y a d'une part les techniques de l'allocation de ressources (monnaie, prix, ...). Il y a d'autre part la répartition du pouvoir d'allocation de ressources entre les agents (privatisation, intermédiation, décentralisation). Il y a enfin l'adoption d'un nouveau regard de la société sur les règles et les implications de la nouvelle modalité d'allocation de ressources. Dans tous les pays, cette triple modification (technique, institutionnelle, culturelle) est amorcée. Mais le problème essentiel est que le délai de maturation et de stabilisation de chacune d'entre elles est variable dans le temps, relativement bref pour la première, plus long pour la seconde et surtout la troisième. De ce décalage dans les temps de maturation naissent les troubles, les incertitudes et le retard dans la mise en évidence de l'efficacité du changement, et donc les risques de sa remise en cause ou de sa dérive. Pour l'heure, il ne semble pas que ces risques puissent aller jusqu'à revenir vers l'arrière. Mais les dérapages nés de la déception, eux, ne sont pas exclus. Le maintien de l'assistance occidentale est, de ce point de vue, plus que jamais nécessaire.

* * *

De ce "bilan des bilans", il faut sans doute retenir l'ampleur du chemin parcouru par les pays en transition tout autant que les difficultés qu'ils ont rencontrées. Sur ce point, et quelle que soit la manière dont on regarde cette transition, on retiendra une conclusion qui semble ne faire aucun doute : la rupture avec l'ancien système d'allocation de ressources est consommée. Sans doute l'héritage pèse-t-il encore d'un poids élevé. Mais dans ce voyage de Colomb -dont on ignorait à son départ la durée et l'aboutissement- le point de non retour est atteint.

Que cette traversée puisse réserver encore des surprises ne fait non plus aucun doute. Certaines d'entre elles risquent même de créer de graves déséquilibres nationaux, régionaux, internationaux. Aucune prospective alarmiste ne doit être rejetée. Il reste que l'ancien bloc soviétique est d'ores et déjà inscrit sur une trajectoire de "banalisation" internationale. Ceci signifie qu'à l'intérieur d'une grille de lecture générale -la transition- utilisable encore longtemps pour l'évaluation, chaque composante de l'ensemble devient un élément dont l'approche doit de plus en plus être fondée sur les atouts et les handicaps spécifiques.

PANEL II

Living Standards and Social Welfare

Chair: Daniel George, Director
NATO Economics Directorate

Panelists: Michael Ellman
Lubomir Filipov
Yuri Khromov
Fikret Pashayaev
Domenico Mario Nuti

LIVING STANDARDS AND SOCIAL WELFARE

Michael Ellman

Depending on which international institution's statistics you choose to chart the economic and social evolution in Eastern Europe and the former Soviet Union, the same country can be presented as 'progressing nicely toward full recovery' or 'in serious decline'. The truth, believes Professor Michael Ellman, lies somewhere in between. While most of the international statistics available are produced by professionals using sound methods, they often do not take into account the unreliability and fast-changing nature of the markets they are measuring. Two examples of this are the tendency of producers to conceal part or all of their output to escape taxation and the fact that - in Russia, for example - the networks which provide trade and economic statistics are not in place and do not cover all regions and sectors of activity.

Michael Ellman is Professor at the Department of Microeconomics, University of Amsterdam.

Introduction

It is well known that after 1989 there was a sharp fall in living standards and social welfare throughout the region, with a big difference between countries. Data on this were presented at this Colloquium two years ago by Michel Gaspard.[1] The purpose of this paper is to update his contribution and also discuss certain social indicators which he did not analyse.

Data Problems

The data available to analyse living standards and social welfare are not very reliable. There are three reasons for this; structural change, change in statistical methods, and the survival of old problems.

Statistical time series are most useful when the structure of whatever it is that is being measured remains unchanged. The reason for this is that one can be reasonably sure that a measured change is a real change and not merely a statistical artefact resulting from a change in the structure of what is being measured. In Central and Eastern Europe, however, a number of important structural changes have taken place which makes the meaning of many statistics problematic.

Particularly important structural changes are the ending of shortages and queues, the growth of the private sector and the emergence of a multiplicity of actors in foreign trade. The transition from widespread shortages and queues to the general availability of goods for those with money, means that the conventional measures of "real income" (i.e. money incomes deflated by a price index) do not properly capture the relative incomes of the population before and after this very important systemic change. For example, the IMF has more than once published figures showing a growth in Soviet real incomes (or "statistical real incomes") in 1987-91, despite the fact that welfare obviously declined in this period. The confusion arises because inadequate account is taken of the worsening shortages in the USSR in 1987-91.

Another fundamental structural change has been the growth of the private sector. This has probably led to an understatement of the level of output in recent years, and possibly also to its rate of growth. The reason is that a substantial part of the private sector is eager to conceal part or all of its output/income in order to escape taxes. Furthermore, the end of the state monopoly of foreign trade has also had consequences for foreign trade statistics. Whereas it was fairly easy to collect accurate foreign trade statistics when foreign trade was carried out by a small number of state organisations, it is much more difficult when it is carried out by a large number of actors. This is one of the reasons for the notorious inaccuracy of Russian foreign trade statistics.

The end of communism has been accompanied by important changes in statistical methods. One such change has been the transition from the MPS (material product system) method for the compilation of the national income accounts to the SNA (system of national accounts) method. This change, which began many years ago in Central Europe and which has not yet been completed in parts of the CIS, is a complex matter which raises many difficulties and automatically makes national income statistics from before and after the change non-comparable (unless they are specially adjusted). Another statistical change is the transition from complete enumeration, which characterised the communist statistical system, to sampling. The latter is in general more sensible and produces reliable results, provided that the sample is representative. Naturally, national statistical offices require time to learn how to use the new methods. During this learning period they may fall victim to various childhood diseases.

Some old statistical problems have survived the transformation. For example, the Soviet family budget survey, although based on a large sample, was notoriously unrepresentative and unreliable. The same is true of its continuation, the Russian family budget survey. Similarly, the cause of death data in many countries, derived from death certificates, is of distinctly low quality. For example, an examination by the German Federal Statistical Office of 2,500 randomly selected GDR death certificates found inconsistencies between the examiner's report and the recorded cause of death in nearly 40 percent of cases. In 15 percent of them major errors were evident.[2] It is likely that such errors continue to be widespread in Central and Eastern Europe.

Because of these statistical problems, it is difficult to get a clear and unambiguous picture of what has really happened in the last few years. This is one of the factors explaining why different people and organisations have quite different images of what has happened to living standards and social welfare during the transition. For example, IMF publications show a decline in Russian real wages between 1987 and 1994, but the decline is not very sharp and much less than the fall in statistically measured output.[3] Similarly, in a recent draft paper about Russia two IMF economists state that "Taking into account estimates for street and informal trade, retail sales declined only marginally in 1991 and 1992, and have been rising anew since 1993."[4] On the whole it is fair to say that the IMF picture is of a decline in living standards in some countries in some periods, but basically nothing dramatic. On the other hand, according to UNICEF,[5] "The mortality and health crisis burdening most Eastern European countries since 1989 is without precedent in the European peacetime history of this century. It signals a societal crisis of unexpected proportions, unknown implications and uncertain solutions."

My view lies between these two positions. I do not share the self-satisfied view of the IMF. It seems to me clear that at any rate in some countries there have been serious declines in social welfare which are usually ignored in IMF analyses. (This is understandable in a financial organisation which is primarily concerned with monetary variables.) On the other hand, although I think that UNICEF has played a very positive role in collecting data on social welfare in Central and Eastern Europe and publicising them, I do not agree with some of the colourful adjectives UNICEF has used to attract publicity for the problems. For example, the idea that the recent increase in the crude death rate in Russia is "apocalyptic"[6] is completely absurd in the light of the demographic history of Russia/USSR in the twentieth century.[7]

Inequality

Accurate data on inequality in Central and Eastern Europe at the present time are difficult to gather for three reasons. First, for measuring the relationship between high and low incomes it is naturally particularly important to have accurate data on the highest and lowest incomes. Actually, however, it is usually much more difficult to collect these than to collect accurate data on the middle of the income distribution. The reason for this is that at the top of the income distribution people may be particularly anxious to keep their income from the knowledge of the tax authorities, and at the bottom of the income distribution it may be difficult to get reliable data because the people are not officially registered, move house frequently, are only partially literate, are in trouble with the authorities, etc.

Hence data about the relationship between the highest and lowest incomes are particularly unreliable. Secondly, the transition from a society in which a large part of inequality was formed by non-cash privileges (e.g. access to high quality cheap housing or restricted access shops) to one in which inequality is largely a monetary phenomenon, may confuse interpretation of the data (this is an example of structural change). Thirdly, the existence of substantial price and income differences within a country may generate a spuriously high level of "inequality". This is particularly the case in Russia, where prices (and incomes) vary sharply across that huge country.

According to the World Bank researcher Milanovic, "On average, income inequality has increased by around 5 to 6 Gini points, from about 24 in 1987 to about 30 in 1993, with the greatest increases in the Baltics, followed by Russia, Bulgaria, the Czech Republic and Poland. (The Gini coefficient measures the inequality of income distribution, the maximum being 100 points. Absolute equality measures 0.) This five-to-six point increase is about half of what occurred in the United Kingdom during Margaret Thatcher's ten-year rule. In Eastern Europe and the FSU, however, the change occurred in four to five years, so the intensity of change was about the same. A Gini coefficient of about 30 is still not high, relative to many middle income countries, but exceeds that in many OECD countries, among them the Scandinavian countries, Belgium, Holland, and Germany."[8] In addition to the increase in inequality within countries, it is likely that there has also been an increase in inequality between countries.

Whether or not this "Thatcherisation" of Central and Eastern Europe was desirable, is naturally a matter on which opinions differ.

Employment and Unemployment

The sharp decline in employment in Central and Eastern Europe is a phenomenon to which the ECE in particular has drawn attention.[9] In 1990-92 employment fell by 29 percent in Bulgaria, 18 percent in Slovenia, 13 percent in Poland and 9 percent in the Czech Republic. Partly this led to a growth in measured unemployment, which by the end of 1993 had reached 16 percent in Bulgaria and Poland and 14 percent in Slovakia. (By the end of 1994, measured unemployment ranged from about 3.5 percent in the Czech Republic to 19 percent in the former Yugoslav Republic of Macedonia.) Partly it led to a decline in the participation rate. The decline in employment in industry and agriculture was necessary because of low levels of labour productivity in those sectors under the old regime and the sharp falls in production which have taken place. Further declines in employment and increases in unemployment can be expected in some countries.

Unemployment has become a serious problem for particular groups of the population (e.g. school leavers, gypsies, the elderly), for particular occupations (e.g. missile engineers and coal miners), and for particular regions (e.g. in

Russia for towns in the far north and former military-industrial towns, and in many rural regions throughout the area).

The decline in employment and growth of unemployment can be evaluated in various ways. The emergence of unemployment as an ever present reality throughout the region may well have a positive effect on work effort and motivation. Many people consider that the employment of women under the old regime was excessive and the withdrawal of some of them from the labour force is a positive development. On the other hand, large scale unemployment among young men will obviously stimulate crime and threaten social order. (In 1991-93 the Russian homicide rate doubled, and in 1993 was about three times that of the USA and 15 times that of Italy.)

Similarly, the expulsion of elder people from the labour force has often been very disagreeable for them, harming both their incomes and their self-esteem. Furthermore, the decline in demand for certain skills has naturally hit the people concerned very badly. A positive aspect of the decline in employment has been the recent rapid growth of industrial labour productivity in a number of countries. For example, in Poland in 1994 labour productivity in manufacturing rose by 12.5 percent (this followed increases also in 1992 and 1993). Similarly, labour productivity in manufacturing in Hungary rose by 7.9 percent in 1994 (after rising by 12.6 percent in 1992 and 16 percent in 1993). In the Czech Republic it rose by 5.7 percent in 1994 (after declines in 1990-93). These sharp increases resulted from a resumption of economic growth combined with restructuring.[10] They are positive developments for the international competitiveness of these countries.

Poverty

There are a variety of estimates about the proportion of the population in the region in poverty and the changes in this proportion during the transformation. Naturally, the proportion of a population living in "poverty" always depends on where the "poverty" line is drawn. By drawing it lower one always reduces the proportion, by drawing it higher one increases it. Since the cut-off point is always essentially arbitrary, it is not surprising that there are a variety of different estimates in circulation. One estimate is that of UNICEF, which calculates that in 1993 in Bulgaria 26 percent of the population lived in extreme poverty, and that in 1992 the corresponding figures were 1 percent in the Czech Republic, 15 percent in Poland, 19 percent in Romania and 23 percent in Russia.

Milanovic has compared the proportion of the population of the region living in poverty before the transformation began and after it. He used a common poverty line ($120/month/capita in 1990 international prices). He came to the conclusion that whereas in 1987-88 only eight million people (about 3 percent of the population) lived in poverty, by 1992-93 (or 1994) this figure had risen to 58 million or 18 percent of the population. This result, of 50 million new poor arising from the transformation, is a very striking, and very sad, result. Of these 50 million new poor, more than 40 million live in the three Slavic states of the FSU. In the Czech Republic, Slovakia, Slovenia and Hungary, poverty defined in this way scarcely exists, since the cut-off point chosen is low compared to incomes in these countries. The only positive finding by Milanovic is that, unlike in Latin America, the poor do not - yet - represent a distinct underclass. They are currently reasonably integrated into society. It will require the maintenance of the present situation for some time to generate an underclass that is only weakly integrated into the wider society.

Mortality

In Russia and Ukraine there has been a sharp increase in mortality. A small increase in mortality also took place in Bulgaria (in 1989-93). The crude death rate in Russia has risen from 11.4 (per thousand inhabitants) in 1991 to 12.2 in 1992, 14.5 in 1993 and 15.6 in 1994. This was an increase of 37 percent in the three years 1992-94, a remarkable demographic phenomenon. Although it was partially a result of an ageing of the population, it was mainly a result of increases in the age-specific death rates. This increase in mortality and its ultimate causes, have already given rise to extensive discussion.[11] Two ways of presenting the significance of these mortality data in easy to comprehend forms are to estimate excess mortality and life expectancy.

It seems likely that in 1990-94 excess mortality in the whole of the former USSR arising from the increase in age-specific mortality rates was about 1.5 million. (This is about one and a half times excess mortality in the 1947 Soviet famine.) In 1987-94 Russian male life expectancy at birth fell by about eight years, from 65 to 57. The latter is a very poor figure in international perspective. Not only is it well below the advanced countries, but it is also below the middle income countries such as Turkey or Brazil, at the level of Indonesia in the late 1980s, and only two years above the Indian level of the early 1980s.

The only positive aspect of the Russian mortality data is that it seems to have stopped increasing. In the first quarter of 1995 the crude death rate was 15.7, which was 3 percent below the level of the first quarter of 1994. This gives rise to the hope that Russian mortality peaked in 1994 and will fall this year. (It should however be pointed out that these date are not comprehensive since they exclude Chechnya, where mortality has not declined in 1995.)

These figures are not just a curiosum for historical demographers. It is entirely possible that in the Duma elections in December 1995 and the Presidential elections of summer 1996 the nationalists and communists will make an issue of the "genocide against the Russian people" of which the West is allegedly guilty.

Morbidity

"The past four years [i.e. 1990-93] have witnessed a persistence or resurgence of several 'poverty diseases', including infectious, parasitic and sexually-transmitted diseases. Children are the most likely victims of these ailments. The situation regarding the incidence of diphtheria, tuberculosis and hepatitis started to deteriorate in 1990 and 1991, worsened in 1992, and has now reached epidemic proportions in some areas. There are also signs that these diseases are slowly spreading to previously unaffected areas."[12] Russia is still experiencing diphtheria and syphilis epidemics and a steady growth of tuberculosis. In the first four months of 1995, in Russia the incidence of diphtheria rose by 75 percent over one year earlier, of syphilis by 146 percent and of tuberculosis by 9 percent.[13] As in most welfare indicators, there is a sharp difference both in levels and in trends, between countries of the region. For example, UNICEF has drawn attention to the decline in the incidence of tuberculosis after 1992 in the Czech Republic.[14]

Improvements

The sharp deterioration in welfare in recent years has been one of the results of the collapse of Communism and of the depression. Now that the depression has been replaced in many countries by economic growth, one would expect to see an improvement. Even when the economy grows, however, it is not always the case that consumption also grows. It could be that the additional resources are devoted to improving the external balance (which is necessary in Hungary) or to investment or to government expenditures. Furthermore, even if average consumption grows, it may be that the consumption of those at the bottom of the income distribution may not do so. Nevertheless, if real GDP in a country with a more or less stable population grows by 5 percent or more, then average consumption is likely to grow and also the consumption of most of the population is likely to grow. According to the EBRD *Transition report update* five countries of the region are likely to have a real GDP growth of 5 percent or more in 1995. They are, Albania, the Czech Republic, Estonia, Poland and Slovenia. In all these countries, it seems likely that average consumption will rise in 1995. For a large part of the population in a number of countries, the transformation crisis is receding into the past.

Effects

It seems likely that the situation described above has had and will have four effects:

- It is a tragedy for many of the people directly affected and their relatives and friends. Those who are part of the additional deaths or additional cases of various unpleasant diseases are of course victims of disagreeable social and epidemiological processes.

• This situation is partly the responsibility of the West. Having devoted enormous resources to struggling against Communism, and having encouraged the people of Central and Eastern Europe to destroy Communism, the West declined to launch a "new Marshall Plan" (although it did provide substantial gross resources for the countries of Central and Eastern Europe). With the exception of the former GDR, the people of Central and Eastern Europe did not receive the massive net transfers from the West than many of them had previously hoped for and expected.

• The social costs of the transformation were one of the reasons for the electoral victories of the post-communists in a number of countries (Lithuania, Bulgaria, Poland and Hungary). It seems likely that in the forthcoming Russian Duma and Presidential elections these social costs will also be a factor influencing the results. Russia, however, does not have a post-communist party, but a genuine old-fashioned Communist party. This is the strongest political party in the country and is likely to fare relatively well. So may other nationalist and anti-Western groups as the (surviving) victims of the policies of the past few years express their discontent.

• It will strengthen the self-confidence of the local liberals[15] and of the international financial institutions. The five countries listed above as likely to fare well in 1995, are all countries that have pursued fairly orthodox economic policies, usually in collaboration with the international financial institutions. Those countries in the region which have done something very different have not fared better, usually just the reverse. Officials from the countries which are the principal shareholders in the international financial institutions can be satisfied that by and large those institutions have fulfilled the task assigned to them.

Footnotes

1. M. Gaspard, Incomes and living standards in Central and Eastern Europe and the former Soviet republics: recent developments, current situation and outlook, *Economic developments in cooperation partner countries from a sectoral perspective* (NATO, Brussels, 1993).
2. N. Eberstadt, Demographic shocks in Eastern Germany, *Europe-Asia Studies* 1994, vol 46 no. 3 p. 529.
3. *Russian Federation,* IMF Economic Reviews 16, 1994 (IMF, Washington DC, 1995) table 17 p.78. (This table does show a very sharp fall in real pensions.)
4. V. Koen & M. Marrese, 'Stabilization and structural change in Russia, 1992-94' mimeo March 1995 pp 10-11.
5. *Public policy and social conditions,* Regional Monitoring Report no. 1 (UNICEF, Florence, 1993) & *Crisis in mortality, health and nutrition,* Regional Monitoring Report no. 2 (UNICEF, Florence, 1994).
6. *Public policy and social conditions,* Regional Monitoring Report no. 1 (UNICEF, Florence, 1993) p. 20.
7. It is characteristic of UNICEF's knowledge of Russian/Soviet affairs, that when comparing current mortality increases with World War II, it uses for Soviet excess mortality in World War II not the currently available best estimate (26-27 million) but the Stalinist falsification (7 million). See *Crisis in mortality, health and nutrition,* Regional Monitoring Report no. 2 (UNICEF, Florence, 1994) p.46.
8. *Transition* (World Bank) vol. 5 no. 8 October 1994.
9. *Economic Survey of Europe in 1993-1994* (ECE, UN, New York & Geneva 1994) pp 84-85.
10. For these figures see *Transition report update* (EBRD, London, 1995) p. 9.
11. *Crisis in mortality, health and nutrition,* Regional Monitoring Report no. 2 (UNICEF, Florence, 1994); M. Ellman, The increase in death and disease under 'katastroika', *Cambridge Journal of Economics* vol/ 18 no. 4 August 1994; J. Nell & K. Stewart, *Death in transition: The rise in the death rate in Russia since 1992* (Innocenti Occasional Papers EPS 45, UNICEF, Florence, 1994); J. Shapiro, The Russian mortality crisis and its causes, A. Aslund (ed) *Russian economic reform at risk* (Pinter, London & New York, 1995).
12. *Crisis in mortality, health and nutrition,* Regional Monitoring Report no. 2 (UNICEF, Florence 1994) pp. 54-55.
13. *Zdorov'e naseleniya i sreda obitaniya* 1995 no. 5 p. 19.
14. *Crisis in mortality, health and nutrition,* Regional Monitoring Report no. 2 (UNICEF, Florence, 1994) p. 55.
15. The word "liberal" is used here in the European sense.

THE TRANSITION OF THE BULGARIAN ECONOMY: IS THE SOCIAL PRICE TOO HIGH?

Lubomir Filipov

The people of Bulgaria are paying a high price for economic reform. Three quarters of the population earns less than a living wage; unemployment is high; and social security funds are down. Lubomir Filipov notes that things might get worse before they get better. The high inflation rate (121 percent in 1994) means that the current tight monetary policy cannot be relaxed. The country's only hope is that the private sector will come to the rescue of the economy - but to do so, it will have to get a lot bigger.

Lubomir Filipov is the Deputy Governor of the Bulgarian National Bank, Sofia.

The restrictive monetary policy of the Bulgarian National Bank induced a real decrease in household savings and a sharp contraction of the household credits in real terms for the same period.

At least two questions should be asked: firstly: "Has this price been bearable?"; *and secondly: "Has the outcome been worth the high social price?"*

The answers tend to be negative - in 1994 74 percent of households existed on less than the living wage but the inflation rate (CPI) was 121 percent. Nevertheless the necessity for further financial stabilisation in the country calls for future restrictive monetary and wage policies and future budgetary constraints. Any possible relaxation of the restrictions can be done only on the basis of a rapid increase of the private sector share.

It may seem unusual that a central banker discusses the issues of living standards and social welfare. Simply because - in the developing countries in general - central bankers have always been regarded as being on the other side of the "barricade", and by their restrictive monetary policy "spoil" the living standards. But this is only half true. The central banker is often restrictive in the short run, while aiming for a long-term sustainable growth and hence, an increase in living standards.

Let us see the effect that five years of transition in Bulgaria to a market-driven economy have had on the Bulgarians' way of living. The average real salary in the country shrank in 1994 by 44 percent compared to the 1990 figure. Wages dropped from 5.8 percent of GDP in 1992 to 4.9 percent in 1994 and social security funds from 13.5 to 11.9 percent of GDP. The unemployment rate reached 20 percent of the active population.

What was the responsibility of the central bank for these consequences? In early 1991 the Bulgarian National Bank began the reform with a huge money overhang - the money supply was considerably higher than GDP. More than half of the money supply was held by households. Hence a very restrictive monetary policy was inevitable. Real positive rates on credits were influenced by the interest rate policy of the central bank. The burden of this financial disproportion was so huge it had to be shared between the budget, the banks and also the households. This led to real negative interest rates on the deposit side.

The restrictive monetary policy of the Bulgarian National Bank induced a decrease of household deposit stocks in the banks in real terms, and a sharp contraction of the households credit in real terms for the same period. While the household savings stock in the banks dropped in real terms, the share of the savings in their total expenditure increased.

According to the statistical data, in 1994 the real average wage was 56 percent, and the real average pension 53 percent of those in 1990.

The quasi-fiscal deficits in the form of losses in the real and financial sectors have been only barely reduced. The need for further financial stabilisation in the country means future restrictive monetary and wage policies and future budgetary constraints. A possible relaxation of the restrictions can be allowed only on the basis of a rapid increase of the private sector share. In this area, including in the financial sector, foreign investments have to play a very important role.

However, the very restrictive monetary policy in the second half of 1994 brought some positive results. Since the beginning of the year the exchange rate of the Bulgarian Ley has been rather stable and the average monthly inflation rate (CPI) for the last three months was below 2 percent. For the same period, the rates on household deposits have been positive.

The phenomenon of households being almost net creditors to the financial system must be handled separately by a central banker. On the one hand, in these circumstances the restrictive monetary policy cannot affect that part of the money supply. On the other hand, any further restriction on incomes seems unbearable. So the only possible way to stabilise the monetary supply is to provide incentives for the households to invest in privatisation or in government securities.

CURRENT FOOD SITUATION IN RUSSIA AND PROSPECTS OF AGRARIAN REFORM

Yuri Khromov

Once the post-Soviet Agricultural sector went into a free-fall, the government rapidly recognised that this reform process required special attention - due to its delicate 'food-security' implications. But the government's new role is not to provide food, says Yuri Khromov, but to create the conditions in which private enterprise can satisfy the population's appetite. In the meantime, several million private plots located across the country are filling the gap left by the decline in state production.

Yuri Khromov is the Head of the Economics Department of Russia's Institute for Strategic Studies.

This paper discusses four issues: the crisis in Russian agriculture, the current situation on the national food market, and the status and prospects of agrarian reform, agricultural imports and food security.

For the last four years (1991-1994) the volume of gross agricultural production in Russia fell by 25 percent. In 1994 overall gross production fell by 9 percent, grain output fell by almost 20 percent and the number of cattle decreased by 10 percent.

Per capita consumption of almost all basic foodstuffs has diminished dramatically in the last five years. In 1994, per capita meat consumption fell back to the 1970 level, and the supply of milk products fell to the 1960 level.

Agrarian reform continues in Russia. Almost all former collective and state enterprises were re-registered, 55 percent of them became joint-stock corporations and partnerships, 10 percent were organised as independent cooperatives. There were 280,000 private farms at the end of 1994, and some 11 million ha of land are now owned by private farms (5 percent of all agricultural land).

Grain imports (now on a commercial basis) decreased in 1994 by 19 percent - the year in which the state stopped importing grain. The quality of imported foods in Russia is often very low, and in its current food situation, the country is starting to look like middle-income countries in the Third World.

General Crisis - Russian Agriculture in the 1990s

The structural crisis of Russian agriculture has been underway for the past 10-15 years, before the creation of the "former USSR". Being a large importer of agricultural produce this country was not able to secure high and stable growth rates for national agricultural production that were comparable to other importing countries. Though the former Soviet Union maintained rates of agricultural growth that were comparable to other exporting countries - namely the USA, France and Australia (Table I).

In today's unreliable situation, Russia shows no signs of positive agricultural development. For the last four years (1991-1994) the volume of gross agricultural production fell by 25 percent. The recession in Russian industry was even deeper - 44 percent for the four years. These figures were presented by the Russian Vice-Premier Alexander Zaveruha (in charge of agriculture) at the All-Russian Economic Congress on Stabilisation and Development of the APK (AIC - Agro-Industrial Complex) last March in Moscow. Mr. Zaveruha underlined that in 1994 crop production fell by 22 percent, and the livestock output decreased by 28 percent in comparison with the period of 1986-1989.[1]

Table I
Indexes of agricultural and food production in large countries and regions of the world (1979-81=100)

	Agricultural production				Food production			
	overall		per capita		overall		per capita	
	1980-2	1990-2	1980-2	1990-2	1980-2	1990-2	1980-2	1990-2
FUSSR	100	108	100	99	100	110	99	101
USA	102	108	101	97	102	108	101	97
China	105	163	104	139	104	161	102	137
France	101	106	101	100	101	106	101	100
Egypt	103	141	100	108	103	153	101	117
Brasil	104	134	102	107	106	138	103	111
Australia	95	117	94	99	93	113	92	96
Asia	104	148	102	121	104	148	102	121
Africa	102	128	99	93	102	129	99	94
North America	102	111	100	96	102	112	101	96
Europe	102	107	101	104	102	107	101	104
World	103	126	101	104	103	127	101	105

Source: FAO data. "World Resources 1994-1995", pp. 292-293.

The Russian Minister for Agriculture and Food, Alexander Nazarchuk, has recently made a statement on the rates of recession in the food sector of the Russian economy. For the last four years the volume of meat production fell by 60 percent, butter by 44 percent, milk by 63 percent, vegetable oils by 30 percent, sugar by 23 percent. The Minister named the fundamental factors of crisis in Russian agriculture: budget deficit, disruption of economic ties and cooperation in Russia and the CIS, fall of demand, imbalance of agricultural and industrial prices. Only the last point led to the huge financial loss in agriculture - some 24,000 billion roubles (R24,000 bln) during 1991-1994. In the beginning of 1995 100 large agri-corporations went bankrupt.[2]

Russia's agricultural recession continued in 1994, with gross production falling by 9 percent. The financial situation in agriculture was also in a deep crisis: in 1994 (at 1 October) 47 percent of all farms and enterprises in agriculture had registered a loss. The share of unprofitable farms and agri-corporations in 1993 was only 10 percent. The indebtedness of agricultural producers on 1 January 1995 reached R4,800 bln. In late 1994 the government was forced to reschedule R5,600 bln. of agricultural debts.[3]

A grave problem of Russian agriculture was caused by the so-called disparity of agricultural and industrial price growth. Between 1991 and 1994, prices for inputs grew 3.1 times faster than those for agricultural output. This means that a farmer must sell three times more grain or other products than it was needed four years ago to buy a tractor or a harvester. As a result, many farms and agri-corporations are on the brink of bankruptcy. They have no means to pay wages, to buy fuels, spare-parts and chemicals.

For example, in 1991-1993 prices for industrial goods and services rose 522 times, but agricultural prices grew 147 times. It is obvious, as Dr. V. Volkonskiy from the Russian Institute for National Economic Forecasting wrote, that pure market forces could not secure optimal price correlation and a supply of the inputs needed for agriculture. Abrupt deregulation of agriculture has created destructive consequences in Russian economy that are just as serious as those after the forced industrialisation and collectivisation in the 1920s and 1930s.[4]

Grain Production

Russia was the largest grain producer in the former USSR. At the same time Russia was behind the majority of other Soviet Republics in yield capacity because of natural and climatic conditions (Table II).

Table II
Annual grain production in the former republics of the USSR
in 1990-1992

	Production 1000 t	Yield kg/ha
Armenia	274	1918
Azerbaidjan	1328	2187
Belorussia	6387	2569
Georgia	535	2094
Kazakhstan	23218	1013
Kirgizstan	1432	2500
Latvia	1340	1965
Lithuania	2807	2666
Moldova	2512	3455
Russian Federation	100220	1701
Ukraine	39994	3094
Uzbekistan	1985	1840
Tadjikistan	300	1298
Turkmenistan	571	2398
Estonia	830	1971
All	183731	1779

Source: "World Resources 1994-1995", p. 293.

In 1994 the gross grain production in Russia fell by almost 20 percent. The level of output was less by a third in comparison with the 1990 indicator. The fall in volume of production was a result of both low productivity and smaller crop areas (Table III). In 1994 the grain area (56.2 mil. ha) decreased by 8 percent.

Table III
Grain production and yields in Russia

	1990	1991	1992	1993	1994
Gross Production mil. t	116.7	89.1	106.9	99.1	81.3
average yield t/ha	1.85	1.44	1.72	1.63	1.45

Source: Terentjev, A. 1995, p. 53.

Large agri-enterprises (public corporations, cooperatives, collective farms) produced 94 percent of all national production of grain in 1994. The share of private farms in national grain production was slightly higher - 8-12 percent - in the Volgograd, Saratov, Samara, Chelyabinsk and Omsk oblasts of the Russian Federation.

The plan for state grain procurement (11 mil. t) was fulfilled only up to 20 percent. The Russian Ministry for Finance "found" a small portion of money (1994 budget declared R2,500 bln to buy grain for Federal Pool) and financed only R398 bln to buy 2.18 mil. t of grains. State Regional Pools bought 10 mil. t of grain - 50 percent of the planned volume. Since January 1995 many regions of Russia suffer from a lack of wheat flour for bread production. According to the statement of the Chief of Section, the Government Department for APK and Consumer Market Dr. I. Terenjev, this situation could bring additional social tensions.[5]

In 1994, production of other main crops in Russian agriculture also decreased. The output of sugar-beets fell almost by 50 percent. In case of government support, gross crop production in 1995 is forecasted at last year's level (Table IV).

Grain production in 1995 could easily fall further. The problem is that the winter grain area decreased by 1 mil. ha in autumn 1994. This spring there were no sprouts on 1.7 mil. ha - 19 percent of all the area under winter grain. Sprouts on other 1 mil. ha were very poor.[6] Problems of financing of the spring fields work could result in a 25-39 percent fall of crop production this year. (According to the estimation of the General Director of the Russian Food Corporation M. Abdulbasirov.[7]) Minister, A. Nazarchuk, said that "national food security is now at stake", and that no region in Russia would be able to finish this year's sowing campaign in time - its term should be two times longer than usual.[8]

Table IV
Production of basic crops in Russia, mil. t

	1986-90 average	1992	1993	1994	1995 forecast
Grain	104.2	106.9	99.1	81.3	82.0*
Oilseeds	4.1	3.9	3.4	3.4	3.4
Sugar-beets	33.2	25.5	25.5	13.9	20.0
Potatoes	35.9	38.3	37.6	33.,8	35.0
Vegetables	11.2	10.0	9.8	9.6	10.0
Fruits and berries	2.6	2.8	2.7	2.1	2.1

Source: Terentjev I. 1995, p. 54. (65 mln. t was a final figure)

Livestock Production

The situation in the livestock sector is even more critical than in the crop sector of Russian agriculture. The cattle population decreased from 57.0 mil. heads in 1990 to 43.9 mil. in late 1994; the number of pigs diminished from 38.3 mil. to 25.0 mil. total stock of sheep and goats fell from 58.2 mil. to 35.9 mil. heads.[9]

In 1994 the number of cattle fell by 10 percent - an even greater decline than in 1993 (6 percent). The stock of pigs decreased by 13 percent (9 percent in 1993), and the number of sheep and goats fell by 18 percent (10 percent in 1993). The share of cattle in private hands increased as a result of redistribution of stock between former kolkhoses and households (Table V). But the private sector is still dependent on the supply of calves and yearlings from large livestock enterprises. The Center for Economic Conjuncture under the Russian government forecasts a further fall of all kinds of stock in 1995.

The output of livestock products fell (Table VI) due to lower production efficiency and decreased demand. In 1994 the volume of total meat production fell by 9 percent. The level of 1994 production was one third less than in 1990. Production of fresh cow milk decreased last year by 8 percent. And hen egg production fell by 7 percent. Per capita livestock production also fell. Meat production was 46 kg per capita in 1994.[11]

Table V
Livestock numbers in Russia
(on 1 January) 1,000 head

	1994	1995	1995 B % % K 1994
		cattle	
All	48900	43885	90
in enterprises*	36300	31055	86
in households	12600	12830	102
		pigs	
All	28600	25011	87
in enterprises*	20300	16676	82
in households	8300	8335	100
		sheep and goats	
All	43700	35948	82
in enterprises	35800	18362	71
in households	17900	17586	98

* *agro-corporations, cooperatives, kolkhoses, state farms.*
Sizov, A. 1995

This deep agricultural output decline has caused a depression in the Russian food industry. Food production fell even deeper in comparison with agricultural production: the volume of meat production in the food industry in 1994 decreased by 25 percent, output of vegetable oils fell by 24 percent, butter by 33 percent. There was a 52 percent reduction in the production of canned vegetables and fruits.

Table VI
Livestock products

	1990	1993	1994	1995 Forecast
Production of meat from slaughtered animals, mil. t	15.6	11.9	10.8	10.3
Cow milk, whole, fresh milk. t	55.7	46.5	42.8	40.0
Hen eggs, billions	47.5	40.3	37.4	37.0

Source: Terentjev, A. 1995, p. 55.

According to a forecast for 1995, national production of meat would fall further by 12 percent, vegetable oils output by 25 percent. Every month some 600 factories in the food industry stand idle.[12] Main problems of the food sector are caused by low technical efficiency and strict finances.

The gross fish and seafood catch in 1994 (3.47 mil. t) was nearly 1 mil. t lower than in 1993 (4.37 mil. t). The output of fish for food in 1994 was 2.10 mil. t (2.72 mil. t in 1993). But a large percentage of fish products was exported. For example, only 1 mil. t of food fish was sold on national market - this totals some 50 percent, as compared to 1993.[13]

Food Situation and Consumption Patterns

The supply of basic foods in Russia - bread, potatoes, cow milk, hen eggs, fish - was near the optimal level in the late 1980s. There was only a lack of meat, fruits and vegetables in diets. But Russians did not suffer from any deficiency of proteins, and the average food calorie intake was very high: since the 1950s it was over 3,000 per capita per day. The FAO estimated that food energy supply in the Eastern Europe and the former USSR was 3,380 calories per capita per day in 1988-1990. The number of calories supplied is forecast at the same level for 2010. This is identical to the level of calories supplied in the OECD countries (3,400 in 1988-1990) and well over the food energy consumption in the developing countries (2,470 in 1988-1990). However, average indicators usually conceal facts of malnutrition. For example, there are some 20 million people in the USA who are considered to be hungry and suffering from malnutrition.[14]

The real food consumption problem in the former USSR was caused by low vitamins intake and a lack of some minerals. There was also a lack of animal protein and some imbalance of amino acids in diets. Sporadic forms of protein-energy malnutrition in the former Soviet Russian Federation (RSFSR) could be (although hidden in official statistics) a result of food deficiency in some regions of the country.

Per capita consumption of almost all basic foodstuffs (besides bread and potatoes) fell dramatically over the past five years. According to Russian Ministry for Agriculture and Food data, per capita consumption of meat, milk, butter, vegetable, oils, fish and sugar in 1994 was almost twice lower than in 1990.

Deficiency of food protein is estimated at 35-40 percent, lack of vitamins - 50-60 percent.[15] In 1994 per capita meat consumption decreased to the 1970 level; the supply of milk products decreased to the 1960 level. Nevertheless Minister A. Nazarchuk stated that the Russian Federation has a good opportunity to feed itself and gain "national food security".[16] But the food situation on the Russian market could be even worse in 1995 than it was in 1994 (Table VII).

At the end of 1994, the food market in Russia was again faced with a crisis of short supply, which was especially acute in large cities. The fall of national food production was the main factor of that crisis. Food imports were not able to resolve the problem. The situation on market of imported foods was aggravated by "Black Tuesday" on the Russian foreign exchange market last October, when the exchange rate of rouble to US dollar deflated by almost one-third during one day of trading. Even in Moscow there was a stoppage of butter supply. It was overcome in early 1995 as a result of the sharp increase of consumer prices and emergency imports of butter from Western Europe.

Liberalisation of prices and privatisation of trade have filled shops with many items of foodstuffs never seen by ordinary people in Russia in the Soviet period. Of course, prices are very high. Food consumer prices in Russia reached European levels (except for bread prices). But average wages do not exceed 80 US dollars a month. Some estimates give a proof that 60-65 percent of Russian population is now unable to consume meat products rationally in cause of low incomes.[17] Over half of family households spend some 90 percent of their incomes to buy food.

Table VII
Per capita consumption of basic foods in Russia, kg per year

	1991	1992	1993	1994	1995 forecast
All kinds of meat	69	60	59	50	45
Milk and milk products (fresh whole milk equivalent)	347	281	294	277	254
Butter	5.8	5.4	5.3	5.0	4.0
Vegetable oils	7.8	6.7	6.0	6.5	3.25
Sugar	38	30	32	33	23

Data: Goskomstat and Roskomtorg.

Incomes of 45 million Russians (30 percent of the national population) in the beginning of April 1995 were below official minimal living standards. This marks a 23 percent increase over the past year. The growth rate of this social segment of the population in 1994 was only 5 percent.[18] Nominal average wages per month in the first quarter of 1995 (R326,000) were 2.2 times higher than a year ago. But in real terms, they decreased by 31 percent.[19] A further fall in real incomes would mean a deterioration of the food consumption status in Russia. Taking into consideration possible social consequences the government would be forced to enlarge the scale of aid to the low income population - a hard task in times of budget deficit.

Agrarian Reform: Status and Prospects

Agrarian reform in Russia in the 1990s is aimed at the denationalisation of production and restructuring of former kolkhoses (collective farms) and sovkhoses (state farms) into agro-corporations and independent farmers' cooperatives. The creation of wide strata of private and family farms will guarantee real growth in the efficiency of agricultural and food production. Unfortunately, agricultural reform in this last decade of the 20th century was started without the required preparations, including legal issues. This is contrary to the two previous major agrarian reforms in Russian history begun in 1861 and 1906-1907.

The great Russian reformer, P.A. Stolypin, considered that successful formation of private farms would only be possible in Russia after 20 years of peaceful life without wars and revolutions. But during those 20 years (1907-1927) Russia survived World War I, two revolutions and the Civil War.

In 1992, the first wave of Russian liberal reform was certain that the deregulation and "farmerisation" of agriculture could easily solve all the problems of the agrarian sector. Now there is a more rational approach towards agrarian reorganisation. It does not mean that agrarian reform has stopped. On the contrary there is stable progress of agrarian reform, but this goes on more reasonably and takes into consideration the special features of this sector of the national economy, its cultural traditions, etc.

At the beginning of 1994, 24,000 kolkhoses and sovkhoses (95 percent of all farms) were re-registered: 55 percent of them became joint-stock corporations and partnerships, 10 percent were organised as independent cooperatives, 4 percent as farmers associations, 25 percent conserved their statutes as kolkhoses, and 6 percent as state farms. The number of private households actively producing agricultural products doubled between 1991 and 1994. In addition, there were 280,000 private farms at the end of 1994.[20]

Private Farms and Households

It is now obvious to many people that small private farms will never solve Russia's food problem. They have a chance to survive and flourish only in the framework of close cooperation between themselves, or horizontal integration with agro-food corporations and vertical integration with industry and trade. Some 11 million ha of land are the property of private farms (5 percent of all agricultural land). Over the past five years, 40,000 farmers have left agriculture. In the first quarter of 1995 the number of private farms rose by 4,000, according to the President of the (Russian) Association of Farms and Cooperatives (AKKOR) Vladimir Bashmachnikov.[21]

Russian farmers face such economic difficulties as high taxes, expensive credits, a non-payment crisis, poor marketing. According to the farmers' opinion poll in five Russian oblasts (Rostov, Saratov, Novosibirsk, Orlov, Pskov), 70 percent of them do not have marketing channels, 82 percent are unable to gain credit, 89 percent consider high taxes as the main obstacle to doing profitable business.[22] Because of the financial crisis, farmers have big problems obtaining the necessary funding. This spring, for example, farmers in the Vereschagin region, Perm oblast, could only sow by hand.[23]

Private households and tiny gardens are now a more important sector of Russian agriculture than private farms. There are 45 million privately-owned households and gardens. The share of this sector in national agricultural production rose in 1994 to 38 percent.[24] The part-time "farmers" - 22.5 million families - produce on their tiny gardens (common size of plots is 0.06 ha) some 25 percent of national potato production, 28 percent of vegetables, 37 percent of fruits and berries. These data were presented at the All-Russian Conference of Private Gardeners in late April, 1995.[25]

Government in Agriculture

The sharp fall of state procurement of agricultural produce is a good illustration of the progress in deregulation of the agrarian sector of the Russian economy (Table VIII).

Government support of Russian agriculture fell sharply in the 1990s. The share of the APK in budget subsidies decreased from 23.8 percent in 1987 to 14.3 percent in 1992 and to 8.6 percent in 1994.[26] The volume of budget appropriations to support the Russian Agro-Industrial Complex was R13,100 bln. in 1994 (72 percent of plan). One third of all appropriations was spent for procurement of agricultural produce. The government donated R147 bln. for spare-parts and some other inputs and R850 bln. for leasing of agricultural machinery.[27]

Table VIII

Volumes of State Procurement for Federal and Regional Pools, mil. t

	1993	1994
Grain	28.2	12.1
Potatoes	1.7	0.7
Vegetables	2.1	1.4
Slaughtered animals	6.0	4.6
Cow milk	24.6	18.8
Hen eggs, billion	24.3	21.7

Source: "Delovoy Mir", 14.03.1995.

Answering hot disputes between liberals and the agrarian lobby the Russian Prime Minister Victor Chernomyrdin stated on 5 April 1995 that the overall level of agrarian protectionism would certainly be decreased in the near future. State support should be more oriented to stimulate demand.[28]

Of course, Russia must take into consideration the Final Agreement of the GATT Uruguay Round, because it is necessary for the country to join the World Trade Organisation. But global agricultural liberalisation will continue slowly. Agriculture in the OECD countries, according to the recent FAO report, is still far from being market-oriented.[29] Russian Minister for Economy Euvgeniy Yasin, who is considered to be a prominent representative of "liberal economic thought", underlined that Russian agriculture "should be supported by the State", and this aid must first be aimed at increasing the efficiency of national agriculture.[30]

Agricultural Import and Prospects for Food Security of Russia

The grain and food imports of the former USSR were an issue of security policy during the Cold War period. "Grain weapon" problems were widely discussed in the 1970s and early 1980s.[31] The American grain embargo in 1980/1981 forced the Soviet Union to adopt the Food Programme. Both the grain embargo and the Food Programme failed: the United States lifted the embargo and started to credit grain sales to the "strategic enemy"; the Soviets did not manage to secure food self-sufficiency and fulfil other goals of the national food strategy.

Though Russia stopped all state imports of grain in 1994, food imports continue to be an important part of the country's food supply. The Russian Vice-Minister for Foreign Economic Relations, Vladimir Korostin, said that the cost of food imports in 1994 was 20-25 percent of all imports. Grain import (now on a commercial basis) decreased in 1994 by 19 percent. Volume of import of sugar fell by 72 percent, vegetable oils by 66 percent. At the same time import of meat rose 4.5 times, and import of butter increased by 2.3 times.[32] The bulk of food import goes to large cities. In 1994, 10 percent of all meat on the food market in Russia was of imported origin. The share of imported butter on the national market was 25 percent, with 30 percent for sugar.[33]

The quality of imported foods in Russia is often very low. Russian new commercial food importers prefer to make deals with small firms abroad which do not have a good reputation. A part of this import is below quality and sanitation norms. For example in 1994 Gostorginspektzia (State Committee for Sanitation Control) stopped retailing 35-70 percent of samples of imported meat products (including sausages, cheeses, butter, alcohol, tea and coffee) for reasons of poor quality and dangerous components and admixtures.[34]

It is not only a Russian problem. Western large food exporters should be interested in the Russian market for long term business. But consumers' attitude towards "food import" is becoming negative. Here, the main question is the absence of real competition in Russia's food market.

The current food situation in Russia is beginning to resemble the middle-income countries in the Third World (the Near East, Eastern Asia). So food insecurity in Russia could be raised by the factor studied by Gordon R. Conway and Eduard B. Barber. They wrote: "The lack of food security in the developing countries - defined as the access by all people at all times to enough food for an active healthy life - will arise from a lack of purchasing power of the part of nations and households rather than from inadequate global food security".[35] Some Russian households - roughly 10-15 percent - suffer from transitionary food insecurity, based on high food prices, low incomes, unstable national agricultural production.

Solving the problem of food security could be partially achieved after Russia's possible entering the FAO. Russia was among the founding countries of the FAO in 1945. After a 50-year break it is now time to take part in the global agricultural and food system. But it is the new national agri-business that will be the first sector responsible for guaranteeing food security in Russia. The outcome of its efforts will depend on Russian bankers' readiness to invest money in the agrarian sector of the Russian economy. The government role is to support research centres and to aid low-income consumers.

Footnotes

1. Russian Information Agency (RIA). Novosty Rossiiskoy Economici. "News of Russian Economy". 17.03.1995.
2. RIA "News of Russian Economy" 16.03.1995.
3. Nazarchuk, A. The APK at the Modern Stage of Economic Reform. "Economist". Review of the Russian Ministry for Economy. Moscow. 1995. N3, pp. 15, 16.
4. Volkonskiy, V. Agriculture in Time of Market Reform. "Delovoy Mir". Moscow. 18.10.1994, p. 4.
5. Terentjev, I. 1994 Results of Activity of Agro-Industrial Complex. "Economist". Moscow. N4. 1995, p. 54.
6. Ibidem, p. 55.
7. RIA "News of Russian Economy". 16.03.1995.
8. Ibidem.
9. Terentjev, I. Op. cit., p. 55.
10. Cizov, A. The recession in the livestock production will not be stopped this year. Finansovye Isvestya. "Financial News". Moscow. N30, 27.04.1995, p. II.
11. Terentjev, I. Op. cit., p. 55.
12. Ibidem, p. 56.
13. Ibidem, p. 58.
14. Food and Natural Resources, ed. by David Pimentel. San Diego, 1989, p. 422.
15. "Economist". Moscow. N3, 1995, p. 83.
16. Nazarchuk, A. Op. cit., p. 20.
17. Stepanov, V. Lalutenko, B. Meat in Russia: Whether to Produce or to Import. "Delovoy Mir". Weekly. Moscow. 11-17.07.1994, p. 7.
18. RIA "News of Russian Economy". 21.04.1995.
19. Ibidem.
20. RIA "News of Russian Economy". 05.04.1995; Nazarchuk, Op. cit., p. 18.
21. RIA "News of Russian Economy". 03.05.1995.
22. Nikonov, A. Agrarian Reform - The Vital Necessity. "Rossiiskiy Sotzialno-Pjliticheskiy Vestnik". Moscow. 1995, N2, p. 22.
23. "Isvestya". Moscow. 17.05.1995, p. 1.
24. Nikonov, A. Op. cit., p. 22.
25. RIA "News of Russian Economy". 27.04.1995.
26. Kieselev, S. On Monitoring of State Regulation of Agriculture. Rossiiskiy Economicheskiy Zhournal. "Russian Economics Journal". Moscow. N2, 1995, p. 16.
27. Terenjev, I. Op. cit., p. 52.
28. RIA "News of Russian Economy". 05.04.1995.
29. Agriculture: Towards 2010. FAO 27th Session. Rome, 1993, pp. 30, 31.
30. RIA "News of Russian Economy". 26.04.1995.
31. Brown, L. U.S. and Soviet Agriculture: The Shifting Balance of Power. WorldWatch Institute. Washington. 1982. Porter, R. The U.S.-U.S.S.R. Grain Agreement. Cambridge. 1984, etc.
32. RIA "News of Russian Economy". 17.03.1995.
33. Sotzialno-Economicheskoye Rasvitije Rossiyi v 1994. "Social-Economic Development of Russia in 1994". Moscow. 1995. p. 75.
34. "Delovoy Mir", 24.05.1994, p. 8.
35. Gordon R. Conway and Eduard B. Barber. After The Green Revolution. Sustainable Agriculture for Development. L. 1990, p. 60.

Bibliography by Yuri Khromov

Grain Import: Will Russia Overcome the "Heritage" of 70s and 80s? "Delovoy Mir". Weekly, 4-10 October 1993, Moscow.

How to Lessen the Burden of Foreign Debt. "Delovoy Mir", 1994.

Global Economic Triangle and a Place of Russia. "Delovoy Mir". Weekly, 28 February-6 March 1994.

Foreign Countries' Approaches for National and International Food Security. "Strategic Problems of Economic Reform in Russia". RISS, Moscow. Quarterly Review, N1, 1994.

Social Vector of Russian Reform as a Factor of Economic Security. "Strategic Problems of Russian Economic Reform", N2, 1994.

Economic Restoration: What Kind of Capitalism Does Russia Build? Ibidem.

Russian Interests in the Global Economic Triangle in: "Western Europe on the Eve of the Third Millenium". RISS, IMEMO, 1995.

Issues of Food Security of Russia. "Society and Economy". Monthly, Russia Academy of Sciences, N10, 1994.

Russia Food Security: Inner and International Dimensions. RISS, Moscow (in print).

LIVING STANDARDS AND SOCIAL WELFARE IN AZERBAIJAN

Fikret Pashayev

Azerbaijan is rich in natural resources, but it is still finding the road to a market economy heavy going. Wages are trailing prices, with the result that three-quarters of the population are living below subsistence level. Fikret Pashayev says economic reforms create an economic transformation in the long term - but at the moment, it's a question of 'all shock and no therapy'. He also points out that in managing its reform programme, the government has done its best to protect the most vulnerable - and to help the one million refugees from the conflict in Karabakh.

Fikret Pashayev is First Secretary at the Department of International Economic Relations, Ministry of Foreign Affairs of Azerbaijan Republic, Baku.

The Breakdown of the Economy

Azerbaijan, as one of the republics of the former Soviet Union, was closely integrated in the intra-soviet "market" which was based on command economy principles and regulated by the central authorities in Moscow. After the dissolution of the Soviet Union and emergence of newly independent states the traditional economic links were destroyed. Since all industrial enterprises were public and did not have the flexibility for adaptation to the new market conditions, dramatic falls in output have occurred. The problem was aggravated by the reform policy, especially by the liberalisation of prices, inflation, political and economic crisis, and the emergence of the giant refugees' army.

Rich natural resources, particularly oil and gas deposits, iron and alunite ores, sources of building and other materials, as well as water and land resources have allowed Azerbaijan to create a well-developed industrial and agricultural infrastructure.

At present more than half of the Gross National Product comes from the republic's industries. The republic has facilities for advanced oil and gas extraction, oil refining, and chemical complexes, to meet local and export needs.

More than one-third of the national income is produced by agriculture. Traditional crops include cotton, grapes, tobacco, tea, vegetables, fruits and various subtropical produce. Of the country's total arable land of 134.3 million hectares, some 1.4 million hectares are cultivated.

In spite of a series of developed production facilities, the first years after gaining independence were critical for the economy of Azerbaijan. In 1994 the fall in industrial output was 24.8 percent in comparison with 1993. According to the "Economic Survey of Europe in 1993-1994" (UN, ECE, 1994, pp. 52, 63), the fall in GDP in Azerbaijan in 1992 was 28.1 percent, in 1993 - 13.3 percent. The fall in agricultural production in 1992 equalled 25 percent, in 1993 17 percent. According to the special report of the Ministry of Labour and Social Security of the Azerbaijan Republic (Baku, 1995), food production declined more intensively (30.4 percent).

Production of food has further fallen, for several reasons. Among these are:
• The crisis of agricultural relations and previous forms of land ownership in agriculture (which was based on collective property - kolkhoses and sovkhoses).
• The rising price of agricultural machinery, equipment, mechanisms, stores, fertilisers.
• The loss of 20 percent of the Republic's territory as a result of external aggression.
• The presence of more than one million refugees and displaced persons, a substantial number of whom are rural workers.

The table below shows some figures which illustrate production trends for the main food products in recent years.

Production of some food products (in thousand of tons)

	1992	1993	1994
Meat	28.2	17.8	9.9
Fish	31.2	22.2	19.2
Milk	81.1	49.8	40.3
Oil	22.5	14.2	9.6
Butter	2.9	2.3	1.4
Sausage	7.7	9.5	3.9
Macaroni	16.9	14.3	10.0
Sugar	18.8	11.7	3.5
Salt	21.9	3.8	6.9
Cheese	9.5	7.6	4.6

Source : Special Report of Statistical Committee of the Republic of Azerbaijan, Baku, 1995

As a result of a fall in food production and restrictions in imports, the consumption of some products has declined. For instance, the decline in meat consumption in 1992-1994 equalled 32 percent, milk 11 percent, sugar 14 percent, eggs 27 percent.

In recent years, some steps have been taken to reform the economy, such as: liberalisation of prices and decentralisation of management of enterprises; creation of a national currency; the birth of a private sector; and a number of other measures to transform the totalitarian system of management.

Reform Measures: 1990-1994

Between 1990-1994 a number of radical measures were undertaken to reform the economy. These include: 1990-1991 witnessed the reform in management of enterprises aimed at increasing their authority to determine their economic programmes. It was the first step toward setting up market relations. In 1992, central planning of production was terminated. That created favourable conditions for flexible management of the economy in conformity with market conditions. Accordingly, enterprises were given the right to regulate salaries and wages as well as the number of employees. Since January 1992, prices and tariffs of all kinds of production and services, except bread, fuel and public transport, were liberalised. As a result, inflation has grown.

The average monthly rate of inflation rose to between 15 to 20 percent, while individual incomes increased no more than 7 to 9 percent. All this resulted in a considerable decrease in the standard of living - and along with that, the process of polarisation caused by aggravated disparities in incomes - caused more than 75 percent of the population to have income levels below the minimum subsistence level. The difficulties of the transition period had a negative impact on the different aspects of social life.

Social Infrastructure

Under these circumstances the minimum wage has to correspond to the minimum consumer budget of the population. In 1991 the minimum wage equalled 41.8 percent of minimum consumer budget, in 1992 it was 24.5 percent, in 1993 - 10.8 percent, in 1994 - 2.8 percent, in March 1995 - 2.3 percent. In March 1995 the value of the minimum consumer budget in Azerbaijan was an estimated $54, the average wage - $11, the minimal wage - $1.2.

The introduction of a national currency (the Manat) - initially gave the opportunity for the government to ensure through emission the appropriate quantity of money for covering expenditures on wages, but the critical situation in production brought high inflation. The financial difficulties did not allow the government to pursue the adequate indexation policy. In 1992-1995 the index of consumer prices has risen 239 times, but the average wage 57.5, and the minimum wage 22 times.

In the period between 1993 and 1994, along with the increase in prices which were regulated by the government, specifically for bread and fuel, the state carried out measures to protect the more vulnerable strata of the population including students, pensioners and families with many children. The strategy of economic reform is focused on revamping of property relations based on principles of economic pluralism and conversion from the strictly centralised command to a regulated market economy.

Coordination of economic and social policies is needed to protect the welfare of the people. Though it is obvious that in the long term, the reformed economy will pull the country out of this current plight, a shock therapy may result in grave social consequences. In Azerbaijan, with more than one million refugees and 20 percent of its territory under occupation, this problem is especially real. From the strategic point of view, the first priority is to maintain a minimum of social security for the population, to ensure the irreversibility of reforms and a minimum standard of living for the vulnerable strata of the population.

There are plans to increase transfer payments to this vulnerable strata of the population - pensioners, students, families with children. The social protection of these strata will be mostly provided for from the funds realised by the sale of state property. In the draft law of privatisation presented to the parliament it is planned to allot 25 percent of the proceeds from the of selling state enterprises to the fund for the people's social security.

Azerbaijan's economic policy for 1995, as worked out jointly with the International Monetary Fund, is based on the premise that economic and financial stability can best be achieved by a gradualist social policy, as well as by cutting the state expenditures and freezing investments by government.

The problem of creating programmes aimed at fighting poverty, and assisting the socially vulnerable strata of the population, remains unsolved.

Social Security Policy

The radical changes to the life of the country caused by the transition to the market economy call for the entire existing social security system to be transformed. Therefore, a new system of social guarantees is needed.

Azerbaijan developed a system to regulate salaries and wages on a 19 point scale. It pays special attention to creating a durable legal base for the social security of the population.

The Azerbaijan parliament has adopted a law on guaranteed pension rights, social security of the disabled, and vacations. A new system of social guarantees would grant pensions, allowances and compensations to low-income families and the disabled. In view of the liberalisation of prices and the growth of inflation, certain groups (soldiers and veterans, teachers, pensioners, the disabled and others) have been granted discounts for use of municipal utilities, telephone, and public transport.

Today the system of obligatory social guarantees in Azerbaijan embraces 1,200,000 pensioners, about 300,000 invalids, 1,000,000 refugees and displaced persons, 2,000,000 children and about 130,000 students.

A great part of the system of social guarantees is financed by taxes on companies. The minimum wage level has been reviewed to account for inflation and other factors. Salaries, pensions, stipends and allowances are indexed to the minimum wage.

The present social security system based mainly on centralised government financing is inadequate. The population is not protected from rampant price inflation. Therefore, to build an effective welfare structure the state has focused on controlling inflation and overcoming the economic crisis by reviving production, attracting foreign investment, and creating conditions for private entrepreneurship.

Employment and Unemployment

Since gaining its independence, Azerbaijan has joined a number of international organisations including the International Labour Organization (ILO) and has ratified 57 ILO conventions. On the basis of these conventions, it has worked to solve the unemployment problem.

In 1991 the law "On the Employment of Population in the Azerbaijan Republic" was adopted, and labour boards were created. Since then, 151,000 people have applied to the appropriate state authorities, of whom 79,500 found jobs, 65,000 entered retraining programmes, and, 36,000 were registered as unemployed and provided with unemployment benefits. All these measures are financed from an employment fund supported by taxes on business.

For a long period, especially in the 1980s, job creation did not keep up with the growth of the workforce, leading to the steady growth in the number of unemployed. According to some estimates which do not provide a detailed breakdown, the number of unemployed exceeds a million. Application of international statistical standards may improve the estimates. Azerbaijan is traditionally regarded as a republic with abundant labour resources. The problem of unemployment is aggravated by two factors connected with the external aggression - on one hand over 250,000 jobs have been lost in the occupied territories, on the other hand, the arrival of more than 1,000,000 refugees and displaced persons worsened the strained situation in the labour market.

Up to now Azerbaijan has not foreseen any assistance in managing its unemployment problem. But serious work has already begun. With UN and ILO aid, a project, entitled "A review of Manpower in the Azerbaijan Republic" has been launched to refine definitions and estimates of unemployment. It is evident that solving the unemployment problem depends on economic growth.

91

Only in this way can the peoples' right to work be guaranteed by legislation. Azerbaijan needs to attract foreign investment, encourage duty-free commerce, and obtain lower barriers to the free migration of labour.

Demographic Situation

The Azerbaijan Republic's population totals 7.5 million, 53 percent living in towns and 3.5 million (47 percent) living in rural areas. In the past years, growth of the population has been only attributed to the birth-rate, which indicates a positive demographic situation. On average 180,000 children are born each year, about 500 children per day. In previous years, Azerbaijan maintained a high birth-rate. Lately, this figure has decreased because of the economic situation and external aggression. In 1994, the index per 1,000 inhabitants dropped to 22, while in 1985 it stood at 27. The annual average rate of growth of population stood at 3 percent between 1959-1970, 1.8 percent between 1970-1979, 1.5 percent between 1979-1989, 1.1 percent between 1989-1994: the negative tendency of decrease is evident.

Azerbaijan has long been characterised by a relatively low and stable rate of mortality. However, the present situation has resulted in heavy human losses, and consequently a considerable increase in the mortality rate. In 1993, 52,800 deaths were registered at a rate of 7.3 in 1,000, compared to the figure of 6.8 in 1988. Stresses and shocks suffered by pregnant refugee women, lack of elementary sanitary facilities, systematic malnutrition of future mothers, shortage in medicine and food for infants - all these reasons determined the growth of infant mortality. In 1992 the infant mortality per 1,000 live births equalled 28.2.

The mortality figure is reflected in the indicators for average life span, at 70 years compared to 71 in 1959. The average life expectancy for men is 65 years, and for women 74 years. Azerbaijan has, since ancient times, been considered a country with exceptionally long lives. The oldest man in the world, as recorded in the Guinness Book of Records, is 162 year-old Shirali Muslumov from Azerbaijan. But the number of long-livers has sharply decreased in the recent years.

Ecology and the Environment

In Azerbaijan, major ecological problems have accumulated in all the spheres of industry and life. The policy of the former Soviet Union on environmental protection was aimed at intensive exploitation of natural resources. All spheres of economy and industry developed their production at the cost of intensified consumption of raw materials. In doing this, the problems of resources and energy supply were not paid proper attention. Less than half of the Republic's cities have water treatment systems.

The state of the water supply and sewerage system is generally unsatisfactory. The environment in Sumgait is particularly grave because there has been an intensive expansion of chemical enterprises without corresponding levels of environmental protection. The transition to a market economy must exert a positive influence, as a whole, on the efficiency of exploitation of resources, as well as on the state of the environment. But in the very period of transition the ecological situation is becoming even worse.

Among the factors polluting the environment in the republic the worn-out equipment and obsolete technology must be mentioned. Discarded oil industry equipment scattered throughout the Absheron Peninsula, continues to pollute the environment and deform the landscape. The problem of recultivation of land polluted with oil is very critical.

This is why environmental protection and questions of ecology have become a crucial part of state policy. Based on the principles adopted by the world community, a number of fundamental documents, namely, "Ecological Conception of the Azerbaijan Republic" and the "Law On Protection of Nature and Use of Natural Resources" were drafted in a short period of time and ratified in the parliament. Unfortunately, solutions to ecological problems are being carried out under the present circumstances of an economic crisis and acute budget shortages. It is evident that the necessary financing to resolve ecological problems it not available.

The entire Baku Bay and 36 percent of coastal waters are subjected to complex pollution. More than half of the rivers (65.3 percent) of 100 km. length are heavily polluted. The inhabitants of the republic's lowlands are affected by thermal, biological and chemical changes. Lakes of the Absheron Peninsula and Kur-Araz lowland with a total area of 190 sq. km. are in a critical state.

The level of the Caspian Sea increases by 144-168 mm per year, or by 12 to 14 mm per month. The entire seacoast of Azerbaijan, 830 km. is flooded along its entire length. The depth of the maximal flooding is 25 to 35 km., and for subflooding is 35 to 45 km. All the towns, settlements and economic facilities situated in this region need anti-flood protection, or relocation from their current sites.

Seven cities - some 35 settlements with more than 120 buildings of cattle breeding, recreation and storage facilities, homes, recreation areas as well as a total population of about 700,000 - are situated in the area that will suffer catastrophic effects. It is predicted that by 2010, the water level will increase to 26.0 metres. Some 150,000 people - 22 percent of the population - inhabit the territory immediately affected by this increase in the sea's water level.

According to preliminary estimates of experts, the investments required to restore the environment in excessively polluted areas range between $3 to $4.5 million.

Education

Azerbaijan has a long history and tradition of learning. At present there are 22 higher schools, 72 colleges, 162 technical-vocational schools. Now there are 4,419 schools functioning in Azerbaijan, including 2,328 secondary schools, 969 primary eight-year schools and 522 pre-school institutions. There are 1,434,500 pupils in the schools of the republic and they are taught by more than 152,600 teachers. The system of private educational institutions is being developed.

Specialised secondary schools play an important role in training more than 70,000 pupils for specific jobs.

The most difficult problem of education today remains the extremely low salary of teachers in public and higher schools - $10-20 monthly. Other problems include systematic malnutrition of students, absence of necessary food for children in kindergartens, shortage of textbooks, furniture and buildings. The student hostels of higher and technical secondary schools in Baku, Ganja, Sumgait are occupied by refugees. In the territories neighbouring the occupied lands for a long time it has been impossible to organise a full scale education programme as the buildings are occupied by refugees.

With the assistance of humanitarian organisations, an interim solution of building prefabricated small houses as school buildings has been organised. However, the problem is still far from being solved. Many children of refugees and displaced persons are suffering from war trauma and need special counselling and instruction. Unfortunately, this has not been made available because of more pressing problems faced by the republic. Azerbaijan has 242 pre-school institutions for 12,000 children, 616 schools of general education for 117,000 pupils, four colleges for 21,000 students and one high school in the occupied territories.

Health Protection

There are 735 health centres, 1,624 ambulatory services and polyclinics, including 757 ambulatory facilities and 2,288 maternity centres in the republic. Azerbaijan has lost 5,920 hospital beds in the occupied territories; among the refugees there are 1,416 doctors. The number of hospital beds totals 76,900 or 104.4 per 10,000 - well above European Community levels. But these quantitative indicators which were the main criteria for planning and financing, do not reflect accurately the state of affairs in public health. Some 90 percent of hospital beds in rural areas are in buildings unfit to be called hospitals. There is an acute shortage of medical equipment and medicine.

Health receives 4.5 percent of the state budget. In circumstances of economic crisis and inflation, these allocations do not even meet minimal requirements. There are inadequate resources to maintain current facilities or to improve them. Thus they cannot provide care in adequate volume or quality.

Recently, the incidence of diseases associated with social factors has risen greatly: tuberculosis, infectious-parasitic diseases, etc. Annually about a million cases of acute chronic diseases are diagnosed. Inadequate sanitary conditions have led to high percentage of "invalidism" among people with diseases. The indicator in Azerbaijan is very high, fluctuating between 60 percent and 80 percent. Health care management still follows in part the rigid Soviet model and is in need of gradual decentralisation. The search for new financing means will have to include three ways to provide health care - free state care, insurance, and patient payments. Economic and social criteria will determine the mix among these options.

Extensive redesign of the health care network, as well as retraining of personnel, are also needed. For all this Azerbaijan requires the consultative assistance of international institutions.

Key medicine and equipment shortages include: insulin, anaesthetics, blood substitutes, blood-transfusion equipment, disposable syringes, injections, vaccines, serums, anti-TB and cardio-vascular medicines and cancer preparations. As a whole, specialists consider health care in Azerbaijan to be in a critical state. The transition from a centralised to a market economy will definitely facilitate decentralisation of the health care system as well.

Social Status of Refugees and Displaced Persons in Azerbaijan

The President of the Azerbaijan Republic, the Supreme Soviet (the Parliament) and the Cabinet of Ministers adopted a number of significant decrees and resolutions aimed at the problems of refugees and displaced persons. All the issues related to them are covered by the "Law on the Status of Refugees and Displaced Persons", adopted on 29 September 1990. Under this Law, refugees and displaced persons will be provided with an allowance and accommodation to meet their most urgent needs; employment and education of their children are being considered and solved at governmental level.

At present all refugees have been accommodated, they have jobs and are citizens enjoying full rights in Azerbaijan. However, over 200,000 refugees forcibly deported have not been paid compensations for their damages, abandoned houses, constructions, property, cattle, or all the things they had accumulated over the decades they lived in the region. This problem is waiting for its urgent solution.

Displaced persons who total 143,000 families (650,000 people), including 106,666 children up to the age of five years, 357,562 women, and 86,383 pensioners have been accommodated in sanatoriums, boarding houses, hostels, office buildings, in houses of friends and relatives. A part of them are living in tent camps, dugouts, straw houses, fabricated small cottages built by international organisations and in plywood barracks.

The State Committee for refugees and displaced persons and other governmental bodies dealing with the refugee problems are in need of technical and organisational support. The assistance rendered in the form of subsidies and humanitarian relief of international organisations is not enough to meet all the demand of refugees. The main source of their incomes must be their own labour.

Hard living conditions and a lack of basic sanitary norms have encouraged the spreading of various diseases among the refugees. This is due to the chaotic accommodation of displaced persons and a loss of control of sanitary measures - a lack of baths, soap, detergents, and essential medicine. Most of these people have no medical documents. This all worsens the task of medical personnel.

It is evident that the return of refugees requires the solution of a range of complex of problems - beginning with the economic issues and ending in the restoration of a destroyed infrastructure. The problems of stimulating the small business, farming, creating the system of training, re-training of personnel in new methods in managing agriculture are very important.

References

Asian-Pacific in figures, Seventh edition, November, 1993, UN, New York, 50 p.

Economic and Social Survey of Asia and the Pacific, UN, New York, 1995, 156 p.

Economic Survey of Europe in 1993-1994, UN, ECE, 1994

Trends in Europe and North America, UN, The Statistical Yearbook of Economic Commission for Europe, Geneva, First Edition, 137 p.

The socio-economic situation in Azerbaijan Republic in Jan.-May of 1994, Baku, 1994, 60 p.

Special Report of Statistical Committee of the Republic of Azerbaijan, Baku, 1995

Special Report of the Ministry of Labour and Social Insurance of Azerbaijan Republic, Baku, 1995

Social and Economic Indicators of the Black Sea Economic Cooperation Countries, Ankara, 1993, 156 p.

LIVING STANDARDS AND SOCIAL WELFARE IN CENTRAL AND EASTERN EUROPE

Domenico Mario Nuti,
.

Official statistics don't tell the whole truth about improvements in the quality of life in Central and Eastern Europe, says Professor Domenico Mario Nuti. They record the fact that the queues have vanished, and that the shops always have well-stocked shelves. But even so, the truth must be faced. Unemployment is high and set to remain high, and an increasing number of people are falling below the poverty line. In the short term, active labour market policies will help even out the benefits of the reform policies. But the only viable long term solution, he says, is a massive boost in economic growth.

Dr. Nuti is Professor at the University of Rome "La Sapienza" and visiting Professor at the London Business School.

Between 1990 and 1995 the systemic transformation of Central and East European economies has been accompanied initially by a drastic and sustained fall in real income and living standards and the rapid rise of mass unemployment. These trends are now being reversed in the Visegrad countries, which undertook an earlier significant and accelerated growth of real income. Other Central and East European countries have only just began to recover, while former Soviet republics, which started later and less decisively, are experiencing further output decline; unemployment has been delayed but is poised to grow rapidly once capacity restructuring is undertaken. The rapid decline of investment which accompanied the recession allowed a smaller decline of living standards (except for housing), and an earlier recovery with respect to real income. At the same time, investment levels must be substantially raised for economic growth to be sustainable.

To some extent the picture offered by official statistics is distorted. Some of the output reported as lost may have existed only on paper, or have been accumulated as unsaleable inventories, or have been subtracting rather than adding value at international prices. Output and employment in the private sector, now legalised and rapidly expanding, are likely to have been under-declared or otherwise under-recorded; thus some of the unemployed may be engaged in productive activities. Tangible improvements in living standards, - created by the ready availability of a greater range of consumption goods instead of old style endemic shortages and queues - by their nature are not included in national income statistics. At the same time, much non-economic output has continued while the decline has also affected unprofitable activities which still

99

produced some value added. Private sector growth is bound to have been over-estimated, as already existing activities are now surfacing into the legal economy. Some of the unemployed may not register as they lose their entitlement to benefits and are discouraged from seeking a job. An unrecorded decrease in welfare now comes from the misery of the unemployed, the job insecurity of the employed, and generalised exposure to higher criminality and risk of disease. By and large, the distortion of official statistics cannot be deemed to reverse or even alter dramatically the assessment of economic performance during the transformation. An enquiry into the causes of this disappointing performance would raise controversial issues and is outside the scope of this paper.

Within five years from the start of transition, registered unemployment had leapt from zero - indeed from the labour shortages typical of the old system - to almost 10 million in mid-1994, of which 7.5 million were in Central and Eastern Europe, 1.9 million in the CIS and 160,000 in the Baltic states. Unemployment rapidly converged to the European average of 12 percent, replicating a simular range and dispersion. Unemployment rates in the former Soviet Union and the Czech Republic appear to be an exception but they are currently underestimated, about to rise, and conceal underlying results from a combination of slow labour shedding and an even slower process of unemployment absorption, leading to a large, growing and - above all - stagnant pool of unemployed. Current prospects foresee continued and sustained high unemployment rates.

In general, unemployment benefits have been set at relatively generous levels for a limited period. A wide range of social services which typically were provided by state enterprises - such as housing, education, health, holidays, recreation - were curtailed, transferred to local authorities or left to the private sector on a market-driven basis. Food subsidies (which used to be of the order of 5 percent of GDP) have been cut sharply. Many of the social costs have fallen more heavily on women, given their higher proportion among the unemployed and the sharp fall in child care provision. Health trends vary, with infant mortality rising in the former Soviet Union and Bulgaria and falling decisively everywhere else; the death rate rising spectacularly in Russia, Ukraine and Belarus, and falling in Poland and the Czech Republic.

The fast, variable and unanticipated rates of inflation obviously had adverse effects on income distribution, as naturally the weaker groups lost out with respect to those able to assert their relative strength. Everywhere an increasing proportion of the population has fallen below the poverty line - no matter how this is defined. Using a single absolute poverty line of $120 monthly per capita income, a World Bank study indicates an increase in the number of poor from 1989 to 1994, from eight million (3 percent of total population) to 58 million (18 percent of total population), i.e. 50 million new poor in a population of 320 million.

Various groups have suffered to a different extent in different countries. For instance, while everywhere pensioners lost out *in absolute terms*, in some countries they have been able to maintain their *relative* position (e.g. Slovakia, Hungary) or even improve it substantially (Poland - contrary to appearances). In all countries, children have been the heaviest losers in the transformation, with significant increases in the percentage of children under 16 living in households under the poverty line (according to UNICEF data for 1989-92).

It is well understood that the ageing of the European population in the next few decades will place a heavy burden on national economies. This is particularly the case for some Central and East European economies, especially Poland.

In the short run, transformation can be made more equitable by standard instruments of economic policy used to contain unemployment - such as employment subsidies, other instruments of active labour policies, and public works. These are precisely the progressive policies that even, indeed most of all, Vaclav Klaus - for all his Thatcherite rhetoric - has shrewdly implemented to contain unemployment in the Czech Republic. Looking further ahead, the best way to make post-communist transformation more equitable is through the resumption and acceleration of economic growth.

For the West, these trends imply: a large-scale need for external assistance (though not through support for the unemployed, as was initially suggested, due to their chronic nature); the great importance of improving trade access - still greatly restricted in spite of Association Agreements and other agreements with the European Union - and raising direct foreign investment (still very small relative to both needs and to developing countries); and for members of the European Union, the high cost of accession for potential Central and Eastern European members if these were entitled to the same kind of income support (through structural funds and other sources within the European policy of pursuing "Cohesion") enjoyed today by the weaker European regions.

SPECIAL LECTURE

A Two-Edged Sword
The Impact of Ecological Threats
on Economic Reforms
and
The Impact of Economic Reforms
on Ecological Issues

Murray Feshbach

A TWO-EDGED SWORD: THE IMPACT OF ECOLOGICAL THREATS ON ECONOMIC REFORMS AND THE IMPACT OF ECONOMIC REFORMS ON ECOLOGICAL ISSUES

Murray Feshbach

There is a direct link between ecology and economy, says Murray Feshbach. The ecological problems left after the break-up of the Soviet Union have today reached acute proportions - bordering in some areas on the ecological destruction of the population. From the view of the governments of the former Soviet Union, virtually everything needs fixing - so the population's problem is where to start. The West's dilemma is where to start funding - as the cost of cleaning up only part of the region's environment will run into tens of billions of dollars.

Dr. Feshbach is Research Professor at the Department of Demography, Georgetown University, Washington DC.

The impact on potential economic activity due to the environmental legacy from the Soviet regime is devastatingly bad, or as I have called it elsewhere, Ecocide. That is, Ecological Genocide of their own population, and therefore of the economy. Recently, a Russian friend told me, "Everything is going wrong, everything needs repair, every problem is connected to some other problem. We don't know where to begin and we have no money". A senior AID official put the dilemma in similar terms after a State Department briefing I gave on the ecological and health problems facing the former Soviet Union: "Your data are compelling; my problem is how to do all the tasks needed with limited funds available." Indeed, statements like this highlight one of the potential dangers of the Western approach to this problem - policy paralysis.

"Green" issues became a rallying point in the late Soviet period. Today, in the post-Soviet period, "green" issues have once again brought people out into the streets. Today's green issues are not the same as those that were dominant during the perestroika years. The great concern over "green" ecological issues has now given way to great concern over "green" dollar issues. People are finding it difficult not to be overwhelmed by the disastrous economic environment in the former Soviet Union. And the preoccupation with "green" dollar issues has greatly detracted from any progress on "green" ecological issues.

The task becomes even more complicated because the two green issues are now competing for the same funds and this may well prove to be counterproductive. I would argue that the two issues - ecological reform and economic reform - should not and cannot be separated. To attack one without simultaneously attacking the other is meaningless or, perhaps more appropriately summarised as "Soviet". An effective strategy must account for both. The question today is to find the right mix of ecological and economic goals.

• Priorities must be set among the overwhelming problems.

• Short-term goals must be dealt with separately and long-term goals concurrently initiated as appropriate.

In my previous work I have highlighted the severe impact of the highly centralised, irrational and shortsighted economic planning of the former Soviet Union on its ecology. That is, the goal of producing military weapons and heavy industrial output regardless of cost - economic, human or ecological - and the major side effects on the health and environment of the population. Today the problem has taken on new dimensions or new scales not seen anywhere else in the Eastern or Western world. The former Soviet Union remains mired in ecological disasters and economic obstacles. Each of these in turn negatively impacts the ecology of the former Soviet Union and simultaneously threatens productivity leading to economic growth and economic reforms. However, today wide-scale ecological disasters even threaten the very process of economic transformation. These disasters jeopardise economic reform because in financing clean-up projects, money, resources and manpower are diverted away from investment and other economic stimulation activities that are vital for a successful economic transition.

Funding ecological cleanups from internal sources is very limited and external funding is being questioned more and more. Moreover, multilateral, bilateral, and unilateral funding may still be insufficient for the total agenda and needs.

For example, (from *Ecological Disaster*) one of the most serious ecological threats today, the continued operation of first-generation RBMK - and VVER-type reactors will take years and cost many billions of dollars to repair or to replace. Jonathan C. Brown, the World Bank's Division Chief for Infrastructure, Energy, and Environment, estimates a price tag of between $6 billion and $8 billion. Ivan Selin, Chairman of the United States Nuclear Regulatory Commission, has judged that the cost may eventually climb to $20 billion. Private estimates run even higher.

Another example (from *Ecological Disaster*): the Norwegian government set aside 20 million Norwegian kroner (about $2.6 million) for the modernisation of the Russian nuclear electric power station on the Kola Peninsula at Polyarnyye Zori. Separately, the Finns have allocated 9 million markkas (about $1.5 million) for modernisation of the Polyarnnye Zori and Sosnovy Bor (near St. Petersburg) stations. Finland authorised 6.4 million markkas the year before (1992) for inspection, planning and determination of priorities.

In addition (from *Ecological Disaster*), Baltic Eco Association experts estimate that more than 28 billion Swedish kroner (about $3.8 billion) over a period of 20 to 30 years would be required to restore the Baltic Sea to its 1950s state. If the control centre for designing and implementing is Moscow city, and if the reports and interviews with a former chief of the Moscow City Directorate for Nuclear and Radiation Safety Oversight of Gosatomnadzor (their Nuclear Regulatory Commission) are correct, and if Vladimir Mikhaylovich Kuznetsov is not totally biased against his former employer, after being relieved of his position when he ordered 10 nuclear reactors to be closed after classifying them as dangerous to the inhabitants of the city, and if he is not exaggerating, then nuclear dangers may amount to a much more dangerous situation than considered heretofore. Work reliability and safety at 80 percent of the 63 nuclear research reactors in Moscow city and the immediate region surrounding the city, according to his information and evaluation, is such that they should be shut down, since none fully meets modern safety requirements, and only one specific reactor of Kurchatov Institute's 28 nuclear research reactors is a potential killer of 100,000s of persons. (Kuranty, 25-26 March 1995, pp. 1,4.). How hyperbolic or correct is he? Hopefully the former, but...

Again, for example, the Norilsk Nickel Plant and its subsidiary in Nikel' on the Komi Peninsula, had been one of the most, if not the most, profitable enterprises in the Russian Federation. This tremendously "profitable" firm produces some of the most devastating environmental side effects which threaten not only life and limb within and without Russia, but the viability of economic reforms. The total fallout of all pollutants in Norilsk is 85 tons per capita, 35 in Nikel and "only" 0.6 in Moscow - those of us who are familiar with Moscow, have witnessed firsthand the terrible impact on environmental conditions produced by industry and automotive transport. Moreover, until recently there were more than 600 radioactive toxic waste sites (mostly cleaned up, but 50-60 new are found each year). According to V.A. Rikunov, head of the Department of Management of Radiation Safety in the National Economy of Gosatomnadzor, there are 700,000 radioisotopic sources in operation in the Russian Federation. At Kurchatov Institute in Moscow, three nuclear reactors can be found, as can some 50-odd other reactors in the city. And if a major accident occurs? What will be the impact in a large city? Not a Chernobyl, but a clearly serious incident, to say the least. Hopefully funding will be sufficient for this nuclear regulatory commission to monitor and control safety and operations throughout all of Russia as well. So far this does not seem likely.

Returning to Nikel', in large part because of nickel production in Monchegorsk in Nikel', life expectancy at birth has declined to a shocking low level. In Nikel' life expectancy was only 34 years of age at birth, and 44 for the population of the city as a whole.

Since economic reform cannot be carried out from the grave, the impact of a declining life expectancy could be very serious for economic reform. Moreover, what is the incentive to work there and complete the task of reform in such a life-threatening environment? In fact, it is very premature to speak of successful democratisation, privatisation and marketisation in such cities as those which are very heavily polluted or environmentally threatened. For example, cities with heavy civilian and/or military chemical facilities are numerous and reforms are difficult to implement (See Murray Feshbach, Editor-in-Chief, Environmental and Health Atlas of Russia, Moscow, PAIMS, 1995, chapter IV. Available from Center for Post-Soviet Studies, Chevy Chase, MD. 20815, U.S.A.).

About the only positive aspect of the reform to date is that these polluting industries are now producing less because of the disarray in the market and in the supply system, and also because of the lack of money to pay wages.

Furthermore, there has been a brain drain of the scientists and skilled workers at these facilities who might have been the individuals supporting economic reform. On the other hand, those leaving probably will live longer than if they stayed and "fought" for such reforms. And if reforms do take place, and productivity is increased, perhaps output will increase again to its former levels … but will pollution abatement equipment be installed in the interim? Will money be spent by the Russian government, by the local government, by the industry, by the enterprise, or will they hope that the Norwegians and Finns affected by dangerous trans-boundary pollution pay for these pollution-reducing installations in order to save themselves, and the Russians as a derivative benefit? Will they have enough money for this activity, that is the Norwegians and Finns? And then what about numerous decaying ships containing radioactive waste in the fjords of the Kola Peninsula? What if a major accident occurs draining further everyone's funds, not to mention the potential impact on health and the attendant costs to treat and cure those affected. What about the dozens of nuclear-related facilities on the Peninsula?

Environmental and economic security for countries in and around the FSU are uncertain. If another Chernobyl-type accident occurs say on Kola Peninsula and large numbers of people flee across the borders to Norway, it could be devastating to the economy of the country of refuge. How would Norway (and therefore NATO) react, if one million persons flee across the border and become some 1/4 of the population of the country? What does this mean not only in economic terms, but also in general population and health issues that impact on the potential for economic growth? In another view, why did UNICEF conclude at the end of 1993 that if the figures they had at hand at that time were correct - and they were largely worse by the end of 1994 - the potential for social disintegration in Russia is high, and if social disintegration occurs, what does this mean for the organisation of production, the health of workers, and for economic growth? Essentially it means that economic reforms will not be successful, to say the least.

There are also some demographic trends that will negatively impact the future labour supply and that will demonstrate the current declining health of the workers. Overall the expectation is that we will see a major decline in the natural increase of the population of the Russian Federation. The number probably would decrease even further if there was not any forced migration, refugees, and illegal entrants (if counted), which have so far led to some migration of the decline in the population's size. Population increases because of forced migration, refugees and illegal entrants also will come at a cost to house, treat and employ them. Reduction in the growth of the absolute size of the population in Russia is not the result of positive trends, but of negative trends. Infant mortality has increased, maternal mortality has increased, the health of the already severely declining number of new-borns has been worsening, a growth in infectious diseases has been spectacular and will shortly produce a major increase in the number of all deaths in Russia.

The overall level of deaths - especially from extraordinary increases in the rate of diphtheria and probably from tuberculosis, cholera, plague and other diseases which are all relatively low in the West are starting to indicate alarming trends. Looking at the transparencies showing birth and death rates and life expectancy at birth - now 58.9 for males, but may go down to low 50s on average, statistically comprehending, therefore, a range of life expectancies from the 40s to 60s for males - and even a major decrease for females. Population projections made internally for the Russian government show a medium-term projection dropping from 148 million in 1995 to some 139 million persons by 2005, while many countries in the Western and in the Third World are attempting to slow population growth. The former Soviet Union already has such a pronatalist policy in place, but like the Western and Third World its official choices can be frustrated by human decisions and behaviour patterns. However, the consequence of years and decades of not linking decisions on military and industrial production has resulted in a population with serious health problems now and in the future, and again, problems for their potential productivity on the job.

From the point of view of economics, illness, as well as deaths in the prime working ages (increasing by 30 percent between 1992 and 1993) leads to drops in labour productivity, i.e., of output per person employed, and therefore to the reduction of potential economic growth and the economic reforms intended to allow growth to be facilitated in the future. In addition, due to corruption, money designated for environmental pollution abatement equipment and procedures is not being used as anticipated. And the enterprises do not have funds to spend on such equipment or procedures to guarantee current repair and maintenance of this equipment.

I will not go into too many details about the spread of problems, from widespread radioactivity - not only from the Chernobyl accident - chemical products such as dioxin, DDT and benzo(a)pyrene, and the spread of heavy metals at levels many multiples of the entire EEC, toxic waste of human, industrial, agricultural and military origin, and of air, land and water pollution. Perhaps one quote will suffice : the former Russian Minister of Health said

"To live longer, breathe less!" Water pollution is virtually universal and at a serious level.

The principal issue, then, becomes establishing a set of priorities to deal with these problems created by internal causes through external funding agencies, governments, and international organisations. I have attempted to provide such a list of priorities based on an enormous amount of new and better information in my recent book, *Ecological Disaster : Cleaning up the Hidden Legacy of the Soviet Regime* (published by the Twentieth Century Fund (New York) in February of this year). Long before the terrible event in Japan with use of sarin, I had been concerned about chemical weapons, and the book, for example, provides a list of the 53 cities that test, produce and/or store chemical weapons. If I lived in Udmurtiya's Kambarka why should I care about the reform unless the reform - political as well as economic - allows me to have an input into the decision-making process about what to do with these chemical weapons and their remainders?

What if DDT and PCBs wash into the Arctic Sea from coastal sources, and perhaps dumping reaches the United States and Canada? How will this affect health and environmental security in Alaska? Where will the money come from in the former Soviet Union to treat these problems, and do they want to know?

Legacies from the past affect the amount of resources available to implement economic reforms. It will cost billions of dollars to remediate the stock of chemical weapons, remove and properly store nuclear reactors and rods, as well as the liquid radioactive waste from submarines; the Aral Sea, which also affects weather and health in Russia; the Black Sea with revenue from fish catch declining dramatically - the annual catch dropped by two-thirds in a recent seven year period. Thus in 1985, 1.5 million tons of fish were caught; in 1992, 500,000 tons; and since then, according to the Washington Post, only 100,000 tons in 1994. Reduction in the mackerel catch, the former backbone of the fishing industry, has occurred also in the Sea of Azov. Ukraine's interagency environmental commission found that environmental pollution and impact on health of the population caused by the Black Sea fleet operations amounts to 19.4 billion US$ (Kiev, Narodna Armiya 17 Feb. 95, pp. 1-2), and who is to pay for it? Russia? the West?

Oil and gas spillage including accidents and flaring of by-products from oil processing lead to a loss of 7 to 20 percent of all output of oil and gas, and therefore of enormous quantities of income foregone for domestic use, which leads to continued use of Chernobyl-type reactors; hard currency income lost is not helpful as well. Revenues are not available which could have been used to improve the economic as well as ecological, health and political situation.

Transportation network - pipelines, railroad, intercity, transport, and so forth: What will be the costs to foreign investors? The EBRD and other foreign organisations have agreed to contribute funds for repairing the Usinsk pipeline, for example.

The injection of large sums of investment from abroad are deemed to be necessary for a successful reform of the Russian economy. The ecological threat involves variants for foreign investment in Russia. First of all, international companies may be discouraged by the current state of environmental decay in or around Russian industries, especially natural resource industries such as the diamond or oil industry. If a foreign oil company wants to invest in the Russian oil industry, it must consider the current state of disrepair of the Russian oil pipelines, the lack of adequate infrastructure, and the possibility of radioactive contamination of oil fields such as those in Kazakhstan. In any case there will be an environment of uncertainly for the investor. Second, foreign investors may have difficulty finding personnel and employees who would be willing to relocate to a dangerous area because of the environmental situation.

Foreign investors need not only clear and consistent rules of the game, but also firm banking, contract, and tax laws, as well as a cleaner environment, as noted here. To return to the "radioactivity issue" for the moment, it is important to point out that there are incremental costs in developing oil and diamond fields suffused with radioactivity from underground "peaceful, national economic" atomic explosions. These were asserted to be perfectly safe. We now know from Minatom Minister Viktor Mikhaylov, plus others from Kazakhstan and from the Sakha Republic (Yakutiya), that 30 percent of the underground explosions vented some radioactivity, (according to Mikhaylev), as well as from medical research and evidence in Kazakhstan and Sakha, per VM.

Another sector which must develop to stimulate successful economic reform in Russia is agriculture. Currently, Russian agriculture lags behind other developed countries due to poor farming techniques, inadequate infrastructure and widespread environmental pollution and devastation. The result of all these factors has been a decrease in the productivity of land. In response farmers have resorted to cultivating more and more land to try to produce the same crop yields. As a result there has been an extensive use of marginal land, which is not only less productive but also prevents it from being used for other economic activities. Increasing amounts of pesticides and fertilisers were used to stimulate bigger crop yields. This exacerbated the pollution problem and also jeopardised the healthiness and quality of the food produced. Agricultural reform - if it works, and leads to an improvement in the farm situation - will make farms more profitable, the farms or private farmers will be able to afford the purchase of pesticides and fertilisers as they had not been in the last few years and will pollute the land and the food grown in these lands as in the pre-reform period. Thus, a negative result may ensure from a positive development.

Some of Russia's most "profitable" industries i.e., timber, fishing, oil, gas, may be affected by new environmental regulations if they are truly enforced.

There is a cost of enforcing environmental laws and a cost for training people in environmental laws. Environmental law was slow to develop and environmental lawyers and law schools teaching environmental law are, therefore, rare in

Russia. (World Bank, Staff Appraisal Report Russian Federation Environmental Management Project, October 19, 1994, p. 19). Early costs, however, may lead to positive results later. However, as a World Bank study indicates, "Responsibilities for environmental quality management are dispersed among many government agencies. They are poorly coordinated leading to conflicts between agencies and inefficient use of limited human and financial resources available" (p. 19, World Bank).

Moreover, "There is a danger that well-trained and experienced personnel in pollution abatement and nature protection will seek other occupations in order to survive the current economic crisis" (p. 19, World Bank).

Increased regional autonomy can have negative as well as positive features. Coordination of economic reform and environmental regulation in the regions is necessary. For example, how will one section of a river flowing through Chechnya affect those regions below them if war conditions lead to pollution of rivers? One Oblast may be willing to spend money to clean it up and regulate it and another may not.

In sum, a two-edged sword hangs over their heads at both the macro and micro levels. Hopefully, the recently concluded Congress on Ecology and Sustainable Development held in Moscow from 3-5 June, 1995, will lead to improvement in the ecology of the country and therefore enable economic reform to succeed. While it is advisable to remain sceptical, one also can be hopeful that it will succeed. If so, it will also lessen environmental security threats to our countries as well.

RELATIVE HAZARD COEFFICIENT,
BY CITY, RUSSIA: 1992

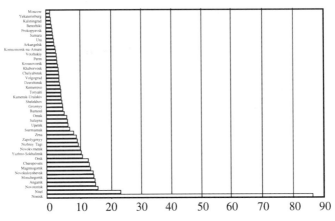

Source: Zdorov'ye naselenlya i khimicheskoye zagryazneniye
okruzhayushchey sredy v Rossli, Moscow, 1994, p.10

REGISTERED CASES OF DIPHTHERIA IN RUSSIA
1985 TO 1994

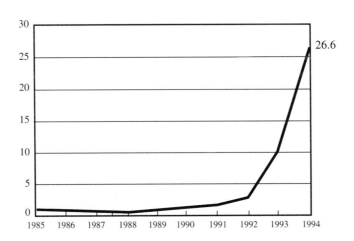

CASES PER 100,000 POPULATION

Sources: Goskomsanepidnadzor Rossii, Zdorov'ye naseleniya i sreda obitaniya, No.1, 1994 p. 22.
Goskomstat Rossii, Zdravookhraneniye v Rossiyskoy Federatsii, Moscow, 1992, p. 20.
Goskomstat Rossii, Narodnoye khozyaystvo Rssiyskoy Federatsii 1992, Moscow, 1992, p. 279.
Goskomstat Rossii, Okhrana zdrov'ya v RSFSR v 1990 g., Moscow, 1991, pp. 77-105.
Minisierstyo zdravookhranenlya SSSR, Zdravookhraneniye v SSSR, Moscow, 1989, pp. 9-10.
Morbidity and Mortality Weekly Report, Vol.44, No. 10, March 17, 1995, pp. 177-181.

113

LIVE EXPECTANCY IN RUSSIA: 1958-1959 TO 1993

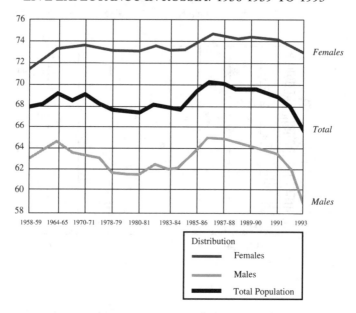

CHANGES IN THE ARAL SEA 1960 TO 1989

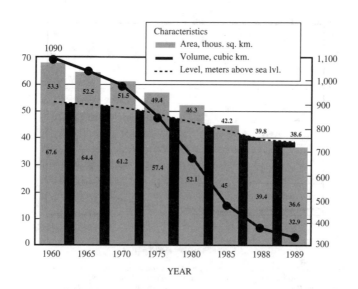

Source: Lyakhin, Yu.I. Sovremennoye ekologicheskoye
sostoyaniye morel SNG. Sankt-Peterburg, 1994, p. 8.

PANEL III

Privatisation and Industrial Restructuring

Chair: Reiner Weichhardt, Deputy Director
NATO Economics Directorate

Panelists: Michael Kaser
Niko Glozheni
Leonid Kosals
Anna Zatkalíková
Peter Rutland

THE PRIVATISATION PHASE OF INDUSTRIAL RESTRUCTURING

Michael Kaser

Privatisation in the West took place within a detailed legislative framework and a free-market culture. Professor Michael Kaser confirms that Central and Eastern Europe's transition is quite the opposite. The direct costs are measurable - paying for restructuring, recapitalising banks, and absorbing old debts. The indirect costs are harder to quantify, but they reflect the chaotic environment in which the reformers have to operate. Their aim, according to one economist, is 'a normal Western market economy'. The problem is that they must create one in a world where literally everything is for sale.

Professor Kaser is working at the Institute of German Studies, University of Birmingham, UK.

Political Factors in Restructuring

Sir John Hicks, the first British Nobel Laureate in Economics, identified the competitive market as the principal institutional contributor to economic development and contrasted it with the only two other mechanisms for the exchange economy - a customary economy (with complete "belowness") and a command economy (with complete "aboveness").[1] He was following through an earlier insight[2] that a price mechanism was not a created institution, but an inherent characteristic of an exchange economy. Among command economies of the past, he cited that of the Mongol Empire of Genghis Khan and his successors, which significantly affected the medieval Russian economic system.[3] The Soviet-type command economy is the only system of modern times in which the nationalisation of productive assets was aimed at the elimination of political and economic competition. Governments of market economies in wartime, and totalitarian regimes have imposed all-embracing controls over the employment of such assets; those governments applied coercion and asset confiscation to enforce their control, but they did not arrogate to themselves the entirety of ownership: the facility of private ownership was not withdrawn.

When political competition replaced the monopoly of a Party oligarchy in the revolutions of 1989-92 and competitive allocation was sought for the factors of production, the choice was inevitably for private ownership of a substantial part of productive assets. Legislatures and executives undertaking that systemic transformation based their privatisation programmes both upon an economic case - to enhance domestic efficiency and external compatibility with trade and

117

factor flows with established market economies - and upon the political case - to build a mass constituency of owners whose stake would dissuade them from surrendering it in any systemic reversal.

The participation of political objectives in government-directed ownership change has of course also been evident in most Western industrial economies, as phrases such as "rolling back the state" and "a property-owning democracy" testified during the 1980s and since. But everywhere, markets were operational within a detailed legislative frame and a pervasive "market culture". By contrast, the privatisation of post-communist governments took place as both political and economic systems were in flux.

This paper seeks to offer a comparative assessment of the progress of privatisation of 30 economies in transition. Three of these are constituents of a contemporary state (the Eastern *Länder* of Germany and two republics of Yugoslavia[4]); 21 are states created by the break-up of federations (15 from the Soviet Union, four others from Yugoslavia and two from Czechoslovakia) and only six continue integrally from communist times (Albania, Bulgaria, Hungary, Mongolia, Poland and Romania). In the majority of transition countries, therefore, the political centre-periphery relationship thus altered on the eve of, or during, the reshaping of the economic centre-periphery relationship, and each reform was radical. Taken in conjunction with personnel changes throughout the political and administrative hierarchy, a fast pace of political readjustment has accompanied the rapid transfer of productive-asset ownership.

The speed of political change has nevertheless been moderated in three ways. First, virtually no changes have taken place in regional and local boundaries, other than in the former GDR which was required to establish *Land* governments to obtain unification with the Federal Republic. Secondly, the previously ruling communist parties have reformed themselves as social-democratic parties: in five states, after a break in opposition, they have re-entered coalition governments (Bulgaria, Hungary, Lithuania, Poland and Slovakia) and in one (Mongolia) they have remained the government throughout. Thirdly, in 11 countries leadership by the president has tended towards the authoritarian, with the result that economic policies may be implemented without too scrupulous a regard for dissent: this is the case in varying degrees in the five states of Central Asia (Turkmenistan the most and Kyrgyzstan the least); of the Caucasus (Azerbaijan more than Armenia and Georgia); Albania, Romania and Serbia. The concentration of political power led the Vice-President of the European Bank for Reconstruction and Development, Ron Freeman, publicly to observe while in Uzbekistan that the Bank can accept and keep as members ("countries of operation") only those countries which adhere to "the fundamental principles of multi-party democracy".[5]

One political development which is the result of privatisation is the enhanced influence of enterprise management in local administration. Under the command economy, state enterprise directors were subordinate to an "industrial ministry" in the capital city and deployed their efforts to obtain and fulfil "easy" material and financial plans (within the "cosy relations" Kornai so aptly described[6]), and regional and local authorities were almost wholly dependent on centralised finance. Lateral contact was largely informal, with factory chiefs associated within the local *nomenklatura*, although some "dual subordination" existed in budget-financed institutions. The mutual relationships after privatisation are much more specific: enterprises generate local tax revenue, profoundly affect local employment and have discarded many of their social-support functions for local authorities to re-establish as best they can. In Russia, in particular, the influence of local management on local government is both ways: a "Council of Directors"[7] exerts pressure on local councils and the latter often have shares in local enterprises.

Such economic restructuring as has taken place has in general happened later than the political reshaping just described, and has followed privatisation (but partly and substantially preceded it in Germany). Some salient features of the changes are noted in a concluding section, but less comprehensively in this paper than with respect to privatisation.[8]

The Privatisation of Non-Farm Assets

Once the policy of asset divestment had been adopted, electorates, parliaments and governments had to choose the recipients of property. Political considerations were taken into account in three ways. The first was to offer restitution or compensation to previous owners. Termed "re-privatisation" (as Zatkalíková† describes it in this volume), the process was especially directed towards households; corporate and institutional owners other than churches and charities were usually excluded. Land and residential property is in process of restitution in the Eastern Lander of Germany, Albania,[9] Bulgaria, the Czech and Slovak Republics,[10] Estonia, Latvia, Lithuania, the former Yugoslav Republic of Macedonia, Poland, Romania and Slovenia. Hungary, by contrast, offered only compensation, but this was in the form of vouchers which could be traded or exchanged for shares in privatised equity or housing. The second was to allow the staff of the enterprise to select the mode of privatisation (or in one republic, Serbia, re-nationalisation). In describing such "decentralised implementation", Rutland, in this volume, cites it as "privatising the privatisation process". The third, and most significant, was to give free, or virtually free, vouchers to citizens to buy equity in state enterprises and in some cases housing. Among the voucher schemes used, or planned, the denomination in most was money, but in a few it was points.[11] The idea of vouchers originated in Poland[12] but the initial schemes were launched in Czechoslovakia and Mongolia.

Nine governments decided against free vouchers, but all 30 states initiated privatisation with some disposal of small state entities - shops, personal service units and artisan workshops - usually by auction, but often by a procedure which allowed existing employees to take over.[13] There is a quasi-voucher scheme in Hungary in interest-free loans for the purchase of shares; its privatisation had originally been on a case-by-case basis but from May 1995, it has been much extended - receipts amounting to $1.2 billion are expected in the first year. Four governments are selling on the model of Western privatisations - the Treuhand in the new German *Lander*, and Estonia which emulated its practice, Azerbaijan (after the post-coup government reversed its predecessor's voucher scheme), and Uzbekistan. In Tajikistan, civil unrest has precluded an overall scheme but much of the state sector which actually operates is run locally.

Macedonia has similarly allowed small firms to drift into private hands, but by mid-1995, nearly 300 larger ones should have been transferred. Because the Yugoslav Federal Assembly has not yet enacted a law on privatisation, it fell to the Montenegrin and Serbian legislatures to authorise ownership change: under the series of laws since 1951 on worker self-management, it is the staff who have been choosing and a substantial proportion have opted to become state property.[14] Croatia also inherited worker self-management, but its law (of 1991) merely formalised such property rights as joint-stock companies, leaving them to sell shares as they chose.

Among voucher-issuing countries, Mongolia was a pioneer, giving uniform-value vouchers to all citizens of any age; Armenia and Turkmenistan similarly schedule them for all citizens, but allow a supplement for any purchase of shares in the employee's own enterprise. Ukrainian non-tradeable vouchers are of uniform value, but citizens are entitled to a supplement corresponding to the amount standing to their credit at the State Savings Bank when the Soviet rouble ceased to be legal tender, and accounts were frozen. Moldova differentiated vouchers by the length of the recipient's employment in the country and Albania and Slovenia by the recipient's age. Bulgarian, Georgian, Latvian, Lithuanian and Romanian voucher privatisation began at various dates in 1995.[15] In the latter, uniform (non-tradeable) vouchers had been distributed in 1992, but because their face-value had been deeply eroded by inflation, a further allocation is being made with a higher value (equal to double the average wage). The Russian and Ukrainian schemes had envisaged deposits in escrow accounts in the State Savings Bank on which the beneficiary could draw only to buy equity in privatised firms, but, in the event, only Kyrgyzstan adopted this procedure.

Ninety percent of Russian tradeable vouchers distributed in 1992, also of a uniform value, were used in the allotted period (to July 1994) together with auction and cash purchases. Forty million shareholders were established in that first stage of large-scale privatisation. Military and dual-purpose industry was nevertheless largely excluded: Kosals, in this volume, notes that government control was maintained in three out of four such plants at the end of the first stage. The second stage, for which money purchase is the sole channel, is intended to be concluded in 1995 and was foreseen as bringing nine trillion roubles ($1.8 billion) to the enterprises being sold (with a smaller payment to local and central government). However, a mere 50 billion roubles ($10 million) had been paid by the end of March 1995, largely because households had no more savings to spend (after the earlier "small" and first stage of the "large" privatisation) and because the corporate and banking sectors preferred to buy Treasury bills. These raised 5.7 trillion roubles in 1994 and should cover the bulk of the 1995 budget deficit of 32 trillion,[16] but to the evident detriment of privatisation in that second stage. The scheme allows some concessions to employees.[17]

The principal reason for denominating vouchers in "points" was to prevent them increasing the money supply and thence inflation. In the united Czechoslovakia, booklets of points were sold at a very low charge and were used in a first round of sell-offs. Ninety-six percent of the aggregate number of shares on offer were taken up. But whereas the Czech Republic maintained the procedure into a second round, Slovakia, after much political controversy, which Zatkalíková† recounts in this volume, discontinued it in early July 1995.

Belarus graduated points on scales related to age, employment and social situation; it made provision for such vouchers to apply to half the state-enterprise equity to be privatised during 1994-97, but by late 1994 only 3 percent of state enterprises had been privatised.[18] Kazakhstan differentiated points by urban and rural residence, favouring the latter.

Most governments which issued vouchers permitted them to be traded, and all allowed them to be pooled in investment funds. In Poland, however, the 15 National Investment Funds into which citizens may invest their vouchers are the pillars of the scheme. Instituted as long ago as December 1993, the Fund management (consortia of Western and Polish financial companies) obtained their first state-enterprise controlling equity in July 1995. Of the 413 state enterprises accepting selection for this first round, 28 were offered at that time, and in a second phase it is hoped to persuade another 300 enterprises into the "pool". The Funds get 60 percent of the state's equity; 15 percent is given gratis to employees, 15 percent is held for social uses or given to pensioners, and the residual 10 percent stays in government ownership. Although Funds may relinquish their holding before term, they are meant to hold their shares and manage the holdings efficiently for ten years. If they perform according to long-term gain, they can leave with 15 percent of the terminal value of the assets under management. In all voucher-issuing states, shares in investment funds could also be bought, but lack of regulation led to a number of fraudulent flotations, particularly in Georgia and Romania; as Glozheni records in this volume, Albanian legislation on investment funds is imminent.

The Russian legislation under the first stage allowed state enterprise personnel to choose among three variants and one of these assured 51 percent of the shares to be allotted to them: it is not surprising that nearly four-fifths of enterprises selected this path to "insider" control.[19] In the second stage, the government has ruled out sale of its controlling holdings in many major companies (the gas and telecommunications monopolies and the biggest oil concerns) and has passed management control in others to a consortium of large banks against a very large loan to reduce other provision for the public borrowing requirement.

De-collectivisation

In Poland and ex-Yugoslavia, collectivisation was never imposed; Bulgarian and Hungarian co-operative farms were at the most liberal extreme and the Albanian form of quasi-state collectives were the most repressive. The privatisation of farmland is virtually complete in Central and Eastern Europe and the Baltic States (with some exclusions of entitlement of foreigners to ownership). Complications have been inserted by legislatures into some procedures - restitution to former owners (as noted above) and leasing rather than outright ownership. Many difficulties have been experienced in the demarcation of properties where an official survey was not maintained on a property basis or was contested. These problems were at their worst in Albania, but were also manifest in Bulgaria and Romania (where a law is in course of enactment to permit the private ownership of land, including by foreigners). The situation in the many Bulgarian and Slovak co-operative farms which continue by their members' wish is complicated by absentee-ownership.

In some countries, notably Russia, Ukraine, Belarus, the Central Asian states, Bulgaria and Slovakia, collective and state farms have remained largely as before. A complex series of reasons accounts for members' unwillingness to establish themselves as independent farmers. Among these in Russia is the strength of conservative elements (from the village *nomenklatura* up to the Agrarian Party in the Duma and the "agricultural lobby" in the government, led by Deputy Premier Aleksandr Zaveryukha) and the difficulties individual farmers face in obtaining supplies, finance for investment and marketing outlets free of corruption and crime. There are similar conservative interests in the other predominantly Slav states, but whereas President Leonid Kuchma decreed Ukrainian private land ownership soon after he took office (though progress is slow on implementation), President Aleksandr Lukashenka remains cautious and only leasehold is yet permitted in Belarus. Elsewhere in the Commonwealth of Independent States (CIS), change to private land ownership has been most comprehensive in Armenia, but is also under way in Kazakhstan, Kyrgyzstan, Moldova and Uzbekistan. Georgia, Tajikistan and Turkmenistan, however, only permit leasehold, and Azerbaijan has not yet taken any measures.

Restructuring

Privatisation is usually the first phase of "restructuring". It constitutes a legitimisation of the political and economic system, and it fosters a more efficient use, and a decentralised mobilisation, of resources. It involves both measures which enterprises normally take in market economies as costs and sales conditions and prospects change, and those which are indicated (though not necessarily implemented) by the systemic change itself. The introduction of a market and especially the liberalisation of incomes and prices evokes effects and responses in both spheres. A difference between the "normal" and the "extraordinary" is that the role of the state is much greater in the second than in the first. This is partly because the state is divesting itself of microeconomic functions and must therefore undertake a specific regulatory function, and partly because the state possesses more funds and more powers to implement change than a private corporation (particularly if inflation and/or recession have weakened the financial, investment and managerial potential of the latter). The state has, as in all circumstances, a duty to execute policies conducive to macroeconomic stability and development and to facilitate (and/or to protect from) external economic transactions.

Among the measures which restructuring has been applying in East and Central Europe and in the post-communist Asian states are:

• The "unbundling" of groups unsuited to, or undesirable for, a market economy. Large combines were especially favoured by planning bodies and communist leaderships as a reaction to the short-lived experiments in managerial devolution of the mid-1960s; monopolies were established under the auspices of Comecon or as national protection and by search for the economies of scale within quasi-autarkies; most state enterprises undertook social-support functions.

• Following any break-up, new organisational forms are required: an important development characterising Russia is the "financial-industrial" group. A recent study by a Russian economist lists the pros and cons of the policy embraced since December 1993, by the Russian State Committee for Industrial Policy (Goskomprom) to foster these, subject to two binding conditions, viz., that no participating corporation should be admitted if its equity were more than 25 percent in state hands and that no financial institution should own more that 10 percent of the shares in a participating corporation or invest more than 10 percent of its assets in participating corporations. There are a number of conditions the relaxation of which requires approval by the relevant government regulatory body, such as the Anti-Monopoly Commission.[20] The danger perceived is that some such groups are motivated by survival through mutual protection and preferential subsidisation rather than by the gain of competitiveness or of foreign participation.

• Capitalisation in many forms includes particularly the recapitalisation of banks (both state-owned and private) and clearing the accumulation of bad debts from enterprise balance sheets. A very substantial literature exists on this topic. Inter-enterprise indebtedness remains substantial in all CIS member-states and in Albania, Bulgaria, the former Yugoslav Republic of Macedonia and Romania. Hungary, Latvia and Lithuania have a special problem because their bankruptcy laws (of 1993, 1991 and 1992 respectively) do not impose a requirement that companies with overdue liabilities should cease trading. Nation-wide loan-restructuring among enterprises and banks was largely completed in Poland in 1994. The clearance of non-performing debt and the laying of sound regulatory regimes have been carried out in Croatia, Czechoslovakia, Estonia (but only after a banking crisis in 1992), Hungary, Latvia, Poland and Slovenia, but remain to be fully developed in most other states. New capital formation is also required for implementing decisions on market forecasts (see below) and may be provided by foreign investment by direct implantation, as portfolio purchase or the flotation of new shares.

• Management may be changed, for those more capable of directing an enterprise (often in a new size and shape) under the new conditions. The dominance of "insider" shareholding (in particular Russia and Mongolia) may weaken such flexibility.

• "Resizing" the workforce may not always, but usually does, mean redundancy. The growth of the private sector to absorb those laid off reduces the need for a state "social safety net". State funding for the externalities of training and continuing education is required to reskill the labour force.

• The reassessment by the restructured firms, their management and their workforce of new prospects for costs, sales and investment includes change in marketing and advertising methods and openness to the development of foreign markets.

• Environmental repair and protection is a significant area for restructuring because of the prevalence of output priority in the previously-supply-driven plan systems. As Feshbach points out in this volume, private owners of former state enterprises are unlikely to have funds both for new investment and for environmental repair, and foreign investors would be deterred by the cost of such repair or even by an unwillingness to live in heavily polluted areas. Another issue is the division of such costs between the state (either as previous owner or for the common good) and the post-privatisation owner.

• There is, finally, the very broad consideration of adjustment to market-based regulatory, prudential and conventional legislation and practice. Again, there is a substantial literature on the necessary infrastructure and the process of monitoring change in it.

The direct costs of privatisation are being experienced under three headings - expenditure on the privatisation process; financial and physical restructuring; and subsidisation, including recapitalisation of banks and the absorption of inter-enterprise bad debts. Indirect costs are emerging because of inadequate legislation on titles and their exchange, poor regulatory procedures and criminality; standards are far from acceptable where a contract killing is cheaper than settlement of a debt, or where a majority of banks do not reach legal reserve ratios or are party to capital flight or money-laundering. Restructuring ends when the aim is achieved (in the words of the architect of the Polish economic transition, Leszek Balcerowicz, a few days after taking office in September 1989) of "a normal, Western market economy".

Footnotes

1. Hicks (1969, p. 21); see also his reply to critiques in Hicks (1977, pp. 181-4).
2. Hicks (1960, p. 707).
3. Kaser (1978, p. 426).
4. Montenegro and Serbia, which have separate privatisation programmes in the absence of any Federal legislation.
5. Cited in *Financial Times*, 31 May 1995.
6. Kornai (1992) and earlier works.
7. In historical perspective, the council (*sovet direktorov*) descends from the merchants' hundred (*kupecheskaya sotnya*) of medieval Russian towns and the Petrine guild (*gild'iya*) (Kaser 1978, pp. 426, 448).
8. This is because the present writer had in recent research compiled more comparative information on privatisation than on restructuring (Kaser 1995a; 1995b).
9. A form of co-ownership was instituted by a 1993 law where non-agricultural land had already been privatised (EBRD, 1994, p. 16). Glozheni, in this volume, notes the legal disputes raised by the restitution of farmland.
10. Industrial property was also included in the restitution law of 1990 for the united Czechoslovakia, and church property in a Slovak law of 1993.
11. The descriptions of schemes follow EBRD 1994, 1995, and ECE 1995; IMF *Economic Reviews*; and documents on East Germany, Mongolia and Yugoslavia.
12. Frydman and Rapaczynski 1994, p. x.
13. For a comparison of 'small privatization' in Russia with the Czech Republic, Hungary and Poland, see Friebel, 1995, and in the latter three Earle et al., 1994.
14. Petrović 1994.
15. As only 434 enterprises were concerned, there are approximately 2,200 shareholders per (rather small) enterprise; data from Mongolian Chamber of Commerce and Industry, 1995, p. 8.
16. The *Financial Times*, 12 June 1995, commented: 'In contrast to Russia's infamously ramshackle equity market, the market for government bonds has won acclaim for its sound trading and settlement arrangements.'
17. For the three variants, see Kaser 1995, pp. 17-18.
18. EBRD 1995, p.53.
19. This short paper is not the place for a full discussion; see particularly Birn, Jones and Weisskopf 1994, pp. 272-6; Kaser 1995, pp. 40-4 and Young and Reynolds, 1994, pp. 39-40.
20. Starodubrovskaya 1995, p. 11.

References

Birn, A., Jones, D. and Weisskopf, T. (1994), 'Privatization in the Former Soviet Union and the new Russia', in Estrin, 1994, pp. 252-78.

EBRD (1994), *Transition Report 1994*, London, EBRD.

EBRD (1995), *Transition Report Update*, London, EBRD.

Earle, J. S., Frydman, R., Rapaczynski, A. and Turkewitz, J. (1994), *Small Privatization: The Transformation of Retail Trade and Consumer Services in the Czech Republic, Hungary and Poland,* Central European University Press, Budapest.

ECE (1995), *Economic Survey of Europe in 1994-1995,* New York and Geneva, United Nations.

Estrin. S. (ed.) (1994), *Privatization in Central and Eastern Europe*, London, Longman.

Friebel, G. (1995), 'Organisational Issues of Trade and Services Privatization in Russia', *Economic Systems,* 19 (March), pp. 25-58.

Hicks, J. R. (1960), 'Linear Theory', *Economic Journal*, 70, pp. 671-709.

Hicks, J. R. (1969), *A Theory of Economic History,* Oxford, Clarendon Press.

Hicks, J. R. (1977), *Economic Perspectives*, Oxford, Clarendon Press.

Kaser, M. C. (1978), 'Russian Entrepreneurship' in *Cambridge Economic History of Europe,* VII, Cambridge, Cambridge University Press.

Kaser, M. C. (1995a), *Privatization in the CIS*, London Royal Institute of International Affairs.

Kaser, M. C. (1995b), *The Central Asian Economies after Independence*, 2nd edn, Washington, the Brookings Institution (forthcoming, revision of 1st edn, London 1992, in Allison, R. (ed.), *Political and Economic Challenges in Post-Soviet Central Asia and the Transcaucasus*).

Kornai, J. (1992), *The Socialist System*, Oxford, Oxford University Press.

Mongolian Chamber of Commerce and Industry (1995), *Review of the Mongolian Economy in 1994*, Ulaanbaatar.

Starodubrovskaya, I. (1995), 'Financial-Industrial Groups: Illusions and Reality', *Communist Economies and Economic Transformation*, 7 (March).

Young, P. and Reynolds, P. (1994), *The Amnesia of Reform: A Review of Post-Communist Privatization*, London, Adam Smith Institute.

ECONOMIC REFORM, PRIVATISATION AND INDUSTRIAL RESTRUCTURING IN ALBANIA

Niko Glozheni

Albania is a small country with big problems, says Niko Glozheni. It emerged from fifty years of isolation under the harshest of Europe's communist dictatorships with its economy in ruin and its people on the brink of starvation. Despite this, the reform programme is working - inflation though still high, is falling, and price controls have all but vanished. The currency is strong, and privatisation is steaming ahead, with the full backing of all political parties. Economic reform will be difficult and painful - but, judging from the progress so far, the worst may be over.

Dr. Glozheni is Executive Director, Albanian National Agency for Privatisation, Tirana.

Economic Reform, Privatisation and Industrial Restructuring

Although it is small, Albania has all the characteristics and problems of a big country. 50 years of isolation and totally wrong economic and technical education policies mean that foreign technological and intellectual investment is much more necessary here than in the other countries of Eastern and Central Europe.

It is said and accepted that privatisation is not only an economic process. To guarantee its success there is a great need for political support from the government, Parliament and the political parties. In Albania it is a very significant fact that most of the politically aware are conscious of the importance of this support. Starting from the President of the Republic, who without doubt is the most positive person concerning the progress in privatisation. Ministers and members of parliament strongly support the process and are an important instrument in implementing the objectives of the economic programme - and particulary of privatisation.

The programme has three main objectives:
• Speed of the process.
• Social justice and transparency.
• Development of small and medium-sized enterprises.

Privatisation in Albania, as in all countries of Central and Eastern Europe, is the most important problem of economic reform. Increasing the economic efficiency of the productive resources; encouraging competition between the different economic activities of the enterprises; reducing budget expenditures for subsidising loss-making enterprises; and increasing the participation of foreign investors in the different economic sectors, are some of the goals of this process which Albania started in August 1991 by passing the Law on Privatisation.

The democratic government which took office in Albania in March 1992, inherited an economy in profound crisis. Industrial production had declined drastically since 1989, with most of the enterprises either closed or operating at a small fraction of their capacity. The country at that time relied on humanitarian aid to avert malnutrition.

Dynamism was to be found in construction and retail sectors. The government was committed to a courageous stabilisation programme with tight monetary targets and price liberalisation. Most of those targets were being met. With IMF and World Bank financing, the government achieved a dramatic fall in inflation from 300 percent to 30 percent in two years. Most agriculture had been privatised and production was expanding dramatically. Housing and small-medium enterprises were returning to the private sector as well.

During 1992 the situation worsened as compared to 1991, but in the succeeding years the situation has stabilised. As the result of the economic policies, a GDP increase close to the goal set of 8 percent (50 percent in the agricultural sector) was achieved.

The inflation rate continued to fall, reaching its lowest monthly rate, 19.5 percent, in August. The monthly inflation rate by the end of 1994 was estimated to be 15.8 percent. A monthly growth in income of 14.2 percent and a monthly increase in expenses of about 16 percent caused the budget deficit to grow.

Great improvements were achieved in price liberalisation. One of the first steps in the implementation of the reform programme was the lifting of price controls for 75 percent of consumption articles in the cities. In April 1994, 96 percent of the basket prices were liberalised. Except for controls on some basic food articles and a limited number of the other-than-food articles brought into circulation by state entities (energy, medicine, telecommunications, urban transportation, and some housing construction), all other wholesale and retail prices have been freed. The government has taken steps to even out prices of basic goods and other controlled articles as close as possible to their real cost.

Another development worth mentioning is the introduction of a uniform and free exchange rate. At the time of unification, the Albanian currency was devalued to the rate of 130 leks=$1. By the end of 1993 as well as during the first three months of 1994 the lek was exchanged at rate of 100 leks=$1. Afterwards the lek became somewhat stronger and by the middle of 1994 it had reached the rate of 90 leks=$1.

Due to its indispensable role in the progress of economic reform and to the dire financial situation of state-owned enterprises, privatisation is considered of vital importance by all the political parties. Nevertheless, despite this unanimous approval, there are some differences of opinion among the different parties regarding the methods, forms and speed of the privatisation process, and concerning issues such as the scope and depth of privatisation, the balance between privatisation and restructuring, and other factors.

Legal Framework

As I mentioned, the basic law on which privatisation is based is the Law on Sanctioning and the Protection of Private Property, Free Initiative and Privatisation of 10 August, 1991. This law is considered as very liberal and very broad, in the sense that it allows enough space for functioning within the government's decisions. It defines the National Agency of Privatisation as the central institution responsible for the transformation of state property into private property, which sets the rules of the entire procedure of privatisation up to the total transformation of property.

Another important law covers the "Protection of Foreign Investments". This is considered as the most liberal for foreign investors, with its main aspects being:
- Elimination of bureaucratic barriers in transactions.
- Arbitration of disputes (regarding joint ventures) in foreign courts.
- Free transfer of capital to banks outside Albania.

There is also a law "On Restitution", which clearly stipulates the amount of formerly private property which will be returned to ex-owners, their definition and the institutions responsible.

The law "On Commercial Companies" defines the organisational forms of registered companies in the Republic of Albania. It clearly defines the relationship between partners in various types of companies. The law "On Transformation of State owned Enterprises into Commercial Companies" and the Presidential decree "On Issuing and the Distribution of the Privatisation Vouchers", are also relevant.

Privatisation and Restructuring

The relationship between privatisation and restructuring for the enterprises in the process has been clarified. Since speed of privatisation is the basic criterion, it has been resolved that privatisation will guide restructuring. In some complex or large enterprises, commissions of experts are to decide on splitting off sections that have little or no technological connection.

If one considers the existing macroeconomic and technical barriers, privatisation's priority over restructuring is indisputable. It is widely accepted that restructuring can be better managed by the private owner himself.

In the end, a state-guided restructuring, however elaborate it may be, would not turn out to be efficient, as market priorities may change considerably in the dynamics of the vigorous macro - or microeconomic changes in the country.

Still, a few enterprises will undergo a process of restructuring according to a special programme funded by the World Bank. The Enterprise Restructuring Agency was set up to help this process.

Privatisation Results

Since the time of its mandate in 1992, the government took measures for fast privatisation in the most rapidly emerging sectors. The retail trade was privatised totally as well as services, road transport, fishing. Later in 1993, the wholesale trade, agroindustrial sector, hotels and other areas were successfully privatised. 1994 marks the high point of small and medium enterprise privatisation to date. Here, most of the construction sector, the foreign trade enterprises, the tourism sector, industry and agriculture were privatised. This process of privatisation is still going on for other sectors as is the privatisation of state-owned assets. (The standard privatisation methods used are auctions, or the favouring of certain social strata.)

The privatisation of apartments is completed and the restitution of the urban land to ex-owners is being finished. Agricultural land has been divided among the peasants.

Mass Privatisation Programme (MPP)

Apart from the points mentioned above, the Ministry of Finance, National Agency of Privatisation and National Bank, immediately started the study, drafting and implementation of a Mass Privatisation scheme. In a very short time it was drafted, as well as a privatisation scheme of joint stock companies and a distribution scheme of compensation vouchers for the population.

The Presidential decree of March 1995 for the distribution of privatisation vouchers marked the start of mass privatisation. Vouchers will be distributed to all Albanians over 18 years old; they are divided into three age groups and several phases. The Bank of Albania will be responsible for printing vouchers and the Savings Bank will be responsible for distributing them to the eligible population.

The medium and large enterprises to be privatised through share auctions need to be transformed into joint stock companies according to the Law On Transformation of SOEs into Commercial Companies which passed 20 April, 1995.

The share auctions will be held at the national level over a maximum period of several weeks. Enterprises will be offered for sale when their preparation is completed and restitution claims are settled. The enterprises which will be offered for share auctions will be announced in advance and basic information on the enterprises will be available.

In the Mass Privatisation Programme, voucher holders will have the choice of investing their vouchers into investment funds. The investment funds are established as joint stock companies which are under preparation.

The privatisation programme is a critical element of the government's economic reform programme. Information on the privatisation programme is designed to raise public awareness of privatisation. Information will be widely disseminated on the following: how and when eligible citizens can pick up their vouchers; auction times, places and processes; and basic information on the enterprises and assets which are being sold.

The privatisation of strategic sectors such as the power sector, telecommunications, water supply, etc., will be made after the special laws for them have been drafted. The groups within the ministries will cooperate with the commission created for the mass privatisation programme.

This is an outline of the economic reform in Albania and privatisation as a crucial element of it. What is happening in Albania is similar to the processes of all the countries of Eastern Europe. Of course, each country has its specifics and differences, but in general the reform in all these countries is going through the same stages with different delays in time.

Albania has suffered under the most brutal dictatorship in Europe, so it is understandable that economic reform in Albania is being carried out with difficulty and is a rather painful process. Despite this challenge, the Albanian government is optimistic about the results of the reform and its achievements.

RUSSIA'S MILITARY-INDUSTRIAL COMPLEX: PRIVATISATION AND THE EMERGING NEW OWNERS

Leonid Kosals

A free-market culture is slowly emerging in Russia's military-industrial complex (MIC). To date the government has been careful to keep overall control: three-quarters of the MIC are still in state hands despite the privatisation programme. But a new managerial attitude is emerging, reports Dr. Leonid Kosals. And this new breed of managers comes not a minute too soon, as this industry is in desperate need of a firm hand to help its companies develop and innovate. Today's big question is whether the governments will actually allow the MIC companies to follow this path to restructuring and conversion.

Dr. Kosals is a Senior Researcher at the Institute for Population Studies, Russian Academy of Sciences, Moscow.

Goal of Paper and Information Used

The goal of this paper is to provide an answer to the questions 1) whether new owners are emerging in Russia's military-industrial complex (MIC) and 2) if the process of creating new owners has been started, what stage this process is at. To do this we must account for the changes in the problems which enterprises are facing during today's radical economic reforms in Russia.

The information used in this paper includes data from four sociological surveys carried out by the author, together with Prof. R. Ryvkina between 1992 and 1995.

Survey I was conducted in January 1992 at the start of the radical transition. Some 312 directors of defence enterprises were polled in all main regions of Russia. We focused on the problems which directors faced and their plans to restructure their enterprises.

Survey II (July 1994) included the opinions of 11 experts on the directions of changes in different parts of the MIC. We revealed whether there was some stabilisation in defence industries or it was only the decay of the enterprises during 1994. Among the experts were the specialists of the State Committee for the Defence Industries, and the League for Assistance to the Defence Enterprises, as well as the directors of the biggest military enterprises.

Survey III (June-December 1994) was carried out by mail with the support and participation of the League for Assistance to the Defence Enterprises.

135

Eighty-five directors of the military enterprises in different regions were polled (216 questionnaires were sent out). The aim of the survey was to analyse directors' changes of attitude related to market reform at the enterprise level, and particularly their opinion about privatisation.

Survey IV, was also conducted with the support and participation of the League for the Assistance to the Defence Enterprises in May 1995. Fifty directors gave answers to the questionnaire about government policy in the MIC, as well as about the problems and prospects of the military enterprises.

None of these studies was representative in the strict statistical sense. The samples were provided by experts because of the secrecy of statistical information concerning the MIC, and the difficulties of managing large-scale investigations of the subjects in question. However, according to competent experts, we have managed to grasp the main problems of defence enterprises because the surveys embraced a large number of organisations belonging to different branches of the MIC, situated both in the centre and in outlying regions, with both relatively good and bad economic positions.

The methodology for these surveys was created by the author together with Professor R. Ryvkina. All possible errors and inaccuracies are the responsibility of the author.

Troubles of Defence Enterprises: From Central Planning to Market System

All enterprises involved in the central planning system in the former USSR were faced with specific problems. The most important among them was the total dependence of enterprises on the ministries and the shortage of material resources. In contrast with managers in a market economy, Soviet directors had no serious financial troubles, nor problems with high taxes, marketing, competitiveness, quality of production, or survival of the enterprises.

In order to know whether defence enterprises are involved in the market reforms, we compared the problems which enterprises were faced with in 1992 and 1994. During Surveys I and III we asked the question: "What are the main problems preventing the efficient operation of your enterprise?".[1] The distribution of the answers is detailed in Table I.

Table I
Main Obstacles to Operation of the
Defence Enterprises in 1992 and 1994 (director's evaluations, percent - [2])

Problems of the defence enterprises	1992		1994	
	percent	Ranking	percent	Ranking
Breaking of the traditional business links between enterprises	80	1	25	6
Shortage of the material resources	44	2	0	11
Instability of economic policy, frequent changes of decisions	23	3	39	4
Too high taxes	22	4-5	77	1
Social tension in the enterprise	22	4-5	14	8
Decline of military procurements from the Government	18	6	60	2
Lack of guarantees for the sales	7	7	32	5

New problems (or old ones which became important under the transition to market economy), specified in 1994

	percent	Ranking
Financial troubles	59	3
Old equipment	17	7
Overdue payments	12	9
Troubles of privatisation	1	10

Towards 1994, defence enterprises had found themselves in a new socio-economic environment, facing new problems, while many traditional obstacles of the Soviet system had disappeared.

Financial difficulties were growing - they occupied the third rank in 1994, while directors did not even mention them in 1992 among the list of important problems. Moreover, the financial restrictions became the key factor in relations between enterprises and government: high taxation was the main problem, according to the directors.

As for the shortage of material resources (one of the major problems in the Soviet economy) - this problem was not mentioned by the directors at all (see Table I). It is interesting that the main obstacle in 1992 - breaking of traditional business links between enterprises - does not matter now. It means the defence enterprises have almost adapted to the economic consequences of the decay of the USSR.

There were serious changes in the economic attitude and behaviour of the directors. Many of them have assumed responsibility for their enterprise. One such director told us during the interviews (Survey II): "The main point is to rely only on my own strength. I know nobody can help us. And I don't expect any assistance - either financial or administrative".

Judging from this comment, we can see that real market reforms have started in Russia: enterprises have been operated apart from the state and the market mentality is starting to emerge among the people.[3]

However, all this is not enough for forming a stable and productive market economy. It is necessary for the efficient owners (who are concerned with long-term prosperity) to gain control of the enterprises.

Ownership Structure of Defence Enterprises

The emergence of the owners was set in motion before the government privatisation programme. This process was determined by many factors operating from the 1980s: the adoption of market-oriented laws (the USSR Law of Cooperation, the USSR Law of the Enterprise, etc.), the policy of "*glasnost*"; the downgrading of ideology; the breaking of the Communist Party's monopoly of political power; and the radical economic changes (liberalisation of prices, liberalisation of the foreign trade), etc. In general all these measures created the conditions for some ambitious managers to operate as *de facto* owners.[4]

Now that Russia has some experience in transition, it is obvious that it will take many years for efficient owners to emerge. First of all, this is because many competitors want to get hold of the former "socialist property". Among them are directors, state officials (federal and local authorities), labour, Russian and foreign entrepreneurs, banks and others. As a result of this competition a clear structure of ownership is emerging, where each owner occupies his own place and has a fixed share of capital. This structure is the indicator of the distribution of property rights determining the enterprise's productivity.

Therefore, we must consider the problem of the single owner, but we have to discuss the problem of a structure of ownership including many agents.

The pace of privatisation is slower in the MIC than in other industries: according to the evaluation of D. Vasiliev, the Deputy Chairmen of State Committee for Property (*Goskomimushestvo'*), 70 percent of enterprises were privatised in Russia by the middle of 1994,[5] but only 53 percent of the MIC (Survey III). Also, half of them were privatised with the different restrictions established by government ("golden share" providing the right of veto by the state, etc.) aimed at preserving state control. Thus, the government had control of the activity of the establishments among all defence enterprises in 1994.

In spite of this, new owners are still emerging in the MIC. Therefore, it is necessary to reveal the real structure of ownership in defence enterprises.

We investigated this during Survey III by putting the following question to directors: "If you establish the value of your enterprise as 100 percent, what are the shares of the different owners?" There was a list of the potential owners and the director had to specify the share of the each owner in percent. The distribution of shares is shown in Table II [6], [7]:

Table II

The owners:	percent
State foundation for property	24
Labour	49
Directors	5
Foundations for investment	8
Private enterprises	7
Russian business people	4
Banks	2
Foreign investors	1
Total	100

Thus, according to directors' evaluations the biggest of the owners is labour, holding approximately half of the property. The second largest owner is the state, controlling a quarter of the capital of defence enterprises. Other owners (Russian and foreign business people, banks, etc.) have the remainder.

Privatisation as an administrative and legal procedure was a relatively short-term action. To know its real results we must investigate the socio-economic consequences of privatisation at the level of the enterprise, in other words, study the changes in management, investment activity, financial position, etc. We asked the directors about these changes (see Table III).

Table III
Director's Evaluations of the
Consequences of Privatisation in Enterprises (percent)

Spheres of enterprise's operation	Position is			Total
	better	worse	not changed	
Freedom of operation	64	0	36	100
Attitudes to labour of personnel	11	20	69	100
Wages	11	18	71	100
Financial position	2	43	55	100
Size of production	7	45	48	100
Quality of production	5	11	84	100
Implementation of new technologies	9	26	65	100
Adoption of new products	49	21	30	100
Conflicts	16	26	58	100
Investment activity	11	25	64	100
Relations with Ministry	7	16	77	100

Of some 11 indicators, positive changes (column 1) were noted only in two cases: directors mentioned the increase of freedom of operation and rise of adoption of new products (64 percent and 49 percent, respectively). In other fields the situation is the same or worse.

According to the directors' estimations, the worst changes are in finance and size of production: 43 percent and 45 percent, respectively, among them cited the negative effect of privatisation.

In general, the negative evaluations of privatisation dominated the positive ones, though in most spheres there are no significant changes (answers saying "no changes" are the most frequent).

Does this mean that one can identify the directors of defence enterprises as the enemies of privatisation?

According to our investigations it does not. For example, answering the question "In your opinion, was the privatisation of your enterprise necessary?" (Survey III) 58 percent gave a positive response and only one-third of respondents said that privatisation was not needed for their establishment (10 percent couldn't give an answer). In informal interviews most of the directors said that it is impossible to refuse privatisation in the current position of Russia's MIC. In spite of negative short-term consequences, privatisation gives the directors the opportunity to become owners and to boost the enterprises.

Finally, the comparative analysis of the position of state and privatised enterprises demonstrates that economic indicators without privatisation would clearly be worse (Table IV, data of Survey III). The investment activity in privatised enterprises is higher and overdue payments are lower than in state enterprises.

Table IV
Difference Between State and Privatised Enterprises in Investment Activity and Overdue Payments (percent)

Economic indicators	Enterprises		In average
	state-sector	private sector	
Investment activity - **was** - **was not**	38 62	57 43	49 51
Overdue payments - **was** - **was not**	30 70	21 79	25 75
Size of overdue payments (mln. Rbl.)	5884	4415	5091

The directors know this (though the difference between these two kinds of enterprise is not great). Therefore they estimate privatisation as a lesser of possible evils. This opinion does not depend on the ideological values of the directors - even those who are opposed to the line of the president and the government share this view.

Privatisation has had contradictory results as a reflection of the contradiction in its position within Russian society.

On the one hand, privatisation had to take place in former conditions of social and political stability. Therefore it had to follow to the traditional Soviet values, such as collectivism, social equality and justice, which are still widespread in Russian society now.

On the other hand, the direct goal of privatisation is to create an economy with private property rights, which is oriented towards the criterion of economic efficiency. The current stage of privatisation is a compromise between these two opposite tasks. This compromise shows itself as a replacement of state ownership by labour property. This action provoked only nominal ownership, and although the property was separate from the state, efficient owners have not yet emerged.

The greatest parcel of the shares cannot concentrate real control over enterprises in the hands of labour - although the government cannot control the enterprises either. Meantime, labour and the state have the opportunity to stop the initiatives of directors and outsiders in important questions. In our opinion directors and outsiders perhaps could become efficient owners of most enterprises if they have much more capital than now.

What Are the Perspectives?

Privatisation in Russia is not yet complete. It will take years for efficient owners to emerge in the MIC. Probably there will be two stages in this process.

Stage 1. Redistribution of property into the hands of those who can keep business competitive in a market economy.

This stage can go in two directions. The first direction is the purchase by business people of the shares held now by the workforce. The second one is the sale of shares currently held by the state.

Stage II. Institutionalisation of the owners. The key problem here is social acceptance of the new owners. It is impossible to fix property rights while the greater part of society will not accept them as owners. Without this, they will not have the security needed for the long-term motivation to invest and to innovate, in spite of the fact that they would have the legal property rights.

The duration of stage 1 might be a relatively short period (perhaps 3-5 years), but the social acceptance of the owners will take much longer, 8-10 and even more years, perhaps. This is because the Russian population is now sceptical about the effects of privatisation. Moreover, public opinion is opposed to the privatisation of large industrial enterprises at the moment. According to the results of a poll conducted by the Russian Centre for Public Opinion Research in April-May of 1995, out of 2,000 adults in the sample, only 8 percent said there had been positive results when asked about consequences of privatisation. Thirty percent mentioned that the results were equally positive and negative, and 40 percent of people asserted that privatisation has only negative sides (22 percent did not know). The more disappointing picture is in the answers of people to the question of whether to keep large enterprises in state ownership: 74 percent of the adults polled think that they should be kept under state control and only 11 percent support their privatisation (20 percent do not know).

Negative public opinion about the results of privatisation and particularly opposition towards a genuine separation of the large industrial enterprises from the state, will significantly slow down the process of finding efficient owners for the MIC.

What are the perspectives of the defence enterprises in such a social context?

To know this, in May 1995, we asked in Survey IV the question: "In your opinion, what is the future of your enterprise?" and received the following answers:

Future of enterprises expected by directors:

	%
- **Expansion of production, increase of profits, hiring of labour force**	16
- **Conservation of the current position**	25
- **Slow down of production, losses, lay-offs**	52
- **Bankruptcy**	5
- **Do not know**	2

Thus, most of the directors polled see the future of their enterprises negatively: more than half among them think that its position will be worse. However, there is a group of optimists expecting the expansion of their organisations.

A similar group of optimists was found in other investigations. For example, in Survey III we revealed that there were 13 percent of enterprises where the socio-economic position was relatively good, according to the directors' evaluations. These establishments could overcome one of the main diseases in the Russian economy - reversing the decline of production. Only 9 percent were in a position to do this, but the expansion of production was 31 percent monthly in 1994 (in comparison with 1993), while the production in other enterprises declined by 27 percent.

The enterprises with a relatively good position had much better sales, 23 percent among them had more orders than they could meet (among others those were only 2 percent). The other organisations in good shape could engage 2/3 of their productive capacities and only 29 percent among them were to cut production of some articles (in contrast with 46 percent and 72 percent, respectively, between establishments with severe problems).

When we make the analysis of enterprises in relatively good condition, we mean only *relative* prosperity, because under the current situation in the Russian economy and society there are no completely healthy organisations. Forty-seven percent of these establishments are near bankruptcy, and 41 percent are in no danger (12 percent do not know). But among the others, 68 percent are afraid of bankruptcy, and only 17 percent are not afraid (15 percent do not know).

Thus, there is a group of enterprises in the Russian MIC which could start to adapt to the market. Although these organisations have all the same ailments as the Russian economy has, they want to use the economic freedom to develop production, to innovate and to embark on conversion. Therefore, the government first has to carry out a policy directed at this group of enterprises to create favourable conditions for their expansion.

*   *   *

The processes of distribution and redistribution of the former socialist property have latent and even criminal forms in Russia. It is not obvious what the final state of privatisation and the structure of ownership will be in the near future, nor what will be the influence of privatisation on Russian society. The traditional sociological instruments used in this paper have their own limitations and cannot provide the analysis of many latent outcomes and results of privatisation. The defence enterprises in Russia usually include many units for social services; these enterprises influence the lives of more than 10 million people[8]. Therefore, it is necessary to add to, and to correct, the conclusions in this paper, analysing the consequences of privatisation for different social groups and taking into account possible prolonged socio-economic and political factors stimulating privatisation in the Russian MIC, and the obstacles preventing it.

Footnotes

1. Directors had to choose from a given list of problems. These problems were revealed during the informal interviews with the directors. Since the problem of the dependence on the ministries already did not disturb the directors seriously in 1992, this problem was dropped from the list.
2. Since the respondents could choose more than one item the sum is not equal to 100 percent
3. To know more details about adoption of the defence enterprises to market see: A. Izyumov, L. Kosals, R. Ryvkina. The Russian Military-Industrial Complex: The Shock of Independence. In: *The New Economy,* Vol. 6, No 1, Issue # 25, Winter 1995, pp. 10-11.
4. The process of privatisation in the MIC was partly spontaneous as in other sectors of the Russian economy. See the analysis of spontaneous privatisation in the MIC in: I. Filatotchev, T. Buck & M. Wright. The Military-industrial Complex of the Former USSR: Asset or Liability? In: *Communist Economies & Economic Transformation,* Vol. 5, No. 2, 1993, p. 198
5. *Izvestiya,* 29 June 1994
6. There are some data that privatisation in the MIC has not moved more slowly than in other sectors. See: C. Gaddy. Economic Performance and Policies in the Defence Industrial Regions of Russia. Paper prepared for the Workshop on Russian Economic Reform sponsored by the Center for International Security and Arms Control, Stanford University, 22-23 November, 1993, p.10. This result was obtained concerning the regional level. As for the level of enterprise there are many obstacles to privatisation in the defence sector - very large size of enterprises, many establishments for the social services under them, etc., which particularly prevent privatisation.
7. To compare these data with the results of the polls among the directors in other industries, see, for example, scientific report: L. Kosals, R. Ryvkina. The Owners of the Russian Industrial Enterprises: the Analysis of Director's Opinions and Expert's Evaluations. Moscow, International Centre for Research into Economic Transformation, 1994, pp. 8. This report based on the poll of 426 directors of industrial enterprises in different branches, located in all main regions of Russia and carried out by the Russian Center for Public Opinion Research in 1994. The structure of the ownership revealed by this poll was very similar to the one presented above. The difference between the two structures of ownership is that in other industries the share of labour is a little bit greater than in the MIC, but the share of the state is less.
8. As J. Cooper argued: "They (defence enterprises - L.K.) are not simply production units, but social institutions, often central to the existence of local communities and even whole towns. Yet it is highly unlikely that all will be viable in the new conditions. Closures will be needed and large enterprises may have no choice but to break up, parts separating out as independent companies. Indeed, the latter process has started with privatisation. In these circumstances the generation of alternative employment will be essential." (J. Cooper. The Conversion of the Former Soviet Defence Industry. London, Royal Institute of International Affairs, 1993, p. 38).

PRIVATISING THE SLOVAK ECONOMY: LEGISLATIVE FRAMEWORK AND DEVELOPMENT

Anna Zatkalíková

There was a lack of theoretical preparedness for the huge privatisation effort in post-socialist countries and Slovakia is no exception. In the beginning these processes were in many case implemented "campaign-style" as in the old days, says Anna Zatkalíková, from the Slovak Republic's National Council. Privatisation is seen as the key to helping the economy, and to cementing political reform in place. There is a spirited debate about how to privatise. The voucher method was popular at first, but the people, and successive governments, are ambivalent about it now. This approach spreads share ownership, but it also hinders the growth of strategic owners who can invest in their enterprise and bring about expansion. Other methods, such as management buy-outs, or selling shares to employees, are under consideration. The debate continues...

Mrs. Zatkalíková is working at the Department of Information and Analysis of the National Council of the Slovak Republic, Bratislava.

Background of the Process of Privatisation

Privatisation and restructuring of industry are the main pillars of economic transformation in the post-socialist countries, and an unprecedented process in Europe's economies in transformation.

One of the greatest concerns is the minimal, in fact absence of, theoretical preparedness for this process. As a result of this, the process was in many cases implemented like a campaign - just as the important economic and political decisions were carried out in the former regime - backed by very little scientific theory or elaboration.

The emphasis put on privatisation as a basic pillar of economic transition was based predominantly on economic goals. It was hoped that it would guarantee an increase in production and at the same time cause the entire economy to grow. In the former socialist countries, state-owned property had proved to be unproductive mainly as a result of the fact that it was not aimed at profit, and political and social goals had prevailed over economic aims. Management was not stimulated to attain profit and was not interested in lowering the costs of production.

The biggest priority in choosing methods and forms of privatisation was the rapidity that might guarantee the change from state to private ownership in a relatively short time and simultaneously promote an increase in economic effectiveness. It would at the same time irreversibly fix the desired ongoing social-political changes in the country. The experiences of privatisation of state property in market economies are rather different from our own, primarily because of differences of scale. That is why they could be used as a model and exemplified only to a very limited extent.

Besides the requirement for speed, one of the greatest obstacles in the choice of standard privatisation methods, was the non-existence of powerful domestic capital interested in the privatisation of larger enterprises. Other difficulties were an undeveloped banking system, an almost non-existent capital market and an absence of competition and relevant legislation.

Hence the reason why the novel "coupon" (or voucher) method of privatisation was chosen in the former Czechoslovakia as the preferred method. This was an unprecedented experiment in the process of privatisation. This form of a "nation-wide lottery", as it was popularly called, succeeded in a short time to "denationalise" a great amount of state property.

As for its character, besides economic goals, there were, without any doubt, certain social and political goals which were very important, especially before the crucial elections in 1992.

Coupon privatisation is, and obviously will be, an object of various economic and political analyses for some time to come. As for its success in the privatisation and transition process, opinions are divided. Besides the speed of privatisation its supporters agree with its fairness in enabling the participation of all citizens without discrimination as to job or position. They can decide voluntarily how to manage their shares. The social aspect is stressed, as a compensation for low financial reward for work done in previous years.

Critics and opponents of coupon privatisation state that the biggest shortcoming of this form is that it has not brought about the rise of so called "strategic" owners who are able to effectively manage former national property, invest in it and ensure its productivity.

A great number of individual owners were created but most of these have not been able to recognise the value of their shares and cannot use them effectively. They are not able to orient themselves in the slowly developing capital market. As a rule these owners often try to get rid of their acquired shares very quickly, and below their value, thereby depressing the price of shares on the stock market. According to estimates in Slovakia about one-third of them already have sold their shares and no longer have any portion of the property.

While coupon privatisation was the dominant privatisation form, and several enterprises were privatised entirely by the coupon method, the property remained ownerless, but under the control of management whose behaviour was not very different from that in the previous era.

It is obvious that in the case of such property dispersal this is only a preliminary phase of privatisation, the denationalisation, which will continue by a gradual merging in the hands of an increasingly small number of owners who will begin to behave as understanding and skilled market operators. Such a process will continue more slowly than the proponents of this method of privatisation could have imagined.

The position of investment privatisation funds needs an analysis at this stage. The funds could play the role of the strategic owners of privatised enterprise. The fact that they concentrate the shares of individual shareholders gives them the opportunity to launch a comparatively extensive portfolio. But the insufficient experience of managing investment funds, the obscurity of the entire process of privatisation and insufficient legislation causes the government to see the funds as suspect, and so to regulate and strictly limit their entrepreneurial opportunities. Obviously there is also a fear of the possibility that a small group of proprietors and fund managers, managing the affairs of a large number of investors, could gain a significant amount of both economic and political power.

Legislative Development and the Privatisation Process

The need to transfer ownership of almost the entire state property required large-scale legislative measures, which started to be implemented at a federal level from 1990.

The first Act which set up the conditions for the transfer of the state property to private persons was Act No 427/90, the so-called Small Privatisation Act, several times amended, followed by the widely discussed Act No 92/91, which legislatively set up the process of the so called Large Privatisation.

One of the forms of privatisation and a difficult point of parliamentary decision-making at the time was the restitution of property, implemented in several rounds.

The first stage - the so-called small restitution - was enabled by Act No 403/90 and was aimed at moderating the consequences of some property injustices; citizens could require the return of property nationalised without compensation in and after 1952. In 1991 Act 87/91 widened the scope of restitution also for larger property nationalised between 1948 and 1952.

The privatisation process started to be implemented in 1991 - then in the same way as in the Czech Republic as it existed in Czechoslovakia.

The privatisation process was divided into two phases - small - scale and large-scale privatisation.

The small-scale privatisation began in February 1991 and was completed in the first half of 1993. The programme dealt with more than 9,500 enterprises, the majority of them belonging to the small business sector. From the five thousand restitution claims made, about 2.7 thousand were accepted. The remaining small enterprises were sold at public auction for more than 14 billion Crowns which the National Property Fund acquired. These sales only comprised fixed assets such as real estate and equipment. The sale was only permitted to Slovak citizens.

The so-called large-scale privatisation started with the first wave of coupon privatisation in 1991. It was completed in 1993 when the Federation was already split. Though there were already some different opinions on the privatisation methods among Slovak economic leaders, the first wave was completed in the originally determined way in October 1993. It included 751 of 1,668 Slovakian state-owned enterprises with a total book value of about SK 176 billion - nearly $6 billion.

After the reduction of nominal share capital by 31 billion, and transfer to equity reserves, some 80 billion was sold by coupon privatisation, 48 billion held by National Proper Fund, 10 billion sold by standard methods and the rest transferred to the restituees and the restitution investment fund.

A special problem was posed by the re-privatisation of agriculture. From the very beginning, in 1990, owners' rights to the land were gradually re-introduced. Legislative, organisational and other measures were directed towards the reparation of existing shortcomings and eliminating their consequences. Legislative measures involved specifically the Act on regulation of land and other agricultural property ownership, the Act on land arrangements and Act on the register of real estate assessment. At present all these Acts are to be amended.

The re-establishment of land ownership and its re-activation is based mainly on restitution of original legal relations, in establishing simplified methods in the proving of ownership and its registration in the register of real estate, in the establishment of a state information system on real estate and in the introduction of land arrangements.

The biggest problem of the transition was in the proof of property and land ownership. This was caused by shortcomings in the evidence of ownership in the land register and also by uncertain inheritance provisions.

The transition in agricultural cooperatives was performed in accordance with a special Act. In fact, by the end of 1992, 909 agricultural cooperatives had been transformed. Some 986 succeeding entities have subsequently applied for registration. The first wave of privatisation involved 269 state enterprises in the food and agriculture sector. Some 180 of this number belonged to the food industry and 43 to agricultural purchase enterprises.

The transformation of cooperatives in the sense of the Act above-mentioned is now finished. We can judge from the transition process that many cooperatives followed the law only in a formal sense, without any real internal transition, and the transition in agriculture has not been a big success up to now.

The newly-transformed cooperatives, had, in fact, previously consisted of bodies without land ownership. They now own property shares from the transition, originating from their previous labour. A large part of property shares - about 41 percent - is owned by non-members of cooperatives. Members with land ownership comprise 37.8 percent and members with work participation only comprise 15.3 percent.

An investigation performed by the Statistical Office of the Slovak Republic shows that of the whole amount of cultivated land, coops share nearly 3/4, state bodies share a fifth and the rest is shared by private enterprise. Most of the restitution process took place during 1991 and 1992. With reference to the data mentioned above, 132,692 ha of land were returned to 935,775 applicants.

After the elections in 1992, the Slovak government modified the rapid strategy of the former federal government and decided to slow down the privatisation process. The government doubted the acceptability of coupon privatisation and began to search for other forms. It was motivated by the need to increase the transparency of privatisation, and tried to attain this aim by stressing standard privatisation methods. In the first half of 1993, the process of privatisation was almost halted. The government aimed at public auctions. Just before it lost the vote of confidence the second government of Vladimir Meciar approved a few score direct sales.

In the era of the so-called big coalition formed by Premier Moravcík (March to December 1994) the government inclined again to a quick implementation of the second wave, with a stress on coupon privatisation. The government was preparing property to the value of nearly 100 billion Slovak Crowns for coupon privatisation, later lowered to 70 billion. But in the time at its disposal the government was not able to take more relevant steps as to its implementation, in spite of the fact that 3.5 million Slovak citizens expressed agreement with coupon privatisation by buying the coupon booklet and registering it. It is obvious that this government had no unified attitude towards the apportioning of privatisation methods or to the privatisation process as a whole.

However, there is a paradoxical situation. In spite of the fact that the citizens have unambiguously manifested a positive attitude to coupon privatisation - the number of owners registered in the second wave exceeded those in the first wave by practically one million - in the elections which were held nearly simultaneously with the second wave of privatisation citizens voted for the parties which were critical towards voucher privatisation, and today they continue to neglect it.

After the re-establishment of Meciar's government in December 1994, the government continued in its criticism of coupon privatisation and declared its support of standard methods - direct sale and public auction. However, in the government programme of December 1994, coupon privatisation was not rejected. It was stated to be a fundamental method and it was promised quick implementation dependent on the preparedness of enterprise privatisation projects. In the

Memorandum of Economic Policy of the government (April 1995) addressed to the IMF, the government manifested its willingness to speed up the transition process. The main stress is on direct sale, sale on the capital market or on public auction, and also on the second wave of coupon privatisation. The aim was to sell the major share of every enterprise to "strategic" investors.

According to this document, coupon privatisation had to have company shares valued at roughly 50 billion Slovak Crowns. The whole action, commencing with the pre-run, began on 1 July, and will finish in June 1996. Privatisation by standard methods was planned to finish at the end of September 1995.

These days, however, the government announced a modification of the governmental privatisation strategy. The government intends to implement privatisation by means of standard methods and employees' shares and particularly through management ownership of the enterprises.

The government is of the opinion that management has the best pre-conditions for restructuring enterprises and accelerating their development. The role of workers' participation in privatised enterprise is also being stressed. The government wants, therefore, to give management and workers the chance to privatise business by paying in installments, from the profit of the enterprise.

A list of so-called strategic enterprises has been approved by the government. These enterprises should stay in the hands of government for the time being and will not be privatised for reasons of strategic importance for the country's economy.

The full abolition of coupon privatisation is a very important announcement. However, there is the promise of compensation by state bonds for the nominal value of 10,000 SK, for those registered for the second wave of privatisation.

There are some indications as to how these bonds are to be used - to buy shares on the stock market, for the purchase of appartments, etc. But because this matter is still quite new and unofficial, it is very difficult to analyse.

As a conclusion here are some data on the economic performance of the Slovak Republic in 1994:
- GDP growth reached 4.8 percent.
- Inflation abated to 11.7 percent by December 1994.
- Unemployment had stabilised at 14.4 percent (and it was down to 13.3 percent in May 1995).
- Exchange rate stability has been maintained, the Slovak koruna is convertible for current account purposes.
- The proportion as a percentage of private sector:

	1992	1993	1994
GDP	32.4	39.0	58.2
Industrial production	11.0	20.5	56.3
Construction industry	35.0	58.2	79.3
Retail	73.1	81.5	89.4
Transport	39.0	51.7	57.3

SUCCESSES AND FAILURES: PRIVATISATION IN THE TRANSITION ECONOMIES

Peter Rutland

The solution to Eastern Europe's transition problems lies in implementing the Western economic policy 'trinity' of liberalisation, stabilisation, and privatisation. The first two were relatively easy because governments simply had to stop doing things - controlling prices, and spending money. The third was more difficult, yet it had become an important criterion for measuring the success of economic reform. The key to its success, says Peter Rutland, is strong leadership, good administration, and a clear timetable. They have been a qualified success, he thinks. But the benefits could take years to come through.

Dr. Rutland is Assistant Director (Research) of the Open Media Research Institute, Prague.

Western observers very quickly adopted an agreed framework for analysing the transition from state socialism in Eastern Europe. This framework was essentially teleological in nature. It was assumed that there was a definite model towards which the former socialist countries were headed. In the economic sphere, this was to be a capitalist market economy, to be reached through the speedy unleashing of market forces. There was widespread agreement among Western economists that what was required was the policy troika of liberalisation (lifting controls and allowing market-clearing prices to emerge), stabilisation (eliminating inflation and establishing convertible currencies) and privatisation (the transfer of assets to new owners).[1]

These standard formulae, derived from the principles of neoclassical economics, received a welcome audience in the West. The confidence with which Western economists advanced these prescriptions was comforting to Western governments and financial institutions. It seemed to impose order and predictability on the chaos of the disintegrating economies and political systems of Eastern Europe.

As with the economic prognosis, so it was with the political system. The common assumption was that these countries would all move towards Western-style electoral democracy, again on the premise that there was, broadly speaking, a single model which could be emulated.

Note that both in the economic and political spheres the received wisdom was strongly teleological in nature. It was assumed that we knew where these countries were headed, and that their destination was more or less a single model of social organisation. Behind this assumption there stands a still deeper and less explicit premise: the supposition that, as national economies become more integrated into the global economy, they must necessarily become more alike. As with the expansion of the European Union, it is expected that integration must take the form of the addition of increasingly homogeneous units. While some degree of homogeneity is obviously a precondition to international economic cooperation, global experience over the past 30 years (the success of the East Asian economies, for example) suggests that strong elements of heterogeneity will persist even as countries increase their level of international economic cooperation.

If challenged, Western experts would admit that yes, of course, there are differences between Anglo-American and German forms of corporate governance; or that yes, there were important distinctions between presidential and parliamentary forms of democracy. However, it was implicitly assumed that these were of minor importance, not significant enough to alter one's overall perception of the transition process. For East European economies, this meant that they were expected to pursue a single model of economic transition - and would be assessed in terms of their relative success or failure in pursuing that goal. The East European countries were held up against an abstract model of marketisation and democratisation which few (if any) can actually be expected to realise. This approach carries the danger of engendering frustration among the leaders and peoples of Eastern Europe - a feeling which may be turning into resentment towards the Western countries which are categorising them as "failures" in the transition process.

Beyond the Rhetoric of Transition

As other presenters at this conference have noted, the countries of Central and Eastern Europe have found it very difficult to implement successfully the policies needed to stabilise their economies and introduce market institutions. Five years into the transition process, only half a dozen of the 27 countries in the region can be deemed to be "succeeding". In the remaining countries, one can detect some positive signs, but these are offset by persistent problems. In general, all countries have made considerable progress in liberalising their economies - lifting price controls, removing restrictions on private enterprise, and opening up foreign trade.

Most countries have also made brave efforts to stabilise their economies, by cutting government spending and tolerating a fall in real wages. However, this has usually not been enough to bring the rate of inflation down into single figures. Even in Poland and Hungary, inflation continues at 20-30 percent a year, and the foreign debt overhang remains a troublesome problem. The third aspect of the policy package - privatisation - has seen even more mixed results. While most countries have seen a boom in private retailing and services, the bulk of manufacturing industry remains in the hands of the state. (On this, see the paper in this volume by Michael Kaser.)

Perhaps the most worrying feature of the transition is the deep and persistent fall in GDP.[2] In his presentation to the NATO conference, Professor Michael Ellman offered a list of five countries which appeared to have turned the corner of the "transformation recession", and experienced positive growth in 1994 (Slovenia, Albania, Czech Republic, Poland and Estonia). Optimists would wish to add other countries to the list of success stories, arguing that the fall in officially-reported GDP overstates the extent of recession, because of the expansion of the informal sector. While it is true that the unreported economy has boomed, there have been few systematic efforts to estimate its rate of growth. Its expansion is unlikely to have been sufficient to offset the 40-50 percent drop in official GDP. (Bear in mind also that there was already an informal sector before 1989.)

Five years into the transition, then, few countries in the region can claim the mantle of success. And yet the standard approach to the transition economies is to judge them in terms of success and failure. Analysts anxiously monitor their performance to see who is furthest down the path towards a market economy, and typically draw up scorecard of who is ahead and who is falling behind. This orientation towards success has two deleterious side effects.

First, countries which are showing few signs of progress are told that they must be patient, and are reassured that eventually they will reach their goal. This advice is unlikely to be very convincing for much longer. Five years into the transition, people's patience seems to be wearing thin; as is evidenced by the victory of social-democratic governments in the second round of free elections, in every country save the Czech Republic.

Western observers will have to acknowledge the fact that for some of these countries the transition process has effectively ended, and they must develop new categories to analyse the politics and economics of countries which seem to be "frozen" in transition. This implies that rather than targeting assistance and policy advice on measures to speed up the pace of transition, the West should be more focused on trying to shore up the status quo, to preserve those elements of the economy and civil society which are functioning effectively and provide a bulwark against social entropy.

Western policy for some of these countries may have to start thinking more about stopping a slide back into anarchy and despair, rather than a blinkered focus on the necessity of transition to a brighter future. The West cannot afford to allow large parts of the eastern half of the European continent to slip into a living tableau of "Waiting for Godot."

The second negative consequence of the success orientation of Western analysis is the temptation to analyse events in each country in terms of their progress towards democracy and a market economy. It is particularly pernicious to draw up a scorecard ranking the various countries in terms of the speed of transition they have attained. Observers zero in on a handful of easily-monitored indicators, and keenly report who is ahead in currency convertibility or reducing budget deficits, while Eastern governments anxiously await their latest bond rating from Standard & Poors.

Such an approach is undesirable because it encourages politicians to think in terms of abstract and universal models rather than trying to tailor solutions to local problems. It also plays into the long standing rivalries and tensions between the countries of the region. Repeatedly through their unhappy history they have found themselves competing for attention and favours from the West. On occasion this has caused them to prematurely embrace Western philosophies and alliances, while simultaneously failing to cooperate with their Eastern neighbours. Western states wittingly or unwittingly pick favourites among the Eastern countries, and play out their own rivalries with other Western states on a continental scale. This happened in the 1920s and 1930s, and it seems to be happening again.

Unlike in earlier periods, however, this situation is unlikely to produce sharply negative consequences. There are no attractive alternative ideologies to liberal democracy, and it is hard to imagine communism or fascism taking root in the region once again. However, the fate of Yugoslavia should serve as a sobering reminder of the need to carefully study the situation inside each country in its own terms, rather than holding them up in comparison to abstract models of marketisation and democratisation.

How to Account for Success?

Let us assume for the sake of argument that the success/failure paradigm is a viable approach to the study of the economies in transition. How, within the framework of this approach, can one explain the differing outcomes in differing countries? In particular, can one attribute success to the adoption of correct economic policies? It is our contention here that it is extraordinarily difficult to come up with a systematic and empirically grounded explanation of the relative success and failure of the economies in transition. And to the extent that a pattern can be discerned, it is just as plausible to argue that the policy package adopted by a country's political leaders is not as decisive a variable as is often assumed. Rather, exogenous or circumstantial factors, such as the starting position of the country when it entered the transition process, may be more important in accounting for differences in final outcome.

What features are shared by the five countries identified by Professor Ellman as the most successful transition economies to date (Slovenia, Albania, Czech Republic, Poland and Estonia)? It would be hard to argue that they had all adopted similar policy packages. Each country seems to have implemented a range of measures which differ both from each other and from IMF orthodoxy. Some were able to adopt and maintain wage controls, others were not. Some have carried out a mass privatisation programme, others have not. Admittedly, they have all made progress towards currency convertibility and stabilisation, but the measures adopted have varied from country to country (a currency board in Estonia, a crawling peg in Poland, strict monetary and fiscal policy in the Czech Republic), and inflation in several of them (such as Estonia and Poland) remains obstinately high.

Even if one was willing to argue that one could detect a strong convergence in the policies adopted by these countries, this would beg the question of why those particular countries adopted the requisite package of policies. It should be emphasised that most observers merely assume that because their economies seem to be succeeding, this must be because the countries adopted the necessary policies.

One must pose the chicken-and-egg question: it may be that an improvement in economic performance caused by extraneous factors made it possible for the governments to adopt something resembling orthodox policies. As far as this author is aware, this point about the similarity of policies among the "successful" countries has yet to be shown through a thorough comparative study. Inferring from evidence of success that the country must therefore have adopted the correct policies is an ex post rationalisation rather than an explanation. There is a hint here of the "ants on a log" syndrome. (Ronald Reagan once compared the US Congress to 600 ants on a log, each thinking that it was steering it down the river.)

The key feature in explaining these countries' success would appear to be that they are all adjacent to Western markets. This makes it relatively easy for them to benefit from a rapid increase in cross-border trade and tourism. It also means that it is at least conceivable that they could be invited to join the European Union at some not-too-distant point in the future. One can add that with the exception of Poland all of them are small in size. This means that a given quantity of Western aid goes further than in a country the size of Ukraine, and it means that the impact on the European Union of greater access to Western markets will be relatively modest. (To reiterate, this is less true of Poland - the absorption of her farm sector into the Common Agricultural Policy would be a very costly exercise.)

The point is that for reasons of geography the economic prospects for these countries, short-term and long-term, are more rosy that for larger countries located further to the East, for whom access to the European Union is only conceivable after the first wave of countries have gained entry. Even this tentative explanation has to deal with exceptions, however. Hungary and Croatia are both small countries with a common border with an EU member, yet for various additional reasons their economies have failed to stabilise sufficiently to make it onto the Ellman list.

Does this argument over how to explain success really matter? Well, it is not purely an academic dispute. Western aid and trade has been tied to the assumption that the crucial variable is government policy. Some governments are rewarded for adopting the correct policies, and others punished for failing to do so. Moreover, the debate over transition has come increasingly to be dominated by a horse-race mentality: looking for which countries are ahead and which are falling behind.

How to Explain the Successful Privatisation Programmes?

Privatisation has proved to be the most difficult of all the policies to adopt.[3] Effective implementation of a programme of mass privatisation has in practice been confined to a handful of countries (East Germany, Czech Republic, Russia). In all these cases, the leaders opted for a swift and fairly simple privatisation scheme, where speed took precedence over questions of equity and fairness (about which political debate can go on *ad infinitum*).

However, the more one looks at this question, the more complex it becomes. It is instructive simply to draw up a list of all the factors which could possibly have an important influence on the success of the privatisation process. An evaluation of the relative success of Russia, East Germany and the Czech Republic in implementing a mass privatisation programme would have to consider some or all of the following elements:[4]

Economic factors
* A stable, convertible currency.
* A stable or growing GDP.
* A boom in exports, generating cash for needed imports.
* Modest unemployment, to avoid social tension.
* The introduction of effective bankruptcy procedures, to accelerate restructuring.

Political factors
* The emergence of a cohesive, technically competent team of top administrators.
* Support from strong political leadership.
* Conjunctural factors (a window of opportunity).
* Public support for the programme.
* Consensus among political and economic elites in favour of the programme.

Administrative factors
* General bureaucratic capacity (efficient, non-corrupt civil servants).
* The laying down of a strict timetable.

• Existence of a clear and reliable legal structure to adjudicate disputes and monitor implementation.
• The creation of a separate specialised bureaucracy tasked with designing and implementing the programme.
• Support from international agencies.
• A decentralised process to minimise opposition while maximising administrative capacity.

Note the multiplicity of factors that could be involved. One can draw three broad conclusions about the relative influence of these factors from the countries where mass privatisation was quickly implemented (Czech Republic, Russia and East Germany).

First, economic factors may be less decisive than was initially supposed by many Western observers. In all three countries privatisation was implemented despite the fact that the fall in GDP had not stabilised. In neither Russia nor the Czech Republic has bankruptcy legislation played a very important role, nor has unemployment risen to significant levels. Russia even managed to carry out its programme in the midst of continuing high inflation.

Second, all three countries' privatisation programmes share some common features at the level of administrative design. In each of these countries the programme was implemented in a decentralised manner, and a lot of responsibility for proposing restructuring schemes was delegated to the level of the enterprise. Either the current managers or rival would-be owners were obliged to draw up privatisation projects, which would then be approved by a central clearing house. Another distinctive feature was that in all three countries a special new government agency was created to monitor the process.

This agency was given a specific and narrow mandate, and from the outset the assumption was that it would wind itself up once the assets in the programme had been shifted into new ownership. This meant that the bureaucrats in charge of privatisation had clear instructions to move the process forward as quickly as possible. Countries which tried to involve existing bureaucratic agencies do not seem to have been able to inaugurate programmes capable of transferring a large volume of assets in a short period of time.

As far as the politics of transition are concerned, there were two competing schools of thought as to how best to tackle the problem of political opposition to reform. The central paradox facing the reformers in 1989-91 was that the potential beneficiaries of reform (future capitalists and future generations of consumers) did not currently exist as organised social actors: they had a hypothetical existence, and were dispersed through society.

On the other hand, those who would bear the costs of transition (such as pensioners, farmers, and workers and managers in heavy industry) were already present, were aware that they would be among the losers, and in some cases were well-organised and with a strong political voice. How could one overcome this political imbalance between the diffuse winners and the all-too-specific losers?

There were two schools of thought on this question. The "window of opportunity" philosophy, as represented by former Polish Finance Minister Leszek Balcerowicz, argued that the government must move as quickly as possible: while the old elites are disoriented by the collapse of communism, and while the new government enjoys a honeymoon of democratic legitimacy. The coalition building school argued that compromises must be made in order to neutralise potential adversaries (by offering them side payments) and unite potential beneficiaries by welding them into a coalition actively supporting the reforms. This would necessarily be a protracted process, in contrast to the lighting strike advocated by the window of opportunity school.

The window of opportunity strategy seems to have worked fairly well with regard to liberalisation and stabilisation. These were relatively simple policies whose basic features were well-known from the experience of other countries. They could both be introduced quickly since they involved doing less of something (regulating prices or spending money, respectively). Privatisation was a rather different proposition, since this required doing something positive creating a mechanism for transferring a massive volume of industrial assets into the hands of new owners.

In each country which adopted mass privatisation, steps had to be taken to neutralise potential opponents and to create a political constituency in favour of change. In East Germany this was done through a generous social policy and a commitment to raise Eastern wages to Western levels: a policy which is costing Germany in excess of $100 billion a year in subsidies.

In both Russia and the Czech Republic a crucial component of privatisation was the distribution of vouchers to the general population. This gave the people at large the hope (cynics would say the illusion) that they might personally gain from the programme. More subtly, one can argue that the voucher programmes created uncertainty about who would finally emerge as the new owners of the privatised firms. It was realised that the shares distributed to the general public would not stay in their hands for long, but would be bought up by mutual funds, businessmen, banks and the like.

But the programme did not try to closely regulate the secondary market in shares, and did not predetermine who would emerge as the new owners. This uncertainty was politically useful, since it gave the government a degree of "plausible deniability". In the event that ownership gravitated into the hands of foreigners or unsavoury native businessmen, they could argue that this was not their intent, but that it was the product of the autonomous decisions of individual citizens, selling their shares to the highest bidder. Also, uncertainty over the outcome of the whole process may have encouraged potential opponents of privatisation (for example, incumbent managers) to adopt a wait-and-see attitude, since it might turn out that they will benefit from the scheme.

Lessons Learned

The preceding section argued that it is very difficult to come up with convincing explanations for why some countries appear to be succeeding in transition to a market economy. The main conclusion to be drawn from this is that one must be cautious about making success criteria the pivotal factor in determining one's attitude towards the political and economic situation of a given country.

With regard to privatisation in particular, it is worth reiterating that the complex process of industrial restructuring is not synonymous with privatisation. Closing factories, shedding labour, and investing in new industries with good future prospects are difficult decisions which will not necessarily be solved by the simple transfer of assets from state into private hands. Restructuring begins before privatisation takes place (as state-owned firms are weaned off subsidies and are thus forced to accept "hard budget constraints").

And most of the real struggles over restructuring will occur after privatisation, and will spread over many years. The mere act of transfer of ownership is but one step in this process, and one should beware of exaggerating its importance in the search for signs of positive developments in the transition economies. Also, one should not forget that exposure to market competition (domestic and international) is likely to be far more important in promoting efficiency than the specific question of the pattern of ownership of industrial assets.

Many commentators at this conference have underlined the fact that the countries of the region are politically and economically distinct and should not be subsumed into a "one size fits all" transition model. Many countries of the region have strayed from the preordained transition path, or at least are falling badly behind, and each faces a unique configuration of problems. Successful integration with the global economy in general, and the European Union in particular, clearly does presupposes a certain degree of homogeneity from its component parts.

The record of the past five years in Eastern Europe suggests that heterogeneity continues to be the order of the day. Indeed, in some respects the region's diversity is greater than it was in the socialist period, when the Soviet Union tried (largely unsuccessfully) to impose a degree of uniformity. But the more difficulties these countries encounter in the transition to the market, the more diverse they will become, since problems and calamities tend to emphasise uniqueness. As Tolstoy says at the beginning of Anna Karenina, "Happy families are all alike, but every unhappy family is unhappy in its own way."

From this record of diversity Professor Michael Kaser drew the conclusion that one must call upon the state to step forward and take measures necessary to adapt to the particular problems of the country in question. However, just because each country has a different set of problems, and because each country has its own state apparatus, it does not follow that the state is best-placed to deal with the divergence from the ideal transition path.

One can agree that in most countries the market transition model has failed to bring about the necessary restructuring of large sectors of heavy industry, and has failed to halt the precipitous fall in GDP and living standards.

But just because spontaneous market processes have failed thus far does not mean that the state will be capable of doing a better job. The mere fact that the state is specific to each country does not mean that the national state is capable of dealing with its problems. The evidence of the past 40 years of socialist economics suggests just the opposite - that the state is likely to do an even worse job. If one looks at specific sectors of state activity (such as health care or the education system), one finds that because of budgetary constraints, poor political leadership and general social dislocation, the post-1989 state is performing less effectively than its socialist predecessor. This does not augur well for their ability to mount an effective industrial restructuring policy.

Thus it is still possible to argue that the state that governs least governs best, and that there will be no easy solutions to the economic plight of the ailing transition economies. Non-state actors such as international governmental agencies, international private business and domestic private business, may be more effective at tackling these problems than the national state.

Footnotes

1. For a sample of the transition literature, see S. Islam and M. Mandelbaum (eds) *Making Markets* (New York: Council on Foreign Relations, 1993); L. Csaba *The Capitalist Revolution in Eastern Europe* (London: Elgar 1994); J. Sachs *Poland's Jump to the Market Economy* (Cambridge Mass.: MIT Press, 1994).
2. G. Kolodko, 'From recession to growth in post-communist economies', *Communist and Post-Communist Studies*, vol. 26, pp. 123-43, January 1993.
3. On the general progress of privatisation programmes, see the series of studies from the Central European University, such as: J. Earle, R. Frydman and A. Rapaczynski (eds), *Privatisation in the Transition to a Market Economy* (New York: St. Martins, 1993); and R. Frydman and A. Rapaczynski, *Privatisation in Eastern Europe: Is the State Withering Away?* (London: Central European University Press, 1994).
4. P. Rutland, 'Thatcherism, Czech style: Organized labor and the transition to capitalism in the Czech Republic', *Telos,* winter 1992-93, no. 94, pp. 103-29; P. Rutland, 'Privatization in Russia: two steps forward, one step back?', *Europe/Asia Studies*, vol. 46, no.7, 1994, pp. 110-32; J. Roesler, 'Privatization in East Germany', *Europe/Asia Studies*, vol. 46, no. 3, 1994, pp. 505-518.

PANEL IV

External Economic Relations and Integration into the World Economy

Chair: Graham Sharp, Assistant Director
NATO Economica Directorate

Panelists: Andreas Gummich
Leonid Fituni
Katarzyna Żukrowska
Lazar Comanescu
Zdenek Drábek

THE EXTERNAL RELATIONS OF THE EASTERN EUROPEAN COUNTRIES: A COMPARATIVE ASSESSMENT

Andreas Gummich

The ability of the economies in transition to succeed in their external economic relations can be judged according to some very practical guidelines, according to Dr. Andreas Gummich. Most countries know what they have to do to interact with outside markets. The question is, are they taking action? Those countries that put their policies where their mouth is will be able to create export-led growth, and be able to attract foreign investment - and in the long run increase their nation's wealth, he says.

Dr. Gummich is Vice President, Deutsche Bank Research, Frankfurt am Main.

Introduction

In this paper I will outline eight points, starting with a ranking of the Eastern European reforming economies. Chart 1 is dated one year ago, and today it has become almost obsolete. It shows three groups of countries in the shape of concentric circles. For the most progressive, most advanced among these countries down from the Baltics via Belarus, Ukraine, Moldavia, Romania, Bulgaria, down to Albania, the structure is no longer valid because Estonia among the Baltics e.g. has possibly in the meantime joined the first group. Belarus does not know itself whether it is on the road to reform. Ukraine has started to reform its economy. Romania has emerged as a country with high economic growth in the southeast of Europe, and also Albania has made good progress. So today, therefore, there are a lot of differentiations among these countries.

Let us finally look at the third group of countries, i.e. Russia. This is now 89 different regions and, maybe, has 89 different journeys on the road to reform. Some regions are moving quickly, some of them very slowly; and some of them are not moving at all because they have run out of fuel. But even on the fastest journeys in Russia and its reforming regions, we sometimes do not know who is actually in the driver's seat.

Ranking of Europe's Economies in Transition

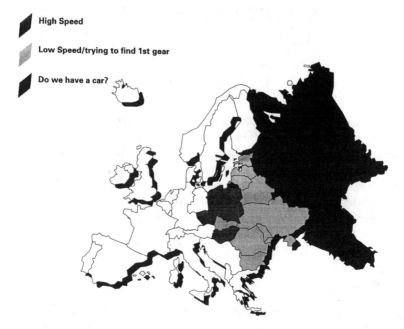

chart 1

My second point is the external comparative assessment for Eastern European reforming countries. Let me give you the following criteria for this external comparative assessment:
- Foreign direct investment.
- Foreign debt.
- The rating by international agencies and, therefore, the refinancing opportunities for the country.
- Volumes, structure, potential and bottlenecks of trade.
- Convertibility.
- Membership in international organisations.

Foreign Direct Investment

Chart 2 shows you the per capita foreign direct investment in several Eastern European countries. Hungary attracted most investment, followed by the other countries that you see here in the chart. How is it that Hungary has been so successful? You know that Hungary is famous for salami, for its paprika, for Rubik's cube and for the New York-based billionaire, George Soros, who lived in Hungary until 1956. But these are not all reasons for the attractiveness of Hungary for foreign investment. The reason was the long-term success as a reforming economy since 1968 when they established *goulash communism*, which was followed by goulash capitalism in 1990. Today they are accused sometimes of implementing goulash gradualism. But this has been sorted out now by the new austerity programme under the new finance minister, Mr. Lajos Bokros, since March of this year. So Hungary has had an easy investment process and, furthermore, it is a country that marketed its reforms properly. It did not make the same mistake as a German pharmaceutical company once made when they wanted to market a headache drug in an Arab country. The company thought that they would launch an advertising campaign and they tried to do it in a major Cairo newspaper. They used three cartoons. The first picture showed an Arab man. Well, you could really see that he suffered. He had headache. He looked not good and he really was in a lot of pain. The second picture showed the same man opening the box with the German headache drug, taking the drug and eating it. In the third picture you could finally see him completely relieved. He smiled, he was relaxed, everything was all right, he had no headache any longer. This advertising campaign was a complete failure. Why was it a failure?

Foreign Direct Investment

($ per capita)

Hungary 700
Czech Republic 300
Estonia 140
Slovenia 130
Poland 75
Russia 27
Ukraine 7

chart 2

It was a failure because the strategists in the headquarters of the pharmaceutical company in Germany had not taken into consideration that in Arab countries you do not read a newspaper from the left to the right.

Hungary has not made this kind of mistake in marketing its abilities and its potential. It has attracted $7-8 billion up to the end of 1994 in foreign direct investment. The exact number depends on your method of calculation. It is followed by Poland with approximately $3.5 billion and the Czech Republic with $3.1 billion. These three countries altogether make up for more than 50 percent of total foreign direct investment in the 26 reforming economies. The whole region attracted $22 billion for investment. That might sound like a lot, but the actual annual inflow of foreign direct investment into the region of $7 billion is about the same inflow as into Argentina alone. And the total accumulated stock of foreign direct investment in the entire Eastern European and former Soviet region, with more than 400 million inhabitants, is less than the accumulated stock of strategic investments in Thailand.

Nevertheless, this foreign direct investment in the East is certainly a success because the countries started only a few years ago and they started from scratch. Chart 3 shows wage levels in the Eastern European region, indicating why these countries are so attractive to foreign direct investors. Wage costs even in the most expensive country amount to less than 10 percent of West German wage levels, including social benefits. It is important to say, however, that these low wage levels make these countries very attractive for strategic, greenfield investors who like to produce and manufacture in the economies. On the other hand, there is a big productivity gap, compared to the West, in all of these countries. So the very low wage level in Russia actually does not mean that the unit-costs are much more attractive than, let us say, in West Germany. No, if you calculate the productivity, the over-manning, the lack of quality and the image gap of products, and the lack of marketing skills, then you end up with the same unit-cost per unit in the West as in some of these countries, as especially here in this example, in Russia.

Monthly Wage Costs in Eastern Europe

(in DM per capita, 1995, including social benefits payments)	
Germany	6800
Bulgaria	180
Czech/Slovakia	400
Hungary	660
Poland	370
Romania	190
Russia	100
Ukraine	45

chart 3

Foreign Debt

My fourth point is foreign debt. In absolute terms, Russia is the most indebted country, with $89 billion worth of Soviet debt. They have also taken responsibility for 100 percent of this debt from other republics. If we add new debt that has emerged since 1992 for Russia, we end up at a number higher than $130 billion. Poland ranks second with $42 billion, Hungary with $28 billion, Bulgaria with $14 billion, Czech Republic with $9 billion, Romania with $4.6 billion and Slovakia with $4.1 billion.

One may use another statistic and measure foreign debt on a per capita base. Here Hungary is in the lead with $2,800 per capita in foreign debt, followed by Bulgaria with $1,800 and Poland with $1,100. Russia comes afterwards with about $1,000 dollars per capita, followed by Czech Republic and Slovakia with $900 dollars per capita and Romania with only $200 dollars per capita.

Bankers tend to use another method of calculating debt burden: the debt ratio. The debt ratio is the ratio of net foreign debt to total annual export earnings. It expresses how many years of exports are needed to repay the foreign debt of a country in full. To give you an example: if a country is indebted to the other countries, to the international markets, with $20 billion and has annual exports worth $10 billion, the debt ratio would be 2.0 because two years of exports would be needed to repay the entire debt. Here, Hungary and Bulgaria are in the (negative) lead with 2.0, followed by Russia with 1.9 and Poland with 1.6; the numbers for Romania, Slovakia and Czech Republic are 0.9, 0.7 and 0.3 respectively. It also makes a big difference whether the countries asked for a rescheduling in the past or not. Poland had a major rescheduling with the Paris Club already in 1991 and had a rescheduling concerning its commercial debt to Western banks only a year ago in 1994. Hungary, the highest per capita debtor, never asked for a rescheduling. In the early 1990s, a lot of Western critics advised them to do so - but they chose to service their debt punctually, which brought them an early seal of approval from the IMF. They were a good debtor country - in contrast to Poland which stopped servicing its debt in 1989, asked for a rescheduling and received a worse international credit rating. And that made it possible for Hungary to attract such a lot of foreign direct investment.

For Russia, the rescheduling question is still open. We hope in the London Club and in the Paris Club to achieve a long-term solution. In both Clubs there are negotiations under way and we are optimistic that we will arrive at a solution for this $89 billion debt which is divided into about $28 billion commercial debt with about 600 banks (London Club) and about $56 billion with the 19 member governments of the Paris Club. The rest of the debt is supplier credits. The non-existence of a long-term international rescheduling agreement puts a big shadow on the creditworthiness of Russia and also on other CIS-States, although Russia accounts for the entire debt today.

Rating and Refinancing

Only three countries in the region have received a rating by Moody's, for example. Hungary has the longest history of refinancing its economy with Eurobonds, but Hungary has fallen a little bit behind now. Poland, just a few weeks ago, as a surprise, received a rating by Moody's of BAA 3, which is the lowest level of investment grade rating for quality-conscious Western portfolio investors. The Hungarian rating (BBB) today is worse than the Polish one whereas the rating of the Czech National Bank is higher. The Czech National Bank is a bond issuer; Poland is going to be one soon and there are rumours that Russia in the third quarter of the year is going to issue Eurobonds again.

Refinancing of these countries is possible when portfolio investors go into the country and invest there on the basis of this rating. You know how portfolio investors can behave in these markets. You know the definition of an emerging market? This definition holds true: an emerging market is a market where you have to be ready to emerge in case of emergency. And this is what portfolio investors tend to do sometimes. In contrast to the positive implications brought into a country's economy by foreign capital this practice endangers the stability of these economies, in extreme situations, by immediate withdrawal of invested capital.

Trade

We have done analyses in the CEFTA countries (Central European Free Trade Association - Poland, Czech Republic, Hungary and Slovakia) and compared the trade structures from 1990 to 1994. The major findings are as follows: the level of openness of these economies is today almost the same as the level of openness of the EU member-countries. The level of openness expressed in the export quota, for example in the Czech Republic compared to Austria - both similar countries with similar sizes of population - is 55 percent today (in Austria) as against 38 percent. If we exclude Czech trade with Slovakia, we still end at an export quota of 37 percent.

Another comparison: Poland and Spain. Those countries have similar size populations, Spain's export quota was 20 percent, and the export quota of Poland was 24 percent at the end of 1994.

All of the countries in Central and Eastern Europe show a higher share in trade with the EU than four or eight years ago. In 1986 their share of trade with the EU was only 27 percent. Today it is 50 to 60 percent and, again, this is almost as much as Spain's or Austria's trade with the EU.

There is, interestingly enough, a reduction in exports of sensitive goods from Central and Eastern Europe to the EU. Producers in sectors like textiles, agricultural products, iron and steel maintain that they have to protect their markets against exports from Central and Eastern Europe and the fact is, if you go into a Belgian restaurant today and order raspberries, they are very likely not from Poland. And this is because the Scottish raspberry farmers have lobbied much more successfully than the Polish ones. Exports from the eastern region in sensitive goods into the EU area have even decreased and, what surprised me most in doing this analysis, there is only a slight surplus in sensitive goods in bilateral trade from Central and Eastern Europe with the EU. There is just a surplus of one billion ECU into the EU regarding iron, steel, textiles, agricultural products; this is just 0.1 percent of total imports of the EU from outside. So there is really not much real danger in imports from Central and Eastern Europe, at least for the domestic industries in the EU.

Russia's trade is a problem. There are poor statistics. Russia is a phenomenon in itself. Winston Churchill, 50 years ago, helped us in saying: We can't analyse Russia. Russia is a puzzle, surrounded by an enigma, wrapped into a mystery". So are the trade statistics. In the far East of Russia a year ago, I saw airplanes packed with Russian tourists. They flew to Hong Kong, Seoul and Tokyo and each of them brought back not just the normal economy class baggage allowance, but a lot of boxes. They (the Russians) are allowed by law to bring back goods worth up to 2,000 dollars tax free. Look at these non-statistical imports. Just imagine that every 15th Russian, namely 10 million Russians, only once a year travels abroad and brings back goods worth up to 2,000 dollars, and you have non-statistical imports of $20 billion. This is more than 50 percent of the imports officially reported from Russia.

Russia - in contrast to other reforming economies - is rich in easily-marketable natural resources. This means Russia can earn hard currency (namely more than $50 billion in annual exports) by exporting oil, gas, gold, diamonds, coal, timber and metals. While gradually restructuring its manufacturing industries Russia, therefore, can bridge the gap, earn money abroad and feed its people. Other countries, not as largely endowed with resources, do not have this opportunity to generate hard cash.

Nevertheless, there are bottlenecks in trade, such as the low technology standards that dominate the Eastern exports, shortages in quality and marketing abilities, and the limited access to Western markets. There is - last but not least - a task for the West, too.

Convertibility

There is a race now between the Czech Republic, Poland, and Hungary as to who gets a completely convertible currency first. All the three countries have already a so-called current-account convertibility, i.e. for commercial transactions. They have fared well with this if we leave aside the deterioration of international competitiveness because of real revaluations.

Today they seem to be unable to wait for full convertibility. Maybe they should go a little bit slower It took Germany 11 years after the introduction of the Deutschmark in 1948 before the currency became completely convertible and the Austrian shilling and the Swedish krona became completely convertible in 1989 and 1991 respectively . So one could argue about this whether a race is right.

Membership of International Economic Organisations

The way towards the European Union is illustrated in Chart 4. We have seen the European agreements. The Czech Republic, Hungary and Poland received these European agreements in December 1991, coming to force in early 1992; Slovakia, Bulgaria and Romania in the meantime. The last countries we have seen receiving that status are the three Baltics. Nevertheless, a good topic for discussion might be when these countries will be able to become full members of the Club.

Toward the EU

European Agreements	
Czech Republic, Hungary, Poland	1991
Slovakia, Bulgaria, Romania Baltics	1995

chart 4

The external situation differs very much from country to country. There are some countries - like Poland and Hungary - that can afford to run a negative current account balance. They can balance this debt through refinancing or by an influx of foreign direct investment. Ukraine, in contrast, has a big problem in bridging the gaps created by a negative current account. It is vital to solve old external debt problems of the Eastern countries, because refinancing opportunities improve and strategic investors will be more willing to invest their capital in the country. Also, badly needed imports to restructure the economy can better be financed.

The overall success on the external front, finally, is both determined and reflected by the total commitments of the respective country to reforms. In other words: those who show clear commitment by putting the right policies in place - including on the external front - will gain from export-led growth, attract foreign investment and will be able to increase the wealth of their nation and will fare better.

RUSSIA: EXTERNAL ECONOMIC RELATIONS AND FUTURE DEVELOPMENT

Leonid Fituni

Russia's participation in international trade and the world economy in general has declined during the current reform period. At the same time, the country has become much more dependent on external economic factors. Private consumption in particular now relies heavily on foreign goods. The positive side of this, says Leonid Fituni, is that the country will eventually become much more closely integrated into the world economy. But he warns that the poorer majority of the population may feel squeezed out of today's new economic order. There is a danger that they will give vent to their feelings of alienation by turning to isolationist politicians - a situation that would be worrying for both Russia and the West.

Professor Fituni is Director, Centre for Strategic and Global Studies, Moscow.

Introduction

This paper offers a comprehensive overview of current trends in the Russian external economic sector. The analysis is given of the current trends in exports and imports. Capital flows into and from Russia are reviewed. Special attention is given to the problem of capital flight.

The paper argues that Russia's participation in international trade and other sectors of international economic relations (except for foreign borrowing) decreased in volume during the years of reform. At the same time, Russia's dependence on external economic factors has increased many-fold. Therefore, future Russian governments will not be able to execute policy without taking into consideration the external economic factor, as domestic economic development is largely dependent on outside factors. Internal consumption - especially in the private sector - relies heavily on foreign supplies, as domestic supply has been severely undermined.

This situation can result in Russia's further integration into the international community and Moscow's greater preparedness to participate in joint efforts to solve major international problems. At the same time it may lead to unprecedented feelings of privation and rejection for the poorer majority of the population, who may choose to bring to power political forces that are more inclined to implement an inward-looking national policy and economic development.

External Economic Relations and Integration into the World Economy

External economic relations are an important sector of Russia's economy. By the level and type of the development of this sector one can judge how far Russia has progressed along the way of market reforms; what is its new role in the world economy, the prospects for accelerating its development.

The changes that took place in Russia's external economic sector are radical and unprecedented. The most far-reaching result of the late perestroika and post- perestroika periods was abandoning the concept of the state currency and foreign trade monopoly. Now thousands of economic units are engaged in both spheres. The volume and the structure of exports and imports changed, too.

Unfortunately, while they are theoretically "progressive", these changes did not bring about increased efficiency in external economic relations. In fact a lot of negative results impeded Russia's development along the lines of a market economy.

First of all, the demise of COMECON resulted in a catastrophic decrease in trade with its former participants and reduced the amount of available resources for economic reform and for maintaining the standard of living of the population. By the end of the 1980s COMECON countries accounted for over 50 percent of foreign trade turnover of the Russian Federation; now they account for only about 15 percent.

Second, the anticipated free market breakthrough of Russian goods to Western markets did not materialise. The barriers, introduced by the West against Russian goods, not only remained as in Soviet days, but in some cases became even more intricate. In 1992-1994 two dozen anti-dumping legal procedures were started against Russia in the West. Many traditional markets were lost. The situation was aggravated by unfavourable dynamics of world prices: they fell for Russian export products and increased for imports.

As a result of these developments and trends, Russia's foreign trade turnover in 1994 was only half of that reached in 1990. Raw materials now absolutely dominate exports - 50 percent of the total is accounted for by energy sector products (mainly oil and gas), and 25 percent cent by metals and diamonds. In fact it exactly repeats the composition of Angola's exports in 1973 (with exclusion of coffee). The share of machinery has been constantly falling since 1988.

In 1994, the export value of the fuel and energy complex (FEC) products reached $21.3 billion, up 6 percent from 1993, though its share in overall export volume has been falling since 1992. Russia tries to compensate for the falling efficiency of its exports by increasing the physical volume of exports. But it manages to reach this goal only by reducing prices for its products. Therefore economic efficiency of export is declining. Over the past two years the growth in total export volumes is due to increased deliveries of FEC products and a boost in exports of other sectors. However, the FEC continues to remain a key sector of the economy for hard currency resource provision and export efficiency. The latter is caused by a rather low level of domestic prices - especially for oil and gas, compared to world markets.

1994 witnessed a cut in contract prices for nearly all types of FEC products; compared to 1993 the aggregate index of contract prices reached 0.95. A rise in export value (against the backdrop of reduced contract prices) was due to growing delivery volumes; the physical volume index reached 1.12. In the first quarter of 1994 it stood at 1.07, in the first half-year at 1.11; it reached 1.12 over the first nine months of 1994.

The export structure of FEC products, notwithstanding slight fluctuations over the year, became almost identical to the 1993 structure by the end of 1994. Oil deliveries account for 42 percent of total exports of FEC products. In 1994, oil exports reached 89.4 million tons, up 9.5 million from 1993. The increase in delivery volume amounted to 11.9 percent At the same time, average contract price dropped from $104.7 to $99.8 per ton, or by 4.7 percent. As a result, the export value grew by a mere 6.6 percent to total $8.9 billion.

It is worth noting that oil contract prices underwent nearly the same changes as did contract prices on the world markets; the deviation in average contract price from the world market did not exceed 3 percent in the spring and early summer of 1994; in other seasons this deviation ranged from 4.5 to 6.7 percent. Moreover, 1994 saw a closer correlation between world and contract prices and volume of oil deliveries, which was not typical of 1993.

A boost in oil exports occurred against a backdrop of declining oil extraction. According to preliminary results of 1994 compared to 1993, oil extraction decreased by 11.5 percent. The share of exports in production volumes increased to 30.4 percent against 24.1 percent in 1993. In 1994, 109.7 billion cubic metres of natural gas were exported, up 14.4 percent from 1993. This means that a larger proportion of natural resources is not used internally, but has to be used to secure hard currency inflows, absolutely necessary in order to service Russia's huge external debt

According to the Ministry of Foreign Economic Relations, in 1995, countries outside the former Soviet Union accounted for four-fifths of the $33 billion worth of foreign trade Russia did (in the first four months of this year). Trade with what is called the "Far Abroad" was worth $26.7 billion in January-April, 13.2 percent more than in the same period of last year. Trade with the CIS fell 4.5 percent to $6.5 billion. Russian trade with the countries outside the former Soviet Union has continued to grow over the entire period, despite a 15 percent drop in January-April turnover with Australia and Oceania. Trade with Africa doubled to an albeit still modest $463 million in the first 4 months. The country still does half its trade with the non-CIS nations of Europe - $18 billion in January-April, $2.5 billion more than in 1994.

Overall, in the first five months of 1995, Russia reported exports up 14.7 percent at $20 billion and imports up 11.1 percent at $13 billion, giving a hefty surplus of $6.9 billion. The Commission for Urgent Issues, a key executive body, reported January-April exports of oil at 38.1 million tonnes, 3.7 million tonnes more than in the same period of last year and including 9 million tonnes to the CIS and 29.1 million tonnes to the rest of the world.

The import trends are quite volatile. Until 1992 imports were increasing. Then the government managed to reverse the trend and the volume of imports began to decrease, but since 1994 growth has resumed.

In 1994, considerable changes were seen in distribution of import volumes between sectors and in the composition of imports within sectors: ferrous metals imports, engineering product imports, chemical product imports, foodstuff imports and non-food consumer goods imports.

The share of ferrous metal products in the overall value of imports dropped to reach 2 percent from 2.5 percent in 1993. Some $564 million of imports were purchased.

Compared to 1993, the share of rolled products and steel imports in import values increased, rising from 15.2 percent to 19.5 percent, while imports of pipes fell from 84.8 to 80.5 percent in 1994. $110 million worth of rolled products and steel were purchased, down 10 percent from 1993. In 1994, a total of 569,000 tons of pipes was imported, compared to 812,000 tons in 1993. However, in 1994 purchases were made at higher prices. The average contract price totalled $798.4 per ton, up 16.4 percent from 1993.

The amount of engineering products in overall import value remained at the 1993 level -34 percent. Some $9.6 billion worth of machinery, equipment and vehicles were purchased as compared to $9.1 billion in 1993. The structure of engineering imports has undergone drastic changes (Table I).

The import value of ground transport vehicles, chiefly cars, decreased by $683 million in 1994. Imports of minibuses and trucks increased. The import of minibuses soared, rising by 130 percent. However, the import value did not exceed the 1993 level due to lower contract prices. The average contract price for a car ran at $3,000 in 1994 compared to $4,600 in 1993. The cost of a truck dropped to $34,000 in 1994.

The share of chemical product imports in total import values increased, reaching 4.8 percent in 1994 from 2.1 percent in 1993. Chemical imports reached $1.35 billion, up 140 percent from the 1993 value. This increase is primarily due to increased purchases of medicines. Their share reached 85.2 percent of chemical product imports or $1.16 billion, compared to $300 million in 1993.

The import value of foodstuffs reached $3.4 billion in 1994, which is near 1993's level. The structure of these imports underwent large changes (Table II).

In 1994, some two million tons of grain were purchased compared to 11.1 million tons in 1993 and 28.9 million tons in 1992. $314 million was spent on grain imports in 1994 instead of 1.6 billion in 1993 and 4.2 billion in 1992.

Sugar purchases were also curtailed. In 1993, compared to 1992, imports of sugar, including raw sugar, shrank by 19 percent. In 1994, they fell by another 26.5 percent, to total 2.3 million tons. Imports of white sugar comprised 50 percent of overall sugar imports, the same as in 1993.

Imports of other foodstuffs saw a boom: beet purchases rose 350 percent, poultry imports rose 440 percent, the import of coffee and tea rose 130 percent, fruits (apples and citruses) rose 430 percent, and the import of butter rose 140 percent.

Imports of meat and poultry grew to 32.7 percent of total food imports in 1994 from 5 percent in 1993. Domestic production fell by 23.7 percent.

The import of non-food consumer products fell by 50 percent to total $1.7 billion, compared to 3.5 billion in 1993. The increase in import customs tariffs in July of last year caused a reduction in the import of consumer goods. In the second half of the year the average duty per conventional imported unit (including fabrics, clothes, footwear and furniture) rose to 17 percent from 13 percent. The value of imports dropped as a consequence by 12 percent in 1994.

No drastic changes occurred in the import structure of non-food consumer products (Table III).

During recent years many changes were introduced in the legal regulation of external economic relations. The law on customs tariffs was adopted as well as laws on currency regulation and currency control. A Presidential decree removed privileges given to participants in export and import operations.

A new import tariff is in force. The average tariff is now 5-7 percent higher. In future a gradual decrease of tariffs is envisaged, starting with commodities, the tariffs for which are higher than 30 percent.

In general, as a result of reforms, the system of external trade became more flexible. It reacts adequately to the general economic changes and to the developments in the world economy. But the system is still far from being economically efficient.

Capital flight is an important problem. It significantly reduces the volume of resources available for implementing economic restructuring and securing internal capital accumulation. Gross capital outflows from Russia are currently estimated at about $50 billion, of which capital flight proper makes for $35-40 billion. Though from a free-market point of view this phenomenon may be considered "normal", in the sense that free capital in a free country looks for greater security and higher efficiency, it poses a severe strain on the Russian economy, which in fact feeds overseas countries and territories at its own expense. Capital inflows of all types (including foreign aid, direct and portfolio investment) average $1-2 billion a year.

Russia timber exporters are reported to have concealed 50 percent of their foreign currency earnings in 1994. According to the Federal Counter-Intelligence Service, violations by some of the exporters have been acquiring an "increasingly criminal nature."

About 30 percent of Russia's timber products was exported at dumping prices in 1994, and some areas (such as the Perm region) exported timber even at below domestic prices. Security services uncovered widespread financial violations, involving mostly barter deals (30 percent of all deliveries in 1994 were on barter). Foreign currency earnings were concealed everywhere. The Arkhangelsk pulp-and-paper mill, for instance, concealed $7.8 million of export revenues.

A dramatic decline in production, despite a favourable market situation and widespread violations, have made timber producers themselves demand government regulation of the industry, and by the start of 1995 virtually all timber exports deals were supervised by the state-owned Roslesprom Co. which has in fact been granted the status of a government ministry.

In the meantime, major Western financial institutions have been displaying a great interest in Russia's timber industry complex, paying particular attention to investment programmes including equity in Russian production facilities.

Under existing Russian laws, a foreign investor can currently own up to 35 percent of the stock. However, the Swedish Tetra Laval still managed to acquire absolute control of the Svetogorsk pulp-and-paper mill, and changes in its production policies have already been creating problems for the mill's traditional consumers inside the country.

In general there are a number of channels of capital outflow from Russia - according to MFER at least 10 percent of export revenues are not remitted to Russia under the pretence that the importer refused to pay for the imported goods. But 80 percent of this money is used for import of commodities from abroad. Another channel is deliberate over-invoicing of imports and under-invoicing of exports. The difference is placed in a Russian resident account opened with a Western bank. Still another channel are advance payments against import contracts, which partners allegedly "fail" to fulfil (failed goods deliveries). The sums received by a foreign firm from a Russian partner are placed on account of the latter in a Western bank.

150,000-200,000 permanent residents of Russia opened their private accounts in the West (not an illegal practice, but one normally frowned upon by Russian authorities).

Emigrants from Russia sell their apartments, dachas, cars, etc., for hard currency, asking buyers to place the money on their accounts abroad. The annual outflow in this form is about $1 billion.

The illegal flight of capital from Russia is much higher than the volume of international aid the country received since 1992. Because of internal instability and unfavourable exchange regulations Russian companies and individuals stash their currency earnings in foreign bank accounts rather than bringing the money home and investing it in Russia. In one instance a source in the Ministry of Finance disclosed in August 1992 that "ten to twelve billion dollars came in and they did not know where it was".

The International Monetary Fund is hoping that the tough economic policies it is prescribing for Russia will attract capital back into the country by increasing confidence in the country's ability to pursue painful reforms. However the recent moves by the Russian government indicate that the currency regime may become harsher but it will not compensate for the stability needed.

The last and most important issue to be discussed is how Russia's place in the world economy has changed and what the implications are for internal development. This question is multifaceted and it is difficult to give a simple and clear-cut answer to it.

Our short overview shows that Russia's participation in international trade and other sectors of international economic relations (except for foreign borrowing) has decreased in volume during the years of reform. At the same time Russia's dependence on external economic factors has increased manifold. It means that nowadays no kind of government will be able to execute its policy without taking into consideration the external economic factor. It also means that domestic economic development is also to a large degree dependent on extraneous factors, including external inputs. Internal consumption, especially the private share, relies heavily on foreign supplies, its domestic basis being severely undermined.

This situation can result in Russia's further integration into the international community and Moscow's greater preparedness to participate in joint efforts to solve major international problems. At the same time it may lead to unprecedented feeling of privation and rejection on the part of the poorer majority of the population, which may choose to bring to power political forces more inclined to implement an introvert type of development.

Imports - Table I

		Import in percent 1993	Import in percent 1994	Deviation, $mln, (+increase) (-decrease)
84-90	Machinery, equipment and vehicles, total:	100.0	100.0	523
84	Nuclear reactors, boilers, rel. equipm.	50.3	51.1	336
85	Electrical machines and equipment	18.1	21.3	399
86	Railway engines and rolling-stock	40	3.6	-18
87	Ground vehicles	19.2	9.5	-829
89	Ships, boats and other vessels	3.2	0.9	-202
90	Optical instruments and equipment	5.1	12.9	777

Imports - Table II

	1993 in percent	1994 in percent
Foodstuffs and food elements including:	100.0	100.0
grain	46.6	9.4
raw and white sugar	31.8	21.9
meat and poultry	3.4	14.5
tea and coffee	4.8	10.9
citruses and apples	3.5	18.7
milk, cream, butter and other fats	3.9	8.7
vegetable oil	1.8	1.8
other foodstuffs	4.2	14.1

Imports - Table III

	Second half compared to first half '94 in percent	Structure in percent, 1st half 1994	Structure in percent, 2nd half 1994
Fabrics	97.5	6.1	6.7
Clothes	81.7	54.7	50.9
Footwear	91.8	21.9	22.9
Furniture	98.6	17.3	19.5

PARTICIPATION OF INTERNATIONAL INSTITUTIONS IN THE REFORMING PROCESS OF ECONOMIES IN TRANSITION

Katarzyna Żukrowska

Economic reform of a post-communist economy is not a question of shock therapy, but of direct foreign investement. To create a favourable climate for investors, the groundwork must be laid at the political level, says Katarzyna Żukrowska. Then it is up to the economy to do its work.

Professor Żukrowska is working at the Institute of Development and Strategic Studies, Warsaw[1]

Introduction

There are three options for a transitional strategy: the autonomous and nationalistic approach, involvement of another state (mainly regional power or a superpower), and support from international institutions. Most of the post-communist states have relied on international institutions in their transition strategy. This approach seemed to be not only the most effective choice but also a solution that is politically neutral. Effectiveness of the support towards systemic transformation which was supplied by international institutions derives from its: experience in macro-stabilisation policy; coordination of the steps taken by different institutions; conditionality; and finally knowledge of mutual relations between political and economic forces of each country. Neutrality of the aid is closely linked with the contemporary stage of development of international relations, enough to mention such features as end of the Cold War; victory of democracy and market over the communist experiment; globalization of technology, production and product; liberalization in international trade of goods and services; capital transfers; and finally, the universality of international institutions.

This paper indicates why the role of international institutions is so important in the systemic transformation and how it changes with the advancement of the reforms. It also shows why other strategies for change are ineffective. Poland is used as a best example, indicating how the whole mechanism has been working, when put into motion.

The Scale and Scope of Transformation Changes

Transformation changes embraced parallel changes in both economic and political systems. In a comparatively short time these systems in the post-communist countries had evolved considerably, bringing them closer to the proven mechanisms of well-established Western democracies. Of course there are numerous things that still require mastering or even creation but today's system in the economies in transition is not only comparable but also compatible with the West. As Dahrendorf states: a political system can be changed overnight, economy requires years to change, while an open society can be created by an exchange of at least a generation.

In the case of Poland, systemic changes were achieved by a shock therapy in the economic field and gradual change in the political sphere. Although in the political sphere the impression was that political power was transmitted totally to the opposition as Solidarity won the first free elections, nevertheless, the political division between the old and new elites was made clear:

- First, by the division of power between the President (W. Jaruzelski) and the government (T. Mazowiecki, heading a government consiting of Democratic and Peasants Parties and Solidarity).
- Second, by gradual changes in the central and local administration.
- Third, by the division of power in the Parliament, where the Senate (upper chamber) was overwhelmingly dominated by Solidarity, while the lower chamber represented more diversified political forces.

Trying to complete the political issue in a short and comprehensive manner, it should be said that, within the advancement of the reforms the political power was changing both in the Parliament (Sejm) as well as in the government and at the presidential level. Poland has experienced a rapid progression, through six governments, with at least two failures in creating a government. The parliamentary elections have changed the representation in the Polish Sejm, which generally can be characterized as evolution from a dispersed representation to a more consolidated one. At the same time this consolidation became univocal with 30 percent of the voters - mainly the right wing orientation - not represented in the Sejm. This situation forces further integration of small and medium-sized parties, despite ambitions of their leaders.[2] The effectiveness of such pressure will be seen by the end of the year in presidential elections.

Generally speaking, changes on the Polish political stage cannot be evaluated explicitly. On the one hand a post-communist President (animator of changes) has been replaced by a Solidarity leader and it is difficult to define this shift in terms of political orientation. It is not as simple as change from the Left to the Right or Center. On the other hand, parties represented in the Sejm have changed as well. Changes have occured not only within the parties but also in the framework of relations among them. Colours of the parties were most of all fading away, even some of the MPs were changing their orientation, moving from one parliamentary club to another. Despite this fading of colours, we could see that parties started to differ in their programmes, not only in their rhetoric. The main indicators concerned some domestic issues as well as foreign policy. In the first case the main problem concerned gradual or "shock" changes in the economy, in other words the issue of the engagement of the government and the reform of the administration. In foreign policy the main question dealt with the integration within EU and NATO membership, in other words the sovereignty issue was raised.

Political evolution in Poland, with its accelerated fermentation, has quickly caught up with the stage that is characteristic of contemporary political development in the West. This can be seen by the fact that the division between the political Left and Right has been replaced by division of those who opt for a more liberal approach to the world's economy and further integration leading towards global managerial solutions, and those who opt for more nationalism and sovereignty in their policy. This evolution and changing strength of political power, as well as political egoism of different parties, can be considered as a set of main arguments that support the idea of participation of international institutions in the reform process.

Other arguments can be found in the economic field. Political scientists, who try to present this problem, usually refer to the main question: from were does the first push come: from the political or the economic field? In the Polish case it is clear that the first push towards systemic changes was defined by political decisions. Although, the economy has played a crucial role in this process. With a better economic performance the pressure to change the system would be weaker.

Economic transformation in Poland has been discussed widely not only in the literature but also here, at the NATO Economics Colloquium in 1993, by the author of Polish economic reform, Leszek Balcerowicz. I will briefly repeat that Polish achievements in the reform process can be ascribed to a very simple mechanism: the market.[3] The whole idea of economic changes consisted of combination of a external and domestic, which have formulated the framework for:

• Macro-stabilisation policy.
• Liberalisation of prices.
• Liberalisation of foreign trade.

The aquired strategy had three anchors, being a traditionally heterodox approach:

• Control over the money supply.
• Exchange rate of the Polish zloty.
• Control of the rise of incomes.

The third anchor is considered to be the main difference between an orthodox and heterodox approach. It gives additional guarantees that pressure from employment does not break the tight corset of money supply, bringing a strong impulse in inflationary pressure.

As forces of the Polish market were too weak and warped they have been additionally reinforced by signals coming from the world market, namely from the European Union, EFTA and CEFTA. After a short period, when prices reached their equilibrium on a rather high level, prices have stabilized and the inflation rate fell, although it is still higher than planned. This therapy has enabled a quick departure from the transformation crisis and a return to growth. The Polish economy started to grow in May 1992, that is two and a quarter years after Balcerowicz launched his plan. Now Poland is considered to be one of the leaders in the process of transformation, along with Hungary, the Czech and Slovak Republics.

In summary: the first stage of reform can be labeled as political. There are several reasons behind this: (1) reform was pushed by political decisions; (2) systemic changes required establishment of political and market institutions, as well as the introduction of legal regulations which were in the hands of politicans; (3) the state sector dominated the economy, which has given stagnating impulses towards the strategy to change, as a normal reaction to preserve the old structures; (4) some of the economic decisions were delegated to international institutions, which has eased their fulfillment.

Within advancement of the reform the decisions gradually became dominated by economic reasoning and their political background lost power. The private sector started to dominate the economy; all the economic subjects have adjusted to the tough requirements of the market; and common interests have been articulated - which helped to form pressure groups, or lobbies, which were increasingly oriented towards the future, not towards protecting former privileges.

The Question of a Reforming Programme

All countries in the region have reservations concerning the strategy for change. The first set of questions concerns the touchy problem of sovereignty.[4] It is understandable that each country tries to protect its sovereignty, especially when it has been recently acquired. Countries must calculate what they win and what they can lose in this process. Is the result of such a calculation positive or negative? The Polish experience indicates that it was a calculation with a net gain.

It is clear that in an interdependent world, countries are less sovereign than when the world consisted of more independent states. Such a development explains that all countries lose their sovereignty on a similar scale. Explaining this fact, one has to stress that the reduction of the state's sovereignity is affected by:

• Developments in international institutions and relations among them.

- Developments in the international economy, by globalisation of the product, production and technology caused by internationalisation of the economy, and accelerated by intensifying flows of capital;
- Relations among countries and of countries with international institutions.

Making the decision about a transformation strategy, each country must take into account the fact that:
- International institutions are changing their character and are shifting from closed clubs into universal ones. This motion can be ascribed to depolitisation of the international economy, mainly achieved by the end of the Cold War. Some of the institutions, which were considered to be most effective tools of the Cold War were closed down or replaced by new ones of a more general character.
- Transforming countries are not able to change on their own and there are several reasons behind that: their capital accumulation abilities are limited; their knowledge of how to change is limited; and the burdens of change are rather high and they are totally imposed on the population which in a short term reduces support for the reforms.

A second set of questions tackles the issue of the width of the opening of the economy. Experience in this field shows that the opening should be rather wide. Protection prolongs only the transition period, not necessarily reducing the burdens. Usually, gradualism is accompanied by the same costs as shock, although the results are limited and the time of transformation prolonged. Opening of markets plays a specific role, as was mentioned above, enforcing the signals of the market. Government is not able to point out which branches of production should be developed in the future, and which should be considered as declining. Moreover, such decisions are politically dangerous as they undermine the support of the electorate. Decisions in this field can be made with the support of intensified competition. It has helped to count the costs, and finally it is one of the measures showing that ECE countries compete with traditional factors: exchange rate, labour costs, raw material costs, but their competitiveness is very limited as far as modern factors are concerned. Development apart from the mainstream economy will widen the gap which exists in this specific field.

Moreover, competition is one of the most effective tools which decides the competitiveness of the country, branch, or product.[5] It dictates the elasticity of the economy to change, adapting to the new requirements of the world market. Saying this we have to remember that the economy is a process and does not like stagnation. Stagnation for the economy is equivalent to losing the ground in competition and competitiveness.[6] This finding is fully supported by evidence coming from the contemporary economy. Enough said of the development of former CMEA countries apart from the mainstream economy. This is not the only example supporting this finding in contemporary economic relations.

Poland was one of the countries which despite relatively decentralized external relations was rather self-sufficient economically which in consequence resulted in rather limited openness of her economy. The big distance in this specific sphere had to be overcome in a short period after 1989.

Economies in transition are opening gradually but they have to accept the fact that with time passing and the advancement of reforms, the opening will be wider. It will embrace not only the liberalisation of goods but also liberalisation of capital flows, liberalisation in services transfers and finally liberalisation of the movement of labour. Regulations in those four spheres are mainly reached on a regional level in the institutionalisation of integration processes in Europe. Specifically, this is defined by the EU Europe Agreement and follows summits of the Union, adjusting the association agreements to changing conditions and fulfilling the existing gaps according to the demands of economies in transformation. Regional solutions are not the only unique arrangements in this field. Establishment of the WTO - as an effect of the Uruguay Round - also brings some predictability in regulations concerning international trade. This concerns general rules liberalising world trade i.e. reductions of custom duties and non-tariff barriers. But it also formulates new rules of the game in case of so called "sensitive goods" such as agricultural products, textiles, steel, etc. For the first time in world trade history we are facing regulations concerning capital flows and trade of services, as well as intellectual property.[7] This fact shows that the process of desindustrialization of national economies is also reflected at the level of international relations.

It can be expected that the GATT/WTO can play a special role in international trade, being a safeguard which determines if relations among certain economic blocks of regional integration - namely the multiplying FTAs (free trade areas) - are not turning into blocks of aggressive protection or expansion, creating thus obstacles towards further liberalisation of international relations. GATT/WTO can be considered as a tool in international relations which has a double-fold role to play: (1) it leads towards development of globalism and not regionalism; (2) it can be considered as an institution with a crucial role in the future international relations which can create mechanisms for global management.

In sum: trade - traditionally - is considered to be the best instrument in creating wealth. In such conditions, opening of the economy not only helps to adjust to new market requirements, helps to restructure the economy, but it also acts as a multiplier, giving employment to the domestic labour force and thus increasing the wealth of the country.

The Role of International Institutions

The role of international institutions in transformation of post-communist countries is rather multidimensional in its character. Some of the aspects of this support were discussed earlier in my paper. Now I would like to make some generalisations.

International institutions engaged in transformation of post-communist countries can be divided into several categories, which derive from the role they have played and the purpose for which they were established: (1) financial; (2) integrational; (3) coordinating; (4) guaranteeing security; (5) advisory; (6) defining policy. Their geographical range permits division into: (1) regional; (2) global or universal. Most of the studies present principles of one organization, rarely do they analyse a group as is done in the study, quoted above, called Assistance to Transition.

The list of international institutions engaged in transformation is long as it covers such organisations as: International Monetary Fund (IMF), World Bank, EBRD, European Union, EFTA, CEFTA, PHARE Fund, London Club, Paris Club, International Finance Corporation, OECD, NATO, OSCE, GATT/WTO, G-7, G-24, etc...

The sequencing of aid provided by international organisations forms an extended web in which support from one of the organizations is conditioned by acceptance of the transformation programme by another. Not speaking groundlessly, it should be said that the crucial role in the setting of international organisations is played by the IMF. This organisation, or rather a stabilisation programme accepted by this organisation, opens the door to other international institutions, such as the World Bank or leads to reductions of foreign debt. Moreover, most of the programmes presented within the framework of EU association agreements, where foreign credits were at stake, also required an opinion of the IMF.

Despite the fact that international institutions have played a multifunctional role in the process of systemic transformation in the post-communist region, the depth of their engagement varied from country to country. Moreover, the financial support of those institutions, despite the role they played in the region, is limited and does not exceed 30 US$ per capita on the average.[8] Information concerning this issue are diversified; according to other sources per capita rate of annual support did not surpass US$49.[9] Generally, over the period 1990-93, some $ 22 bn, i.e. just over one quarter of total receipts of external resources was in the form of official aid on concessional terms. Poland with Estonia and Albania are in the group of recipients of relatively big support in comparison with the rest of the transforming countries.

Table I
Western Assistance to Transition in billion US$

Aid and its destination	1992	1993
Total Net Receipts of which	28,6	23,3
CEECs	10,6	8,4
NIS	18,0	14,9
of which Russia	7,9	11,5
Concessional Aid of which	6,8	6,1
CEECs	3,4	2,6
NIS	3,4	3,5
of which Russia	1,9	2,1

Source: OECD. Aid and other resource loans to the Central and Eastern Countries and the New Independent States of the former Soviet Union in 1992 and 1993, Paris 1995. Quoted after Dispatch from Berlin, June 1995, p. 7.

Poland can be considered as the best illustration of the transition strategy that was applied with the active support of international institutions. This strategy is fully adjusted to specific conditions of all post-communist countries which make an attempt to build capitalism without the capital. In such conditions, when home resources of capital are limited, countries have to take into account all possibilities of attracting foreign capital of different forms. This explains why the following comments are derived from the experience gained in this country.

The first phase of the transition was made possible by international institutions as they have supported the economies in transition with:
• Expertise, know-how and experts.
• Financial aid.
• Reduction of the external debt burden.
• Help in restructuring the economy.
• External disciplining role in case of stabilisation policy (as far as the scale of the budget deficit was concerned or the inflation control).
• Reference to other institutions.
• Conditionality.
• Support for the gradual introduction of currency convertability.
• Adjustement of their aid closer to the requirements of the transforming economies.
• Action as an external leverage helping to keep the changes on course.

It would be difficult to present Polish contacts with all the international institutions, therefore I will concentrate on the main international pillars in the transformation strategy: the IMF and the EU. Both those organizations can easily serve as illustrations supporting the above-mentioned functions of international institutions in the transformation strategy.

In the Polish strategy of establishing international institutional contacts, IMF was the first step. The Fund played the role of a specific safeguard for the other Polish partners, as it led towards:[10]

- Creating conditions for the introduction of reforms (establishment of the stabilising fund for currency convertability initially limited to the internal market).
- Improvement of Poland's situation in the eyes of foreign governments, investors and bankers.
- Creating a precondition for loans from the World Bank.
- Creating a precondition for talks with other international organisations.

In return the Polish government had to accept certain conditions, mainly a strict policy on stabilisation. Each piece of the instalment was paid against realization of the consecutive stages of the agreed programme, according to the time-schedule. Any deviation from the rules could cause an adjournment of payments, which has happened twice in the case of Poland. This required further negotiations with the IMF and led towards a new agreement, adjusting the terms of the contract to the new conditions. Hungary, Russia and other East Central European countries experienced similar disciplinary measures, which at the same time indicated the flexibility of approach towards any economic or political constraints.

The agreement with the IMF was a precondition for reducing the debt with foreign creditors grouped in the London and Paris Clubs. Arrangements in both cases were reached on similar conditions, leading towards 50 percent reductions of foreign indebtedness. The first agreement was reached with the Paris Club which groups creditors with state guarantees. The road to an agreement with the London Club was longer and finally ended in 1994. The agreement perceives the ways that the remaining debts are to be repaid, which is conditioned by the economic situation of the market and takes into account the problem of accumulation of repayments. In 1994 the share of scheduled repayments of the Polish debt did not exceed 2,7 per cent of the state budget.[11]

As time passed, when international institutions became convinced that Polish reforms had passed the "point of no return", the conditions were becoming less and less arduous, although they were still imposing some limits on the government. The main principles behind those limits, concerned two aspects:

- Continuation of the reform, according to the formerly worked out and presented agenda.

- Imposing certain limits in "spoiling money" as we have to remember that inflation can be used in a state's policy to reduce the nominal expenditures of the government.

The European Agreement that was signed on 19 December 1991 in Brussels has formulated conditions on which Poland became an associate member of the Community. The document came into force after the full procedure of ratification on 1 February 1994. Until that date the co-signatories of the agreement were bound by the conditions of the Interim Agreement.

Under the conditions of the European Agreement - Poland has started to create a FTA with the Community. The opening of the markets was asymmetric on both sides as it was an agreement between markets representing different levels of industrial development. Conditions of the agreement, generally, are divided into three groups, which concern: (1) raw materials and low processed products; (2) highly-processed products; (3) goods for which liberalisation of turnover is postponed (agricultural products, textiles, coal and steel, etc.).

The European Agreement provided conditions to protect some of the branches of industry that are considered important to the economy and too weak to be exposed to the pressure of direct competition. It also imposed some quotas on imports from Poland - mainly for goods considered to be areas of particular specialisation. The 1993 Copenhagen EU summit has changed the agenda of abolition of those quotas and increased them in many cases. Despite all the criticism addressed to the limitations of Polish exports to the EU market, until now Poland has not taken full advantage of all the existing opportunities. This is supported by the evidence that in some cases of quotas imposed on agricultural products only 20 percent was utilised in 1992-1993.

The argument for increasing the quotas and reducing the time in which they become mandatory was very simple:

- The share of ECE exports covered by the quotas was very small in the EEC turnover, but it was rather high for the ECE countries.
- The share of those goods was meaningful for the ECE countries.
- Industries protected by the quotas imposed by EU were in decline since the 1960s and ECE exports were not the reason for their problems.
- Changes in this field are advantageous for both partners and in both cases they lead towards an increase of wealth.

Opening the market with the European Union has played a crucial role in the process of marketisation of Poland's economy. Generally it has fulfilled four functions:

- It has increased the competition on the market, forcing the enterprises to catch up with Western suppliers, with better quality goods and with a wider range of choice.
- It has helped to balance the gap between demand and supply on the market.
- It was one of the market tools which has actively worked in fixing the equilibrium prices, putting a ceiling on their hikes.

• Finally, the consumers have learned to demand better quality, better choice and better service.

In sum: the role of international institutions was crucial in the first stages of the reforming process. Now, with the advancement of the reforms it will presumably be addressed towards more concrete activities not being limited to macro-stabilization policy. Not always, at the starting point, was the offered aid adequate to the needs of a country, but this was adjusted according to the demands. The possibilities of using the financial aid were limited by the structure of the aid which was very often in disparity with the needs. Some guilt, in low capital acquisition, can be ascribed to the transforming countries, as they did not develop a proper network of information.

Conclusions: The Future Role of International Institutions

International institutions are taking over part of the duties that traditionally belonged to the governments. This is due to the fact that it is very often impossible for the government to implement a decision which is unpopular and which can bring short term disturbances on the market, but which in the long run will accumulate wealth. Such decisions also concern withdrawal of some privileges which were introduced in different political and economic circumstances, while in contemporary conditions they can be considered as factors which simply: (1) undermine the integration process (widening and deepening); (2) act against the Maastricht criteria of convergence; (3) limit the increase in competitiveness.

In such conditions we can face, on the one hand, a development which will lead towards a further limitation of national governments' control over the market and devaluation of the political options of different programmes. On the other hand, we will face the widely discussed problem of global governance, with such questions as: which institutions or countries can play this role? How and under what conditions? Who supports such an idea and who is against it? What are the arguments in favour of such a solution and what can be considered as an obstacle to putting it into practice? Is it necessary to give supranational powers to international institutions in order to achieve global governance? How will this influence the sovereignty of different countries? What are the fields in which sovereignty must be limited?

The main arguments supporting the idea of global governance embrace the following set: growing interdependence of the world; security and stabilising factors; long perspective goals of limiting the development gap between the North and the South; interdependence between new development patterns, based on liberalisation of trade of goods and services, capital flows and intellectual property, and accelerated de-industrialisation of national economies and international relations.

Footnotes

1. Katarzyna Żukrowska is a professor affiliated with the Institute of Development and Strategic Studies, Plac Trzech Krzyzy 5, 00-507 Warsaw. Poland. Tel no.: + (48 2) 693 55 36; fax no.: + (48 2) 625 06 76.
2. P.G. Lewis, Political Institutionalisation and Party Development in Post-communist Poland; V. Zubek, The Reassertion of the Left in Post-communist Poland in: Europe-Asia Studies, formerly Soviet Studies, Volume 46, No.: 5/1994; M. Dehnel-Szyc, J. Stachura, Gry polityczne - orientacje na dzis, Warszawa 1991.
3. L. Balcerowicz, Lessons from Economic Transition in Central and Eastern Europe, in: Poland. International Economic Report 1993/1994, ed. J. Bossak, Warsaw School of Economics, 1994.
4. K.Żukrowska, Szerolie otwarcie. Polska gospodarka w aktywnym otoczeniu miedzynarodowym. Volumen 1994.
5. The Single European Market and Beyond. A Study of the Wider Implications of the Single European Act, ed. D. Swann, London, New York 1992; European Competitiveness, K.S. Hughes, Cambridge University Press, 1993.
6. Growth, Competitiveness, Employment. The Challenges and Ways Forward into the 21st Century. White Paper, 1994, Brussels.
7. P. Bozyk, An Evolutionary Mode of Transformation of External Relations, WERI, Centre for International Comparative Studies, Working Paper 114, Warsaw 1994.
8. Od GATT do WTO. Skutki Rundy Urugwajskiej dla Polski, ed. J. Kaczurba, E. Kawecka-Wyrzykowska, Warsaw 1995.
9. The World Competitiveness Report 1994, World Economic Forum, Lausanne 1994, p. 10.
10. Poland. OECD. Economic Surveys. 1994.
11. Assistance to the transition. Survey. 1995, Institute for East West Security Studies. PECAT, Warsaw 1995.

Bibliography

Consequences of the Uruguay Round for the Polish Economy, in: Transforming Polish Economy 1994, IRiSS, pp. 233-244, 1995.

Participation of the International Institutions in the Transformation of East Central European Countries, World Economy Research Institute. Centre for International Comparative Studies, Warsaw School of Economics, Working Paper No. 123, 1995.

Internationalization and Competitiveness, IRiSS, p. 22, 1995.

Book: Wide Opening. Polish Economy in an Active International Environment. Warsaw, 1994.

Foreign Direct Investment, in: Transforming Polish Economy 1993. IRiSS, pp. 196-206, 1994.

Poland in International Economy, in: Social and Political Dimensions of Polish Policy in the 1990s. IRiSS, pp. 115-124, 1994.

Ownership Changes in the Polish Arms Industry: Security Issues, co-author L. Turczynski, in: Privatization in NACC Countries, NATO Economics Colloquium 1994, pp. 183-194.

Institutionalization of Polish Foreign Economic Relations. IRiSS, p. 42, 1994.

EXTERNAL ECONOMIC RELATIONS AND INTEGRATION INTO THE WORLD ECONOMY: THE CASE OF ROMANIA

Lazar Comanescu

As the global economy develops, it is becoming increasingly clear that no country can progress in economic isolation, says Lazar Comanescu. Romania is having a more difficult transition than most of Europe's economies in transition, precisely because its previous regime - besides being a hypercentralised one - also promoted a highly inward oriented economic policy which resulted in a real isolation from the world. Today, Romania has realised that economic prosperity can only come from active membership in the world economy. One of its first steps in this direction has been to build up a system that will inspire enough confidence for foreign investment.

Lazar Comanescu is Director at the Ministry of Foreign Affairs, Bucharest

Introduction

There is no need to demonstrate the importance of external economic relations for a country's development. In fact, in a world of continuously increasing inter-dependencies, the economic and social development of each and every country and/or region can no longer be conceived and assured without an active participation in the international economic system. The less integrated into the world economy a country is, the less are the prospects for its dynamic development and prosperity. There are a lot of examples to support the statement. Romania's case is one of the most relevant in this respect.

The policies pursued by the Romanian authorities before 1989, particularly during the second half of the seventies and throughout the eighties, clearly point out how counterproductive the autarchic approach is for long-term economic development. It resulted in an almost total isolation of the country's economy, which brought up serious difficulties that add to the unavoidable ones generated by the transition to the market economy.

First, the autarchic approach translated into a strong tendency towards the hyper-diversification of the economy's structure, without any consideration being given to the availability or non-existence of the necessary inputs. The problems the process of restructuring the Romanian economy is confronted with today are to a great extent the result of these industrial policies.

Second, the Romanian economy was almost totally cut off from international technological developments.

Third, as in the case of other former communist (centrally-planned) economies, the priority was given to the producers' needs and not to those of the consumers, with the main consequence being a significant decline in quality.

Fourth, the policy of paying the foreign debt at any cost led to a cut-off from the external financial flows although they were absolutely indispensable for a policy of efficient economic development.

To sum up, the policies pursued before 1989 resulted in a serious decline in the competitiveness of the Romanian economy.

Measures for the Reintegration of the Romanian Economy into the World Economy

Following the collapse of the centrally-planned economic and social system, Romania has rapidly embarked upon the adoption of those measures able to re-establish and assure the functioning of a real market economy and to reintegrate it into the European and world economic flows. Special attention has been given to the setting up of that framework which enables a more efficient use of the (national) resources, while increasing the competitiveness on European and international markets so as to take full advantage of the benefits of an international open trade, which proved to be the main engine of a sustained economic development.

These measures regard both what one could define as the internal level, and the external institutional and legal framework of Romania's foreign economic relations. Internally the measures were conceived as part of the general process of economic transformations and reform that covers simultaneously the norms, the institutions and the mechanisms of the market economy. In this context, priority was given to decentralisation of the decision-making process, de-monopolisation of production and trade, and development of the private sector.

Price liberalisation, an essential step for providing correct signals for the market, has been also achieved. Measures have also been adopted to reform the banking and financial system, to restructure the public sector and to reduce state interference through subventions directed to public enterprises and consumers. Practically, Romanian foreign trade is now completely de-monopolised with the private sector holding more than 35 percent of the activity in the field (see Table 1). Measures were also taken so that at present a currency market is operational. One of the pillars of a genuine market economy - the Stock Exchange - is now a reality in Romania as well.

Table 1
Weight of the private sector in Romania's foreign trade

	Exports	Imports
1990	0.2	0.4
1991	15.9	16.1
1992	25.5	32.8
1993	27.9	28.3
1994	29.0	30.9
1995	33.7	35.9
(Jan-May)		

Sources: Statistical Yearbook of Romania, 1994; Monthly Bulletin of Statistics, 5/1995

Romanian trade policy has been significantly liberalised after 1990. While direct state control and quota trade were the "pillars" of the trade policy of the former regime, after the breaking of the state monopoly on foreign trade in 1990, international transactions can currently be initiated freely by the Romanian enterprises. The Romanian laws assure the non-discriminatory treatment of the economic actors, no matter the nature of their social capital: private or public, foreign or national. On the import side, quotas have been replaced with customs tariffs.

At the external level, the policies pursued and measures adopted were aimed at re-establishing Romania's foreign economic links to its traditional partners, while at the same time looking for the setting up of a solid system of relationships, as part of the overall strategy of reintegration into the European and Euro-Atlantic structures.

After the signature in 1990 of an Agreement on trade and economic cooperation with the European Communities, a Europe Agreement associating Romania to the European Union was signed on 1 February 1993, and entered into force on 1 February 1995 (an Interim Agreement covering the commercial part of the former had already been operational since May 1993). The area covered by the Europe Agreement is by far the largest compared to any other bilateral treaties signed by the EU (and its member states) with a third country. In fact, it covers almost all aspects of the society i.e.: economy and trade, political cooperation, science and technology, culture, social issues, home affairs, justice, etc.

While the Europe Agreement stipulates that a free trade area between the two parties is to be accomplished, at the latest by the end of the decade, its ultimate objective is Romania's full membership of the EU.

Free trade agreements were also signed with EFTA countries, as well as with the Czech and Slovak Republics, while negotiation for similar treaties are being carried out with the other Central European countries associated to the European Union. As regards the relations with the United States, the MFN status was reinstated, though, for the time being, on an annual basis.

One of the most important steps towards the reintegration into the world economy was the reconnection of Romania to the IFIs. Though the country had been a member of IMF, IBRD and GATT since the early seventies, by the end of the eighties, the links with these institutions had been, from a practical point of view, almost totally interrupted.

Another priority was to create the appropriate framework for reconnecting Romania to the international investment flows, thus stimulating foreign investments in the country, which are seen as one of the main instruments to improve quality, technology, management, organisational and marketing skills. It is worth noting that foreign investors are offered important advantages, among which highly trained labour with low wages. A special law on foreign investments was adopted in early 1991 and this was directly followed by a significant increase in foreign capital entries (see Table 2).

Table 2
Direct foreign investments in Romania (1990-1994)
Investments (mil. dollars)

1990	107.7
1991	156.3
1992	269.1
1993	227.4
1994	511.3
TOTAL	1271.8

Source: Monthly Statistical Bulletin, 12/1994

Nevertheless, the level of foreign investments is still low as compared to those in other countries in the region. New stimulating measures have therefore been developed or will be adopted in the very near future. Their main aim is to eliminate the rather complicated institutional mechanism as well as the bureaucracy that prevail today as far as foreign investments are concerned.

Recent Developments and Prospects for the Future

The general reform process as well as the specific measures adopted induced significant, even spectacular changes in the system of external economic relations both at the institutional and the structural level. The number of trade companies participating in foreign trade activities has remarkably increased. Today, 60-80,000 public and private economic actors are registered as international trade operators. One can compare these figures with the 54 state owned enterprises operating in this field before 1990 to realise Romania's huge step forward towards a real open economy.

As pointed out earlier, the role of the private sector in the Romanian economy has continuously and significantly increased. The contribution of the private sector to the GDP has already reached 40 percent and is soon to increase following the implementation of a law recently adopted by the Romanian Parliament regarding the acceleration of the privatisation. The implementation of its provisions will enable rapid privatisation of another 3,000 public companies, so that the contribution of the private sector in the Romanian industry will reach 60 percent. The hope is that the necessary conditions will soon be created so that the process of privatisation and restructuring of the economy will enable a long term economic recovery and growth, and, as a direct consequence, increased export performances.

It is worth mentioning that foreign trade has already become the most dynamic sector of the Romanian economy (see Table 3).

Table 3
Romania's foreign trade (1990-1994)

	Exports (mil.$)	Imports (mil.$)	Trade balance (mil.$)
1990	5775	9202	-3427
1991	4266	5372	-1106
1992	4363	5784	-1421
1993	4892	6020	-1128
1994	5998	6328	-330

Source: National Commission for Statistics, Bucharest, 1995

The point was already made that one of the most significant consequences of the change of system in Romania has been the shift from economic links with the East to relations with the West, from "imposed partners" to "natural partners", the most important one being by far the European Union. Thus, in 1994, Romanian exports which increased by 22.6 percent compared to 1993, were to the extent of 45.6 percent being directed to the EU member states. Romanian imports increased in 1994 by 5.1 percent compared to 1993, 47.7 percent of the imports coming from EU countries, data for the first five months of 1995 indicating that the EU is already holding more than 50 percent of the foreign trade of Romania. With the accession into the EU being Romania's top priority, the prospects are clearly that this trend will continue.

As for the process of accession of Central European countries to the EU, it is often said that "politics is the engine and economy is the brake". I do not share this point of view at least for two reasons: first, the present development of the Union - including the political development - was mainly determined by the continuous strengthening of the economic integration; second, democracy and stability can best be strengthened and preserved by developing a prosperous market economy.

On the other hand, though a significant gap still separates the two parts of the continent, the Central European economies, including Romania's, enjoy, as previously indicated, the important comparative advantage of having lower average labour and other production costs than the EU countries. This situation combined with the high absorption capacity of the Central European markets really opens very good prospects for a sustained economic growth throughout an enlarged European Union into which these countries wish to integrate. It will certainly help strengthen the competitive capacity of the European Union in the competition with other regions of the world. It is, therefore, a logical thing to say that the accession of the associated countries to the European Union is a process beneficial for both sides.

In such circumstances, it is normal for both sides i.e. the European Union and the associated countries - in our case, Romania - to search for ways and means which will enable full use of all the opportunities offered by the Europe Agreement to the development of their mutual trade and cooperation. On the other hand the need appeared for measures to keep in line with developments that followed the negotiation and signature of the Europe Agreement. The adoption of the Essen strategy, as well as the enlargement on 1 January 1995 of the EU and the successful conclusion of the Uruguay Round, are part of these developments. Encouraging steps were already undertaken in this regard, of which mention should be made of the alignment of the liberalisation timetable in the case of Romania (and Bulgaria) to that of the other associated countries and the starting of negotiations of additional protocols to the Europe Agreements.

The analysis of the evolution of trade between EU and the Central European countries associated to the Union indicate additional opportunities for a further and, at the same time, more balanced development of economic ties between the two parties.

Thus, though mutual trade has registered a steady high growth since 1990 (in 1994 only the increase - as compared to 1993 - was 30 percent for EU imports from PECOs and 20 percent for EU exports towards PECOs), the share of the six associated countries was only around 4 percent in the EU's total purchases from third countries, while Switzerland alone accounted for roughly 7 percent (Source: European Commission, 1994).

With the economic recovery in sight throughout the European Union as well as in the associated countries, the fact seems evident that the potential for further development of trade and cooperation is far from being exhausted.

This assertion holds for all associated countries, but in the particular case of Romania - where the GDP growth was around 4 percent in 1994 - it is even stronger. In fact, while in 1994 the value of EU imports from the six countries was of more than 26 billion ECU, that coming from Romania was only of 2.5 billion ECU. As for EU exports, they were 31 billion ECU as a whole, with Romania holding again 2.5 billion.

To take full advantage of the potential mentioned above, the need is to eliminate those constraining factors that still exist.

First, there is room for further liberalisation measures by the EU, particularly in those sectors - the so-called sensitive ones - where the associates have a comparative advantage.

Second, there is need for a substantial improvement in the infrastructure, both the physical as well as the financial and banking one.

Third, but closely linked to the second, a more stimulating environment for foreign investments in the associated countries has to be created. As far as Romania is concerned, new measures were recently adopted in this respect: a significant reduction in the inflation rate (from almost 300 percent in 1993 to less than 67 percent in 1994 and potentially below 30 percent in 1995). Similarly, important improvements were brought to the foreign investment regulations.

One should nevertheless be aware of the fact that, though decisive, the national efforts of each associated country are not enough. They can only be successful when strongly supported by the EU and the Member States within the framework of a genuine partnership for membership.

The full implementation of the objectives set forth in the Essen Strategy - of which those related to investment promotion are among the most important - would clearly be a very significant contribution to the further development of such a partnership.

INTEGRATING CENTRAL AND EAST EUROPEAN COUNTRIES INTO THE EUROPEAN MONETARY UNION: THE MACROECONOMIC ASPECTS

Zdenek Drábek

The Association Agreements that most of the East European countries have signed with the European Union have created a formal level of regular institutional contact and preferential trade conditions for the Eastern partners. While a basic level of reform is required for Associate EU membership, the hard part is yet to come, says Zdenek Drábek. This is the preparation for Monetary Union. In the East, part of the problem could be a lack of consensus as to what form monetary and financial requirements should take. The other side of this coin is the absence of clear requirements from the European Union, on how it sees true monetary union.

Dr. Drábek is Senior Advisor, World Trade Organisation, Geneva.

Introduction

It is well recognised in Central and Eastern Europe that national economies can no longer be closed and protected as in the past. The protection, which typically bordered on autarky, was extremely costly, and the countries in the region now better appreciate the merits of being "open economies". The countries are too small to be closed and too far behind the developed market economies to benefit from the exclusive reliance on the domestic market. It was undoubtedly the understanding of these simple ideas that led them to become associated members of the European Union (EU). It is also without any doubt that these considerations are instrumental in driving these countries to become full members of the EU.

What is far less evident, however, is the understanding in the region of the extent and the nature of the commitments that these countries will have to take on in order to fully integrate themselves into the EU. A part of the problem is the uncertainty about the specific requirements for the establishment of the monetary union in the European Union itself. Another constraint could be the lack of understanding or, maybe, even of a consensus in the region on the type of integration that will be sought by these countries as the next stage after the Association Agreements. The third type of constraints is likely to be the full appreciation of the macroeconomic implications of integration into the EU.

The purpose of this article is to identify the major macroeconomic constraints in the region on the integration of these countries into the EU. We shall seek answers to the following questions: What have been the main perceptions in the region of the integration process into the EU? Is there already a consensus on "full membership in the EU"? Could the political process become one of the constraints? Considering the economic conditions of the region, are the economic "fundamentals" such that they would allow a smooth integration into the EU? If not, what are the main constraints? What policies or institutional changes would need to be adopted to alleviate these constraints?

The scope of this paper covers, in the Central and Eastern European region, six countries - the four Visegrad countries - the Czech Republic, Hungary, Poland and Slovakia and two Balkan countries - Bulgaria and Romania. The focus will be entirely on the relationship of that region with the *European Union*. Excluded will be a discussion of aspects of integration into world trading or monetary systems. We shall, therefore, not consider such important questions as the role of these countries in the context of the WTO, EFTA, international agreements on the protection of intellectual properties, shipping, air or other transport agreements, agreements on environment, etc.

By addressing the questions of macroeconomic constraints we shall focus on the *internal constraints* to the integration process. Discussion of external factors will be excluded but these factors must naturally be considered in future assessments. In general, the constraints on integration could be either internal or external. I do not deny that external factors have played and will play in the future an important role in shaping the integration process. For example, trade protection of EU or its agricultural policies have already determined the content and the shape of the Association Agreements. However, the analysis of the external factors would be beyond the scope of this paper.

Three Fundamental Impediments to Successful Monetary Integration

The full monetary integration - the Monetary Union - implies the integration of all markets for goods, services and the factors of production (capital, labour and land). In addition, monetary integration can take the form of a market with multiple currencies tied to each other through the system of fixed exchange rates or a market with a single currency. The trend is clearly in the EU to set up a single currency market - European Monetary Union (EMU) - and we shall assume that the Central and East European countries will strive towards the EMU as the ultimate aim.

I shall also assume that monetary integration will take place only if three fundamental conditions are satisfied. They include (1) the absence of a fundamental disequilibrium in the countries wishing to join the monetary union, (2) the economies are not too dissimilar and (3) the governments of these countries pursue policies that can be sustained over a long period of time. In theory, nothing prevents countries from establishing a monetary union even if any one of the above conditions or all of these conditions are not satisfied. However, the costs of such a union would be excessive and the union is unlikely to survive under such circumstances, as we shall briefly demonstrate in the remaining part of this section.

Condition 1 : Political Will to Establish a Monetary Union. The first condition states that there must be a political will both in the applicant and in the existing member countries to create a Monetary Union. It is not entirely obvious that the EMU will be created even though the general expectations and widespread belief, of course, are that this will be the case. The objections to the creation of EMU are well known and they range from the dislike by the Germans of the fact that they should abandon their Deutsche Mark as the single currency to more general distrusts of the political implications.

But the problems are also more substantive. The establishment of the EMU will also require an agreement about the political resolution of conflicts that may arise once the EMU is established. This will be possible only if there is a political will to address and settle such important issues as cost-sharing arrangements that may be necessary to sustain the EMU whenever a bail-out of a member country is necessary due to its poor policies. This is a highly controversial assumption to make as anybody following the debate within the British Conservative Party would testify.

The other important issue is the question of the political process in the Central and East European countries and its relationship to the requirements for macroeconomic and structural adjustment. I am concerned about the former, that is whether these countries will accept politically the macroeconomic discipline that is required to control inflation. The difficult problem in controlling inflation will be the ability to control fiscal balances and, in this respect, the containment of social expenditures, especially on health, education and other types of social spending such as support to families with children, maternity leave, or other child benefits.

Even though some countries in the region may have substantially reduced in recent years various types of subsidies (such as food subsidies), others have had a considerably more difficult time to do so. For example, various types of household subsidies were reduced in Poland from 16 percent of GDP in 1988 to 2 percent in 1993. In contrast, the corresponding subsidies in Romania increased from 1 percent of GDP to 13 percent in 1992 and they were cut back in 1993 to 6 percent. In addition, all countries in the region have increased various cash benefits to pensioners and unemployed as a part of their new "safety nets" for those who fall out of the process of transition. Thus, cash outlays on pensions increased from 7 to 15 percent of GDP in Poland and from

5 to 8 percent in Romania. Similarly, unemployment benefits increased in Poland from 0 to 2 percent between 1990 and 1993 and from 0 to 1 percent of GDP in Romania during the same period.[1]

Several observers have also expressed their concerns about these countries' political will to go through the required structural reforms. They point out structural changes in these countries will take many years, and this will also determine the time pattern of costs and, mainly, benefits. However, as these observers also point out, the political cycle in these countries is "only" four years, which is the standard period between two parliamentary elections. It is clear that politicians will seek to obtain some tangible benefits within the term of their tenure and that, as I have noted, tends to be much shorter than the period that is required for structural changes.[2]

Condition 2: The Absence of Fundamental Economic Disequilibrium. It is well-nigh inconceivable that the admission of Central and Eastern Europe into the EMU will take place at the time that these countries experience a "fundamental economic disequilibrium". The meaning of "fundamental disequilibrium" is not straightforward but the following can be suggested. It is possible to distinguish between internal and external disequilibrium. The former is usually defined as inflation and unemployment, the latter may be represented by the level of indebtedness.[3]

Disequilibrium is costly, especially if it is large. The disequilibrium can be either eliminated through domestic policy measures and this will call for domestic macroeconomic adjustment or it must be externally financed. The difference is, of course, that domestic adjustment costs are borne by domestic residents while external financing would have to come from abroad, mostly from the European Union. In the latter case, therefore, the higher the disequilibrium, the more costly will this be for the European Union. The crucial elements of the disequilibrium are, in my view, the rate of inflation, the level of unemployment and incomes and debt - both domestic and external. In sum, the fundamental state of the economy will be crucial for the negotiations on the entry into the EMU.

— *Inflation* must be low and roughly comparable to other member countries at the time of accession into the EMU. The current situation is not very favourable. As we shall see further below, the country with the lowest inflation is the Czech Republic where the inflation rate reached about 10 percent in 1994, or about 3-4 times higher than the EU average. Moreover, the inflation rates have been "stuck" in most countries for some time, which indicates that further reduction of inflation will be difficult.

The inflation rate could be, of course, brought down by the monetary discipline imposed by the Union. However, the risks of failure are high. There are three kinds of risk. First, the adjustment could result in a political backlash in the high-inflation country. The anti-inflationary policy may be deflationary, and this could provoke dangerous political reactions as the costs of adjustment could be "blamed" on the "foreigners". Second, the excessive costs imposed on the applicant country could be mitigated by financial transfers of the existing member countries. However, this, too, will likely lead to strong political reactions from some member countries. Third, the postponement of the adjustment until the accession would most likely increase the costs of adjustment.

— *Unemployment* in the applicant country must be also on a level that does not pose a threat to the other countries. High unemployment encourages the unemployed to migrate, and the possibilities to do so will be considerably increased by the elimination of restrictions on the movement of labour. The incentives for outward migration will be greatly increased in the presence of large differences in real wages and in the level of consumption. In a certain sense, the income differences probably pose a greater threat to the stability of labour markets in the EMU than the presence of unemployment, particularly if countries with unemployment have an effective unemployment insurance policy. Low wages will also attract foreign investment and this, too, may lead to industrial relocation from high-wage to low-wage member countries. These concerns are particularly relevant for Central and Eastern Europe where wages including various social benefits are estimated to be currently more than ten times lower than in Germany.

Thus, it is primarily the income differences that could be a major constraint on the integration of Central and Eastern Europe into the EMU. The larger the differences in the level of consumption, unemployment and wages the stronger the pressures for higher wages and for outward migration from low-wage countries to high-wage ones. In such a case, high unemployment could lead to exports of unemployment to other countries (regions) through labour exports or capital imports. The higher the level of unemployment and the larger the wage differences among countries, the more likely there will be "disruptive" movements of labour and capital. The integration of product, service and factor markets could, therefore, become extremely disruptive in the presence of large differences. In addition, the integration would become too costly for existing member countries, as we have seen above.

— *Debt Management* is the third possible element of domestic disequilibrium. The settlement of debt liabilities of the applicant country raises the same problem as the need to reduce inflation or unemployment, that is the question of debt financing, how much this will come from domestic adjustment and how much this will have to be shared in the EMU by other countries. Clearly, the higher the debt liabilities of the applicant countries the greater domestic adjustment or the greater outside financing will be called for. As in the case of inflation and unemployment, the Central and East European countries can expect that the level of their indebtedness - internal and external - will not be too high to be considered threatening for the stability of the Union. The situation is not so clear-cut in view of large external debt in Bulgaria, Hungary and Poland.

Condition 3 : Credible Policies are in place. The economy may not be in a state of a "fundamental disequilibrium" now but it may get into one with bad policies. There will be plenty of room for "bad" policies to intervene once the countries join the EMU. They can range from fiscal mismanagement or poor management of public enterprises to bankrupt health or pension systems. Moreover, the policies must be also credible at the time when the countries begin to negotiate because their effectiveness will determine the success of the domestic adjustment process. To ascertain what are "bad" policies and distinguish them from "good" ones is not always an easy task. Nevertheless, a few further examples that are actually based on the current situation in the region can be suggested to make the point but these examples are by no means exhaustive.

Introduction of full convertibility may be premature. In other words, the elimination of all foreign exchange restrictions may have taken place too fast. For example, it may have preceded the liberalisation of labour markets or it may have been introduced in the presence of high inflation.

The exchange rate regime can also become a major constraint on growth. A fixed exchange rate regime may not be sustainable if the domestic inflation rate is higher than abroad. On the other hand, an instability of exchange rate will be detrimental to investments. It is clear, for example, that the appreciation of the real effective exchange rate (REER) in the Czech Republic by 40-44 percent between 1992 and 1994 has dramatically increased the costs of labour and will undoubtedly adversely impact investment planning policies of foreign and domestic firms.

Market access, too, may be liberalised too fast if the domestic firms' adjustment to new market conditions is impeded by monopolistic practices in the market or other forms of imperfect competition, undeveloped financial sector, weak infrastructure etc.

Clarifying the Government Objectives

It would be unfair to expect at the present time a clear statement of objectives on the part of the governments in Central and East European countries with regard to the European Union. It may be too soon after the signing of the Association Agreements. After all, it is only at about this time that the countries are getting out of a deep recession. Moreover, the countries are only now introducing domestic mechanisms to study and ascertain the implications of their membership in the Union. Nevertheless, a clear statement of objectives towards the European integration would be highly useful and the statement should go well beyond stating the obvious aspiration "to become a full member of the European Union". By July 1995, all of the Associated Countries have expressed their interest to become full members, and some of them have already formally submitted their applications, the last one being Romania, which did so in June of 1995.

The crucial issue at stake is a clear understanding of full membership, the goals of the integration, the commitments the countries would have to take upon themselves and the realism of the expectations. The discussion of government objectives can be conducted along the following three issues.

Issue 1: *Unclear Goals and Expectations: Types of Integration.* It is well known that integration between the Central and Eastern Europe and the EU can in theory take different forms. The most elementary is (a) free trade area, next come (b) customs union and (c) economic union, and finally we can speak of (d) monetary union. *Free trade area* is characterised by the absence of internal tariff but also by the absence of a common external tariff. Factor markets are not fully integrated. *Customs union* has also no internal tariff but it has an external tariff that is common to all member countries. *Economic union* includes a customs union and an integration of factor markets leading to a free movement of capital and labour plus other forms of economic cooperation. Finally, *monetary union* includes all features of the economic union and a fixed exchange rate mechanism (such as the EMS) in a multi-currency area that allows one's own currency and fiscal and monetary policies to (multi-currency area). Alternatively and more precisely, the monetary union *stricto sensu* is characterised by one single currency for the whole union which implies one single monetary authority.

In practice, however, the free trade area and customs union are probably irrelevant for the Central and East European countries. Their current contacts go well beyond customs union and, at the very minimum, they will seek full membership of the European Monetary Union (EMU). The status of a full member of the Economic Union is, after all, fully guaranteed by the successful conclusion of the transition period as Associated Members of the EU. The question stands, therefore, whether the countries wish to become full members of the EMU and if so when. But it is precisely this question that remains unclear.

First, the messages coming from the countries themselves are often contradictory. In the Czech Republic, for example, the general enthusiasm for the European Union is sometimes confused by the proclamations of Prime Minister Klaus who has often doubted in public the value of closer integration ties. Moreover, the Czech "success" is typically presented by the Czech government as one that does not recognise the need for "structural policy" as if future membership in the European Union required no adjustment on the part of the Czech Republic. It goes without saying that some adjustments will be necessary even in the Czech Republic.

Second, it is at best unclear whether all the implications of full membership are fully understood in the region. What is needed in particular is a sound understanding of the existing "economic fundamentals" and the extent to which they will call for an adjustment that can only be carried out through changes of domestic policy. Such an understanding is virtually impossible at present in view of the unstable nature of the recent and current developments.

Third, some Central and East Europeans contend that they cannot even begin to plan the next legislative, institutional and economic adjustments until they receive a firm timetable for accession. This is a very serious issue, one that is strongly pushed by the Polish government, and the issue will indeed need special attention in the EU.[4] Assuming, for example, that the Central and East Europeans are willing and able to take the necessary steps to adjust effectively, the EU must be ready in time to accept them. It is not possible to take measures that are politically and economically costly without some sort of arrangement between both parties. However, this card cannot be overplayed. The West Europeans themselves must understand what kind of adjustment they themselves will have to undertake in order to offer a firm calendar fro negotiations.

Issue 2: *The Realism and Understanding of Commitments : Unilateral Trade Liberalisation As The First Big Test.* Many countries have liberalised their trade regimes very fast and not necessarily in an economically rational manner.[5] Poland, Hungary, the Czech Republic and Slovakia have offered and been bound to fairly significant concessions in the Uruguay Round since they were already existing members of GATT. However, some of these concessions have been short-lived as all of them, with the exception of the Czech Republic, have been forced very soon to adopt additional protective measures to help their industries and balance of payments. Poland, Hungary and Slovakia have introduced additional import surcharges which have led to requests for waivers from their international commitments in the newly established World Trade Organization.[6]

A similar example is provided by the history of the customs union between the Czech Republic and Slovakia. The customs union was established following the separation of the two republics and the establishment of two independent states. The union also provided for a special payments arrangement based on a clearing mechanism but both the trade and the payments arrangements ran into severe difficulties in the course of 1994 when Slovakia's balance of trade with the Czech Republic began to deteriorate. This was followed by a devaluation of the Slovak koruna and by the introduction of an import surcharge and several non-tariff barriers. These measures have been highly effective, and the trade deficit turned into large surpluses with its partner. Given the presence of surcharges and of the highly distortionary payments mechanism, the Czechs proposed the elimination of the payments system to which the Slovaks responded by threats of abolishing the customs union. All these examples naturally raise the question whether the pace of trade liberalisation in most of these countries has not been too fast.

The unstable nature of trade relations of the region is also evident from the agreement with the EU about the so-called "sensitive products" in industry (mainly steel, textiles and coal). The Association Agreement provides for a gradual elimination of trade restrictions against exports of these products from the region but the need for adjustment in the region is unlikely to end with the liberalisation of this trade. Further competitive pressures are likely to come from new associated members from other parts of Eastern Europe, from improved access of the CIS countries into the market of the EU and also from other low-cost countries in the developing world. Deep adjustments will be also needed in the agricultural and the financial services sectors of the region even though profound changes will be also necessary in the EU.

The other real test of the ability of Central and Eastern European countries to live up to their commitments will be their attitude towards the loss of independence in the conduct of monetary policy. The loss must be politically acceptable in these countries with full implications. This must mean, for example, that virtually any unemployment must be socially acceptable by the country concerned if it believes that nothing can be gained from having independent monetary and fiscal policies but that more will be gained from a single currency market. As is well known, it is precisely the independence of monetary and fiscal policies that separates the "Euro-optimists" from "Euro-sceptics" in the present controversies in the United Kingdom and some other countries. It remains to be seen how the discussions evolve in the region once the governments in these countries are no longer in position to "monetize" excessive growth of wages, large fiscal deficits or high levels of unemployment.

Issue 3: *The Mentality of "Entitlement".* Unfortunately, many Central and East European countries have taken the attitude that "the West owes them a full integration into the major international economic, political and military institutions". This syndrome has been experienced also in the case of their aspirations towards the European Union. I do not wish to comment in this paper about these countries' membership in NATO, which is primarily a military association rather than one that is based on economic considerations that we are discussing here.

This mentality of "entitlements" is very dangerous. The problem is that it can lead to the adoption of policy measures that the countries may not be able to sustain and to the problem of realistic trade commitments as noted above. The example could be an excessively fast trade liberalisation such as the one noted above. As a result, non-sustainable policies of a member country could become a destabilising force for the other member countries and the very integration grouping which these countries have joined. To put it differently, the adoption of "wrong" policies may eventually lead to what economists call "policy backsliding", that is a reversal of those domestic policies that have become the basis for accession into a given integration grouping, and this will lead to a loss of credibility of these governments policies.

Footnotes

The views expressed in this paper are personal and should not necessarily be attributed to the World Trade Organisation.

1. All these figures come from IMF (1995).
2. This point was forcefully made, for example, by Dr. Andras Innotai at the Meeting of Senior Economic Advisers of the Economic Commission for Europe, 19 June 1995.
3. It is possible, of course, to suggest other criteria of economic disequilibrium, such as debt servicing capacity or the current account imbalances that are difficult to finance through external loans, foreign investments and other forms of foreign capital. They are not considered here. One important reason is that external financing cannot be a constraint on macroeconomic policy in EMU.
4. See "Poles await the starting gun to begin race for EU entry"; *Financial Times,* 10 July 1995,p.3.
5. The extent of the liberalisation can be found in the study of Drabek and Smith (1995).
6. The official justification for the new protective measures was balance of payments difficulties. However, several observers have suggested that these measures also had a protective character.

References

Bornsztein, E. and J.D. Ostry: *Economic Reform and Structural Adjustment in East European Industry*, Washington, D.C. IMF, Research Department, Working Paper, No.WP/94/80.

Drabek, Z. "The Czech Economy in an International Context: Fast Successes but a Slow Recovery", Proceedings to the Financial Times Conference, Prague, 6-7 June 1995.

Drabek, Z. and A. Smith: *Trade Performance and Trade Policy in Central and Eastern Europe*, London: CEPR, Discussion Paper No 1182, 1995.

Edwards, S.: *Why are Savings Rates so Different Across Countries? An International Comparative Analysis*; Cambridge, Mass.: NBER, Working Paper, No.5097.

Enders, A. and R. Wonnacott: "How Useful is the NAFTA Experience for East-West European Integration?" Paper presented to the Conference on European Union, Brussels, 10 June 1995, Friedrich Ebbert Stifftung.

Faruqee H. and A.M. Husain: *Savings Trends in South East Asia: A Cross-Country Analysis*; Washington, D.C.: IMF, Working Paper No. WP/95/39.

Feldstein, M.; "The Effects of Tax-based Savings Incentives on Government Revenue and National Savings", *Quarterly Journal of Economics*, Vol.CX, (1995), Issue 2, pp. 475 - 494.

IMF, *Social Safety Nets for Economic Transition: Options and Recent Experiences*; Washington, D.C.: IMF, Paper on Policy Analysis and Assessment, No. PPAA/93/3.

Kierzkowski, H., E. Phelps, G. Zoega: "Mechanism of Economic Collapse and Growth in Eastern Europe"; *mimeo*, paper prepared for the EBRD, 1995.

Kolodko, G.W.: *From Output Collapse to Sustainable Growth in Transition Economies. The Fiscal Implications*, Washington, D.C.: IMF, Fiscal Department, December 1992.

Kouba, K.: "Systemic Changes in the Czech Economy"; Paper presented to the Workshop on European Interaction and Integration, Vienna, 21-25 November 1993.

Möller, K.P.: "Will Eastern Europe be the Loser in the Battle for the World's Surplus Capital?" in *New Dimensions in East- West Business Relations;* Proceedings of an International Symposium of I.P.I. in Hamburg, 12 -14 December 1990, Stuttgart, Gustav Fischer Verlag, 1991.

Portes, R.: *Integrating the Central and East European Countries into the International Monetary System*; London; CEPR: Occasional paper, No.14, 1994.

Rodrik, D.: *Foreign Trade in Eastern Europe's Transition: Early Results*; Cambridge, Mass: NBER, Working Paper, No. 4064, May 1992.

Tornell A. and A. Velasco: *Fixed versus Flexible Exchange Rates: Which Provides More Fiscal Discipline?*; Washington, D.C.: NBER, Working paper, No. 5108.

PANEL V

Conclusions, Perspectives and Security Implications

Chair: Daniel George, Director, NATO Economics Directorate

Panelists: Andrei Zagorski
John P. Hardt
Eduardas Vilkas
Janusz Kostecki, Leon Turczynski
Hans-Hermann Höhmann
Márton Tardos

STRATEGIC FAILURES AND ASSETS OF RUSSIAN REFORM POLICIES

Andrei Zagorski

Vast differences have emerged between Russia's approach to reform and that of her former satellites, says Andrei Zagorski. Russia seems to lack their commitment to transition. The government devotes its energy to placating interest groups, rather than embarking on a full-bodied reform programme. Defence conversion has all but halted because the grip of the military-industrial complex has not been broken. And the old-style industries are using protectionism not to gain time to adjust, but to keep things as they are. The reform process cannot be stopped, but it can be slowed down.

Dr. Zagorski is Vice-Rector of the Moscow State Institute of International Relations (MGIMO-University).

Introduction

The purpose of this panel is to make general points on the progress of economic reforms in the partner countries, and to discuss the security implications of those developments. Without neglecting but rather welcoming the discussions over single and particularly important issues at this Colloquium, I would suggest that, for the purposes of this panel, we turn to the issues which, to a great extent, transcend the particular problems which have been intensively discussed for the last two days.

Our discussions reveal that there is a differentiation among the partner countries. This distinction is explicit in the new categories that have emerged with the end of the Cold War. First, the concept of Central and Eastern Europe (CEE) has been introduced embracing all partner countries. Later on, with the concept of Eastern Central Europe (ECE), nine (now practically ten) of the partner countries have been singled out. This categorisation implies different modes of relations to be developed between those countries and Western institutions.

It is the ECE countries which have signed Association Agreements with EU, thus receiving the prospects for full membership, while other CEE countries have been offered Partnership and Cooperation Agreements implying, for some countries, only the possibility of transforming those agreements into free trade area agreements if the progress of reforms makes it possible. It is the ECE countries which have become associated partners with the Western European Union (WEU) and, with the prospect of becoming EU members, have also the prospects of being admitted to the WEU. It is the ECE countries which are the subject of discussions with respect to the prospective NATO extension, while other CEE countries have little chances of exceeding the level of the Partnership for Peace. There is not only an explicit but also implicit distinction between the CEE partner countries which, though being sometimes vague, largely goes along the border of the Former Soviet Union (FSU) with the exception of the Baltic states.

The purpose of this paper is not to lament that there should be no such distinction and that all partner countries should be treated equally and offered similar options. The purpose is to suggest that we should go beyond the political and bureaucratic criteria and ask ourselves the question: whether that distinction has an objective rationale, *what* is the difference between the two (or even more) groups of countries and what are the implications for the policy toward those countries. Indeed, *if this distinction has a deeper rationale and goes beyond the plausible political and geographic preferences, this would imply that also the substantial priorities and techniques of assisting the transition should differ and go beyond the formal differentiation in the status with respect to various Western institutions.*

The problem appears immense, and this paper does not pretend to provide answers to all the questions. It can only initiate discussion over the issue. Therefore, the paper does not provide for a traditional academically elaborated framework but is merely reduced to raising several aspects of the problem. In the following sections, the paper would elaborate 1) on the cultural-political background of the distinction among the CEE countries, 2) on the strategic problems and failures of Russian reforms which make the difference so important, and 3) on the strategic assets of Russian reforms. In conclusion, some suggestions are developed.

What is the Difference?

One of the distinctions between the ECE countries and Russia (and, indeed, most other Newly Independent States - NIS) refers to the recognition that Russia is "another world", as if it does not belong to the European civilisation or community of values. Many authors note that Russia itself avoids identifying itself as a European nation.

The validity of a universal model of development was explicitly rejected by President Boris Yeltsin in a speech made in February 1994, in which he explained why the leading market-oriented reforms had been left out of the Russian government. Russia is different, Yeltsin said, the national character of the Russian people is not like the other Europeans. He promised that reform would continue, but *reform a la Russe*, not according to the recipes of the International Monetary Fund.[1]

Most recently, Yeltsin has reconfirmed that the reform in Russia would be pursued *a la Russe*[2] whatever that implies. And the issue of belonging or not belonging to Europe, of the applicability or non-applicability of European values and standards to Russia provides an important background for political debates in Moscow.[3] Hence the discussion of the eventual security implications of developments in the FSU: while remaining a major European actor, Russia may either re-emerge as a new imperialistic power, as a European problem,[4] or it may develop as a cooperative partner, as part of the European family and of the European community of values.

Whatever the political importance of this debate, it does not imply the impossibility of a deeper systemic transformation in Russia. While acknowledging the presence and the strength of the traditional culture, one should not imply that traditional culture is not capable of modernisation. The history after World War II reveals that such modernisation is possible. This was largely the case with Germany and especially with Japan, and is largely the case with many of the ECE countries. As admitted by Max Jakobson, before World War II Czechoslovakia was the only democratic and advanced industrial state among the ECE states. All the others were agrarian countries ruled by authoritarian regimes.[5]

Therefore, the possibility of a systemic transformation in (and of) Russia cannot be neglected on the basis of a pure recognition that, traditionally, Russia did not reveal a stronger commitment to European values, although such a transformation should not be taken for granted either. Thus, *though there is a traditional distinction between Russia and Europe, it is not the distinction which, per se, justifies scepticism with regard to Russian reforms.*

What makes a difference, however, is the lack of obvious progress of reforms in Russia. It is a general feeling, apart from particular problems, that reforms in Russia and most other NIS do not advance with the same speed or enthusiasm on the side of the government as in most of the ECE countries. While reforms in the latter (including the Baltic states) are considered rather advanced, at least in the economic field,[6] Russia hardly appears even to have firmly embarked on that road. Indeed, *what is lacking in Russia is the strong commitment to the kind of complex reform which is usually assumed in the ECE countries.*

The lack of such commitment is not due to the abstract cultural gap between Russia and Europe, and it is not due to the lack of expertise (at least at the macro-level). It is mainly due to the interplay of complex factors and interest groups. Instead of revealing a strong commitment to democratic and market reforms, Russian leadership is merely manoeuvring between social, political and economic pressures. To put it in the words of Jakobson, "Russia does have one foot in the open market, but the other foot is stuck under the heavy weight of old structures. The country is straddling two worlds, shifting its weight from one foot to the other in response to conflicting pressures, external and internal".[7]

The following sections of this paper provide a brief survey of several strategic problems and failures, as well as opportunities for further reform in Russia.

Strategic Problems and Failures

Conversion of the military-industrial complex

Early in 1994, the editor-in-chief of the Moscow Journal 'International Affairs', Boris Pyadyshev, while interviewing the President of Lithuania, Algirdas Brazauskas, asked him what had been the major mistake of Mikhail Gorbachev during perestroika, which appeared rather successful in the first years beginning with 1985. The answer of Brazauskas, at first glance, was a surprise:

"First he committed a grave mistake by trusting the industrialists and first and foremost the military-industrial complex. ... By that time it was assumed that it was possible, with a strong desire, to change and turn the car of the defence industry, to make a sharp curve. Thick ordinances of the Union's Central Committee and of the Council of Ministers were issued addressing the development of the machine tools building, food processing, electronics industry etc. ... Gorbachev trusted those people who engaged in this adventure".[8]

Brazauskas knew well what he was talking about. In the early stages of perestroika he was Secretary of the Central Committee of the Lithuanian Communist Party responsible for industry. He could learn himself that it had proved impossible to build upon the expectation that the Soviet military-industrial complex could be transformed from being a burden to the economy into becoming the driving force of its modernisation on the basis of most advanced "golden" technologies developed in this sector. Then and now, the conversion of the Russian defence production, with a few exceptions, has largely failed.

Meanwhile, the Russian government appears ready to make the same mistake and to believe that the inherited military-industrial complex is capable of becoming the driving force of the modernisation of the Russian economy. Though having suffered drastic reductions since 1992, this complex has largely proved incapable of adjusting to market rules and of modernising the civil economy; instead, it appears to misuse its increasing weight in decision-making to preserve remaining capabilities rather than to promote deeper transformation.[9]

Protectionism

In the Russian economic policy, there is a notable struggle between the liberal intention to further open up the domestic economy, and the increasing tendency towards protectionism. Most recently, the debate focused on the protectionist measures taken by the Russian government to impede imports of food.

In fact, protectionism appears to be an important element of the economic policy of countries in transition, with Russia hardly providing an exception. The former Prime Minister of Japan, Yasuchiro Nakasone, pointed out that protectionism was one of the most important features of the "East Asian development model" - a necessary prerequisite of the strategy of any developing country seeking to close the gap dividing them from the industrialised countries. Nakasone believes, following the German economist Friedrich List, that it is only developed industrialised countries which can afford liberalism. The application of a protectionist policy is regarded by Nakasone as an important element of the success of both Japan and other East Asian new industrial countries.[10]

From that perspective, the application of a protectionist strategy may appear not only inevitable but also welcome for Russia. However, the crucial issue is in which environment the protectionist policy is applied and what purposes it serves. In the case of Russia, protectionism is mainly pushed forward by the lobbies representing old industries (and agriculture) which are not competitive even on the domestic market. Protectionism, however, is perceived by those lobbies only marginally as a tool for gaining time for adjusting to the world markets, but mainly as an important instrument for lowering the pressures toward modernisation and structural reform of the Russian economy. Indeed, the protectionist policy of Russia now appears more to serve the purposes of preserving what is remaining of the old Soviet economy (and its system) rather then to promote its transformation.

Reintegration of CIS

The kind of policy Russia develops toward the Commonwealth of Independent States (CIS) again should be raised as a strategic dilemma of Russian reforms.[11] The re-integrationist temptation in Russian policy,[12] the kind of quasi-restoration of the FSU in a new form, or of a quasi-CMEA out of the CIS states strengthens both trends: the increasing role of the military-industrial complex which is unwilling or unable to adjust to the new requirements, and the orientation towards preserving the old Soviet standards of production defended by a protectionist policy.

If the emerging re-integration of the FSU is not replaced by another strategy of "new integration"[13] injecting market criteria into the cooperation within the commonwealth, the currently developed conception of a CIS Economic Union, providing, *inter alia*, for the establishment of a free trade area and of a customs union of the member states may become a serious obstacle for developing cooperative relations of Russia with GATT, European Union, etc. Though the Partnership and Cooperation agreement between Russia and the EU provides for a transition period during which Russia may maintain beneficial relations with the CIS countries, later on it will have to choose the priorities of its policy: either further rapprochement with Europe or further consolidation of the CIS regardless of its compatibility or incompatibility with the world markets.

Strategic Assets of Russian Reforms

Whatever criticisms one may make of Russian policy, the failure of Russian reform should not be taken for granted. There are several developments strengthening the motivation for continued transformation.

Lack of resources
Whatever disagreements develop in the Russian ruling elite, the possibilities for further balancing between real reform and cost-intensive manoeuvring are limited politically, economically and financially. Governmental support for inefficient industries is shrinking, and the competition among the old sectors (and the army) for sharing the shrinking cake is increasing. Despite the ever stronger re-integrationist rhetoric in the Russian elite, for economic reasons Moscow has abandoned far-reaching conceptions of a confederation or a union of the NIS.

The most recent negotiations with the International Monetary Fund over the latest stand-by loan to Russia have revealed both the severe budgetary constraints on Russian politics as well as Moscow's dependence on external funding. This does not imply that reforms in Russia would not go ahead *a la Russe* - indeed, they will in a sense that no one can prescribe the particular shape and features of that reform instead of Russia itself. However, it does imply that there is a space for the basic principles of the market to be integrated into the reform plans of the Russian government.

Self-dynamics of Reforms

Despite the manoeuvring of the government which, so far, has largely failed to meet its declared ends, the short period of shock therapy in 1992, and the introduction of the principle of economic freedom, have released new forces which are continually at work and are expanding market relations in the Russian economy. Many of those developments are reminiscent of "wild capitalism" and entails criminality, corruption and not the "civilised" market which has been expected. However, most important is the fact that, in the end, the still rather narrow entrepreneurial sector is becoming an ever more important actor in the national economy.

The preferences of this sector in favour of an integration of Russia into the global economy are clearly manifested in the dynamics of Russia's foreign trade. Russian trade with the CIS states has dropped from 56 percent in 1991 to 20 percent in 1994, and the EU has become Russia's major trading partner. During the first half of 1994, Russia's trade with the EU[14] amounted to 37 percent of Russia's total foreign trade volume and exceeded the trade with CIS countries by 50 percent.

Russia already has changed and is still changing. Those changes already have developed a self-dynamic and are driving the reform initiated in 1992 even despite the uncertain policy of the government.

Emergence of Civic Society

It is the beginning of a civic society which may be the most important sign of that ongoing change. Though the strengthening of this phenomenon should not be taken for granted - it has often occurred in Russian history but was again and again oppressed - the importance of this development cannot be underestimated. The emergence of a civic society and of economic freedom, two developments which both go hand in hand, are most important for the spread of democratic values in Russia. It may have been the only positive effect of the Chechenya crisis that, though remaining passive, the majority of Russian society did not welcome the adventure, thus abandoning the centuries long tradition of following the government.

Conclusions

The analysis of developments in Russia requires a complex approach and cannot be reduced to traditional categorisation. Russia is neither a true democracy nor a clearly authoritarian state, neither a market nor a planned economy. It is a country in an extremely complex transition, the outcome of which is not yet clear. What trends take the upper hand can be influenced by the outside world only marginally. However, while generating no immediate security challenges, the long-term failure or success of reforms in Russia may have important security implications.

Among possible suggestions for how to promote a more reform-friendly outcome of those developments, only two will be mentioned here.

• Without neglecting the importance of the stabilisation of the Russian state, i.e. through financial support, the emphasis should be on strengthening the emerging civic society and free enterprise in Russia. Though the shift toward supporting private rather than state institutions has been taking shape through the last two years, even greater emphasis should be placed on the activities of NGOs, and the development of the public sector (education, infrastructure, etc.). While designing such programmes, the emphasis should be put not on imposing criteria on the recipients but on jointly developing those criteria in order to meet the real needs of the latter. The major partner for this work should be not the state structures but a body of independent experts both from Russia and from outside.

• While the normative work previously done by the OSCE has been largely overshadowed by security considerations, the OSCE still can return to the important task of promoting the consolidation of the rule of law and economic freedom. It is especially the economic dimension of the OSCE which has been largely ignored by the EU countries. However, combining both the legal and the economic dimensions of the OSCE while elaborating more specific standards for economic legislation, and of an OSCE mechanism for the implementation of those standards - similar to the OSCE human dimension mechanism - could, in a longer perspective, contribute to the development of a more homogenous legal-economic space in Europe including Russia.

Footnotes

1. Max Jakobson, 'Collective Security in Europe Today', in: The *Washington Quarterly*, Vol. 18, no 2, Spring 1995, p. 60.
2. See Interview with Boris Yeltsin in *Izvestiya*, Moscow, 10 June 1995.
3. For a review of this debate see. i.e.: Andrei Zagorski, 'Russia and the CIS', in: *Redefining Europe: New Patterns of Conflict and Cooperation*, edited by Hugh Miall, London; New York: Pinter, 1994.
4. S. Neil MacFarlaine, 'Russia and European Security', in Hans-Georg Ehrhart, Anna Kreikemeyer, Andrei Zagorski (eds), *The Former Soviet Union and European Security: Between Integration and Disintegration*, Baden-Baden, 1993.
5. Max Jakobson, 'Collective Security in Europe Today', p. 60.
6. For a differentiated analysis of the progress of reforms in the ECE countries see, i.e.: Demokratie und Marktwirtschaft in Osteuropa. Hrsg. von Werner Weidenfeld, Gutersloh, Bertelsmann, 1995.
7. Max Jakobson, 'Collective Security in Europe Today', p. 60.
8. Algirdas Brazauskas, ' "Divorce Lithuanian-Style" and After', Mezhdunarodnaya Zhizn, Moscow, 1004, no 4, p. 14.
9. On this see, i.e.: Pavel Ivanov, 'Military Industry and Conversion', in: *From Reform to Stabilization... Russian Foreign, Military and Economic Policy: Analysis and Forecast, 1993-1995*, Edited by Alexander Lopukhin, Sergio Rossi and Andrei Zagorski, Moscow, 1995.
10. Yasuchiro Nakasone and others, Posle Kholodnoi Voiny (After the Cold War), Moscow: Progress, 1993, p. 180-194.
11. See: Andrei Zagorski, 'Strategic dilemmas of Russian reform policies', in: *Economic Developments in Cooperation Partner Countries from a Sectoral Perspective*. Colloquium 30 June, 1 and 2 July 1993, Brussels: NATO, 1993, p. 282-284.
12. See, i.e.: Sherman W. Garnett, 'The Integrationist Temptation', in: The *Washington Quarterly*, Vol. 18, no 2, Spring 1995, pp. 35-44.
13. For the distinction see, i.e.: Andrei Zagorski, Reintegration in the former USSR?, in *Aussenpolitik*, 1994, Vol. 45, no 3, p. 263-272.
14. This data includes trade with the four countries that were expected to become EU members from 1 January 1995. Nonetheless, the negative outcome of the referendum in Norway on the country's participation in EU does not affect significantly the cited data.

A REPORT CARD FOR ECONOMIES IN TRANSITION

John P. Hardt*

How will we know when Eastern Europe and the former Soviet Union have completed their transition to a market economy? When economic performance begins to improve sharply in a stable political and economic environment, says John Hardt. What these regions need to achieve a successful transition, he says, is nothing short of an economic miracle. But it is a dream that can be realised. Exactly the same thing happened in Europe and the Far East after World War II - and in parts of southeast Asia over the past 15 years.

Dr. Hardt is Senior Specialist in Post-Soviet Economics of the Congressional Research Service of the Library of Congress, Washington, DC.

Toward a New Social Contract of Transition[1]

All of the states of Central and Eastern Europe and the former Soviet Union are committed to transition. They are engaged in transformation from central-planning to market-based economies, and from single-party control to political pluralism. The governments have expressed these goals, but the pace of implementation of liberalising policies and laws varies widely, and the ultimate involvement of the newly defined states in the economy is yet to be determined.

No state has reached the point of self-sustaining reform from which the successful completion of the transition may be assured. Even the remarkably successful states in Central Europe and the Baltic states should be considered in mid-course of the transition. Although many new states do not appear to be well off the starting mark none should be written off at this time.

An assessment of where they started, an explicit vision and strategy of where they hope to end the transition and how they expect to get there is needed but lacking in most countries. A more articulated version of the "OECD model" that specifies objectives and success indicators relevant to key players seems appropriate. Likewise, clear identification of the players who judge and contribute to success is useful and necessary. These players are the electorate, the new entrepreneurial classes, the donors and the foreign investors.

In 1994 it was popular to declare some economies in transition successes and others failures. The London Economist had Poland "turning the corner" with an end of its post-revolution recession. Anders Aslund provided a very insightful and useful assessment of 27 countries in the region, finding eight successes and the rest failures. His focus was especially on inflation control with 50 percent per annum price inflation as the cut off and contested elections as a measure of democratic progress to facilitate economic reform.[2]

While achieving these measures of progress is necessary, they do not seem sufficient to make a judgement of success. A broader set of objectives and performance measures would appear to be necessary to obtain support and commitment from the key players to assure sustainable support based on a viable consensus for reform. The sustainability of the changes toward the central objectives of a democratic and market system under a rule of law should be seriously questioned. Moreover, an assessment should be made not only on inflation control and elective politics but as to how much progress has been made toward higher living standards, employment opportunities and systemic changes generating confidence in the electorates and new entrepreneurial classes, satisfying conditionality of donors and attracting foreign investors. Both measures of efficiency and equity need to be served by transition, considerations especially critical to attaining support from the electorate.

For these countries to create a smoothly-functioning market economy, six critical success factors must be met:

• Financial stability.
• Rising living standards.
• Improving employment opportunities.
• Legal and regulatory framework facilitating development of market institutions.
• Openness to the world economy through reduced barriers to trade and investment.
• Pluralistic political systems and international affiliations promoting political and security stability.

"OECD MODEL" - Multiple Objectives and Performance Measures

The "OECD model" implies a number of criteria for judging the successful attainment of the strategic objectives of transition, with an emphasis on rising living standards, employment opportunities and financial stability as appropriate bases, as noted by the OECD Annual Report in 1992:

Today, the failure of the Soviet model strengthens a trend that in fact has been emerging in the world economy for some years. The concepts of pluralistic democracy and the market economy, the essential elements of the "OECD model," have exercised a strong attraction, not only in Central and Eastern Europe but also in certain countries of the rest of the world—to achieve the highest sustainable economic growth and employment and a rising standard of living in Member countries, while maintaining financial stability, and thus to contribute to the development of the world economy.[3]

From the "OECD model", this author adduces six criteria for assessing progress toward the goal of democratic and market systems under a rule of law.[4]

- Financial stability including price liberalisation and budgetary discipline, a low real interest rate and a convertible currency.
- Living standards in both real income and quality of life measures rising above pre-revolutionary 1989 levels and with promise of take-off in living standard improvement by transition's end.
- Employment opportunities from an expanding market economy that recognise the importance of both efficiency of the labour force and equity issues such as income distribution.
- Market Facilitating Institutions development that provides the minimum requirements of a legal and regulatory framework needed to foster commerce, investment and contracting, promote stability, and control corruption and crime.
- Openness to the world market through reform measures and accession to bilateral, regional and international public and private organisations requiring adherence to market rules of behaviour.
- Political and security stability deriving from development of pluralistic political systems that promotes domestic consensus and by national, inter-regional and international associations fostering more secure environments.

The criteria merit more detailed discussion before suggesting a strategy and new social contract and proffering a report card on the economies in transition.

Financial Stability

There is little question that macroeconomic stabilisation programmes need to liberalise prices, reduce trade and currency exchange barriers and adopt budgetary discipline that eliminates the practice of monetisation of deficits, and moves toward elimination of debt at international, national, and inter-enterprise levels. Monetary and financial stability would foster progress in other necessary reform measures, and also would benefit from progress in other reform measures. While reducing inflation below the 50 percent per annum level is important, support from key players is likely to be even more sensitive to other success indicators, especially rising living standards and attracting foreign investment.

Living Standards

Throughout the region the transition started with a recession or deep depression as state support for traditional priority sectors such as defence and heavy industry collapsed and bottlenecks from the breakdown in regional trading systems depressed output. As a result effective employment and real income fell below pre-revolution levels of 1989. With the resurgence of output in services and privatised sectors, income stabilised and started up in some countries. The availability of food and consumer durables revived, but with unequal distribution. The continued fall in the quality of life accentuated by sharply lowered living standards is indicated by each of the following "externality" measures which have been in deepening crisis.

- Environmental quality is poor by all measures: air, water, solid waste criteria. The residue left by military demobilisation and forward deployed Soviet forces adds a newly evident environmental threat. Remedial actions are limited as funding for clean-up has been scarce.[5]
- Health measures: incidence of diseases and infant mortality have increased, while quality of medical care and life expectancy have fallen from low pre-1989 levels throughout the region.
- Housing, always in short supply, became even more critical with relocation of demobilised military and displaced workers. With restructuring labour mobility has become even more restricted due to the housing constraint.
- Educational opportunities and quality have declined. The revolutionary change in the system from command to market has reduced the budget effectively supporting education.

The quality of life measures added to the perceived fall of real income accentuated by income inequality may explain why many polls indicate citizens feel they are worse off than under the old regime and also that the new legal and regulatory systems are against them and favour a new elite.

The central indicators of success in earlier Western industrial economic development were the economic miracles that could be measured in real terms, e.g. the several decades of OECD countries' growth from 1950-1973 found the average real income more than doubled without extreme inequality.[6] Perhaps as persuasive as rising real income and improved living standards in Japan, were general access to consumer goods such as the four Cs: personal cars, computers, air conditioners and colour television sets. Likewise, the shifts from bicycles, radios, and watches to availability in the market and peasant access to motorcycles, television sets, and refrigerators in China were a recognition that rural modernisation was beneficial and a meaningful stimulus to the participants in rural modernisation. The availability of a variety of consumer goods in East-Central Europe and parts of the former Soviet Union has increased substantially, although income distribution does not make the new consumer goods accessible to all.

While the quality of life receded under the old regime standards, paradoxically the burden of social expenditures burgeoned to one quarter of the gross domestic product in the period of 1985-90 for social welfare, education and health. Particularly burdensome has been the cost of maintaining pensions. Ironically, the rise in these social welfare costs were concommitment with liberalisation in reform-oriented countries during the communist period.[7] Now these expensive "entitlements" claim a disproportionate share of tax revenues without an improvement of the quality of life commensurate to the cost.

Employment Opportunities

Statistics on employment are especially unreliable. The reasons illustrate some changes in the economies: many new jobs have developed in the privatised sectors, especially in services and small scale enterprises which tend to understate employment; many state enterprises report employment that includes workers who generate little output, i.e. "concealed" unemployment.

Those countries that find ways to support labour-intensive improvements in their infrastructure and their quality of life (environmental quality, health, education, and housing) will generate productive employment. Foreign direct investment attracted by skilled labour and low real wage costs can generate substantial new employment in large scale enterprises.

According to Machowski and Schrettl:

At present exchange rates, wage costs in the CEE region average only one-tenth or less of western German levels. Even on very optimistic assumptions about growth of labour productivity in the CEE region, a huge wage differential is bound to persist for the foreseeable future.[8]

While employment opportunities may increase, the discrimination developing in employment practices in many countries is leading to a new underclass especially populated by unemployed women and many minority groups.[9] The U.S. Secretary of Labour Robert Reich in the interest of combating discrimination and ensuring equity in the United States called for "a new social contract between business, government and citizens to help millions of Americans in the anxious class survive in today's economic order of down-sizing, reengineering and global competition."[10] This call may resonate in Eastern Europe today. A former chairman of the U.S. Council of Economic Advisors called attention to the trade-off between efficiency and equity that may also seem relevant today in Eastern Europe, "The rights and powers that money should not buy must be protected with detailed regulations and sanctions, and with countervailing aids to those with low incomes. Once those rights are protected and economic deprivation is ended, I believe that our society would be more willing to let the competitive market have its place".[11]

Market-Facilitating Institutions

The destruction of the old, Communist, command economic institutions left a void and the development of the necessary and progressive role of the market friendly state has been delayed in many states, actively opposed in others. Without a legal and regulatory framework both efficiency and equity are adversely affected; crime and corruption are encouraged. Under these circumstances citizens feel the new system is not on their side, entrepreneurial groups - private owners, managers and workers - are not protected from the powerful old party holdovers and new criminal organisations, foreign investors and donors do not have the sufficient degree of economic, commercial and political stability that would attract investment or assistance.

For their world development assessment the World Bank "calls for a stronger orientation toward the market and a more focused and efficient public sector role. History suggests that this is the surest path to faster growth in productivity, rising incomes, and sustained economic development."

From this "rethinking the role of the state" in the transition to market economics, one may conclude that the minimum new institutional developments required for market-friendly institutions, early in the transition, are the following.[12]

- An independent central bank, and efficient private commercial banks.
- A modern tax code.
- A modern system of commercial law and courts and competent law enforcement systems.
- Regulatory agencies to foster competition and protect consumers.

Openness to World Market Economies

Membership in international economic institutions and commitment to assistance programmes fosters the development of open economies with convertible currencies, reduction of trade barriers, and acceptance of rules of the game in the international market place. Membership and programmes with the International Monetary Fund, World Bank and its affiliates, EBRD, and OECD condition assistance on reform progress and adherence to the principles of openness. Moreover, membership and adherence to the World Trade Organization will also require evidence of commitments to open market reform. Although sceptics might say that the countries in transition seek membership solely to obtain loans and access to Western markets, not because of a commitment to reform and open economies; nevertheless, the "dues" for membership are implementation of reforms.

Steps in accession to the European Union or other regional trade and investment agreements suggest not only openness but also development of better statistical systems, harmonisation of laws with those of market economies and acceptance of criteria of free flow of investment, people, technology and credit in both directions.[13] Still, accepting the full body of EU laws in the *acquis communautaire* is not enough, the legislation must have oversight and enforcement.

Bilateral agreements with major trading countries such as Germany and the United States also suggest adherence to principles of international and regional associations, e.g. acceptance of principles of national treatment, protection of intellectual property, protection from expropriations. Access to markets, investment, and technology tend to reinforce the transition to an open economy. East European economies currently with low real wages may find the gap in real income will rapidly close with Western Europe once the transition is completed.[14]

Political and Security Stability

Many in Central and Eastern Europe look to membership in NATO as important for political and security stability, just as membership in the European Union might be for fostering economic stability and growth. Many states of the former Soviet Union encouraged membership and integration into the Commonwealth of Independent States as a measure toward economic integration and political and security stability. Others have sought bilateral agreements with the United States along with NATO membership (or pre-NATO Partnerships for Peace).

Most of the Western industrial economies and economies in transition were signatories or successor states to the Helsinki Final Act and seek a more active Organization for Security and Cooperation in Europe (OSCE). Finally the United Nations as a global organisation may provide some economic, political and security stability. The use of peacekeeping forces represents to some a means for maintaining stability.

The CIS, OSCE, and UN have been criticised for their inability to stop the fighting in ex-Yugoslavia and Chechnya. Nevertheless, these groups may together represent an influence on stability that is greater than the separate impact of any one such group. Indeed, together they may develop the balance between centrifugal and centripetal forces in the region as states strive to retain their sovereignty and separate identity while benefiting from the collective integrating forces that promote economic growth, political stability and security.[15]

Moreover, if weapons production and inventories are down-scaled during restructuring with special attention to weapons of mass destruction, the destabilising threat of a substantial stocks of weapons will be reduced.

The break-up of countries in the former Soviet Union and Central Europe may have some salutary political and economic effects. Ivo Bicanic argues that in the transition as unitary states - from the old communist to the new market-system the regional impacts may be "destabilising, inequality-generating and asymmetric". Such developments provide strong incentives to break from the "convoy effect" of preserving the union and favour the "go-it-alone" or trends toward developing political independence in smaller states. If these divorced or independent states follow more avidly domestic reform and openness as smaller more homogenous sovereign states they may develop a more stable and secure environment than if they had stayed in the larger, diverse union.[16]

This development suggests the advantages of the commonwealth over the confederative approach, e.g. the Tatarstan agreement with the Russian Federation fits more into the British Commonwealth tradition than a more unitary federative approach such as in the United States of America. Likewise, settling disputes within the former Soviet Union in the various independent states could draw on the negotiation formula of the Russian Federation for settlement of the federative issues with Tatarstan, Bashkortostan, and Sakha. The destructive example of Chechnya may be of value.[17]

Vision, Strategy, and the Social Contract[18]

Each of the critical interest groups would be more supportive if the leaders of the economies in transition had a clear articulated vision of where they were going and had a strategy for getting there. Historical experience and current assessments support the importance of a vision and strategy as supportive of relevant success criteria and for general consensus-building among major interest groups. East Europe may reasonably expect a substantial improvement in living standards after the transition, an economic miracle; an economic miracle (Chudo) may also be envisioned in Russia.[19] Objective requirements of the OECD model we defined are met, a substantial improvement in the benefits to major players in absolute and relative terms may be expected.

The report card for economies in transition chooses this version of the OECD model as it reflects the perceived views of groups that make a difference by their support as to whether the transition will be sustainable and successful.

The electorate of the countries in transition must support a set of core principles, should share a vision and understand a strategy for reaching the overall objective of prosperity and peace. The new left has organisational advocates and traditional appeals drawing it toward *status quo ante* but cannot resist the demonstration effect of performance as a stimulus to supporting reform.

The new entrepreneurial groups or classes in the states in transition replace the rent seeking groups that require deficit financing to retain the *status quo ante* by populist measures. The tipping of the balance between new reform "winners" and entrenched "losers" is accelerated by privatisation, restructuring and corporatisation. The new entrepreneurial private groups suffer during the transition from a problem common to many revolutionary changes. Machiavelli warned *The Prince:* "There is nothing more perilous to conduct, nor more uncertain in its success, than to take the lead in the introduction of a new order of things. For the innovator has for enemies all those who have done well under the old conditions, and lukewarm defenders in those who may do well under the new."[20] Especially with privatisation, corporatisation and success the balance shifts. Corporatisation is essential as it requires good corporate management.[21] The new entrepreneurial groups also include workers in privatised enterprises.[22]

Foreign investors and donors may both favour the same criteria with the former replacing the latter in weight and influence as the transition progresses. A vision and strategy for the transition is not yet clearly or credibly articulated by the reforming governments of states in transition to the important actors. A current comprehensive assessment as to where the transition countries have come from, and where they are now, is useful for all participants. Where they expect to end up is a particularly missing piece. Knowing better where they have to go to complete the course would be a stimulus for effective time phasing and coordination and provide a proactive basis for building a consensus wide enough to encourage all groups to stay the course.

The historical processes in Post-World War II development of the Western industrialised economies all benefited by a credible vision of where they were to end up in the transition. The rapid economic growth of the OECD countries from the 1950s to the 1970s in which real income more than doubled was important evidence of a credible economic miracle. Expanding benefits of increased trade and investment within the market economies accentuated the collective benefits. These developments in a stable political and security environment made the promise of prosperity and peace a realistic vision. This vision would likely be persuasive to the electorate, the new entrepreneurial classes, the donors and investors if credible. An explicit strategy and clear success indicators would contribute to more coordination of collective effort and consensus building.

The support of the electorates, entrepreneurial groups and donors have been and are important but foreign investors play a uniquely important role.

The crucial importance of investment for countries in transition has been widely accepted based on historical experience and is the crux of Western assistance policy. While official assistance is initially necessary to fill the financial gap, private capital flows should be relied upon as soon as feasible to supply the funds necessary to maintain monetary stability and restructure the economy.

Foreign direct investment will be the major engine of growth coupled with initially modest but expanding domestic investment. Not only would foreign investment provide new technology, but with it would come modern management and marketing techniques to improve the competitiveness of the economy. Foreign investment provides current account finance without debt, and, as several large investments in Central Europe have shown, indicates broad confidence in the reform process.

Macroeconomic stabilisation, privatisation, restructuring and corporatistion will attract investment, reinforcing further reforms and improving creditworthiness. Establishing a modern commercial code in law and market friendly institutions supports the stability necessary to reduce risk in foreign commitments. Together effective economic reform and establishment of a commercial rule of law tend to attract more investment and greatly improve the ability to obtain finance on international money markets, completing a synergistic *virtuous circle*. Investment

241

is a positive sum process in which the citizens and enterprises of economies in transition and Western countries alike gain substantial benefits in real income, profits and employment, and is very important for integration into the global market economy.

Moreover, mutually beneficial investment is the linchpin of partnership between economies in transition and the Western countries. Foreign investment in many countries in the former Soviet Union and Eastern Europe, to date, has been low largely due to the lack of a stable currency, economic restructuring and an inadequate legal framework; substantial domestic capital has tended to migrate out of many of these countries. Progress has been frustrated by measures intended to redress recession and unemployment, but through deficit financing these measures have destroyed the prospects for monetary stability necessary for reform and attracting investment.

Mistrust in the legitimacy of new leadership and lack of confidence in beneficial outcomes of reform have had a negative effect on support of the new regimes and led to rejections at the polls due to the deepening economic crisis. Thus a *vicious circle* of economic decline, debt accumulation, inflation, uncertainty and inadequate investment has occurred. Temporising and gradualism has proven to be an illusion with either the downward or upward process - the vicious or virtuous cycle - being the operative policy choices, with investment levels as the key barometer of longer term success.[23]

The success indicators, if achieved, could produce a virtuous circle for attaining prosperity and stability. Without a clear and credible strategy a vicious circle of persistent claims of rent seekers, government subsidies and protection, and providing for costly but inefficient welfare systems could undermine reforms.

Mid-term Report Card for the Region

As promising as the changes seen in leading reform countries are, they have not yet passed the threshold of successful and self-sustaining democratic and market change. Labelling any countries in the region as failures is premature, and could lead to unfortunate policy implications of hopelessness in the new states and in non-engagement by the West.

Footnotes:

The authors' views are his own and should not be taken to represent those of the U.S. Congress, Congressional Research Service of the Library of Congress or the United States government.

1. Considerable reliance for specific insights comes from *East-Central European Economies in Transition*, released by the Joint Economic Committee: Washington, D.C., GPO, December 1994, 685 pages. PlanEcon *Review and Outlook Analysis and Forecasts to 1999 of Economic Development in Eastern Europe*. December 1994, 225 pages. PlanEcon *Review and Outlook for the Former Soviet Republics*, Washington, March 1995, 246 p. WEFA Group *Eurasia Outlook for Foreign Trade and Finance*, Washington: January 1995, OECD Centre for Co-Operation with Economies in Transition, *Short-Term Economic Indicators, Transition Economies*, Quarterly Publication. See Selected Bibliography.
2. London Economist, passim 1994; Anders Aslund *Lessons of the First Four Years of System Change in Eastern Europe*, Journal of Comparative Economics, no. 19 (1994), pp. 22-35.
3. *The Annual Report of the OECD*, Paris, 1992, drawing its language from Article 1 of the Convention establishing the Organization for Economic Co-Operation and Development in 1960.
4. The OECD has not elaborated their model in the same comprehensive fashion as indicated by their Short Term Economic Indicator series, op. cit.
5. Quality of life measures as vividly assessed by Murray Feshbach at the colloquium should be explicit success indicators. See: Toward a Western Ecological Agenda, Murray Feshbach, in *Ecological Disaster, Cleaning up the Hidden Legacy of the Soviet Regime*, New York Twentieth Century Funds Report 1995, pp. 79-104. C.f. R. Rybkina, Statistika; sotsiologia, Voprosi Statistiki No. 1. 1995, pp. 3-5 inclusive. [the new monthly journal of the Russian Statistical Agency.].
6. *World Development Report 1991, The Challenge of Development*, Washington and Oxford, World Bank and Oxford Press, p. 14.
7. Jeffrey Sachs, Post Communist Parties and the Politics of Entitlement, *Transition*, World Bank, March 3, 1995, Vol. 6, No 3, pages 1-4.
8. Heinrich Machowski and Wolfram Schrettl, The Economic Impact of Unified Germany, Central and Eastern Europe in JEC, East-Central Europe, op. cit. pp. 412-440.
9. Sharon Wolchik, Gender Issues During Transition, in JEC, East Central Europe, pp. 147-170. Michael Paul Sacht, Ethnic and Gender Divisions in the Work Force of Russia. Post-Soviet Geography, Vol. xxxvi, No. 1. January 1995, pp. 1-12.
10. *Washington Post*, 24 September, 1994, pp. D1 and 2.
11. Arthur M. Okun, "Equity and Efficiency, The Big Tradeoff". Washington, D.C., Brookings Institution, 1975, p. 119. C.f. Ed Hewett, Reforming the Soviet Union: Equality versus Efficiency, Washington, D.C.: Brookings Institution, 1988.
12. Cf. World Development Report 1991, Rethinking the State, op. cit. pp. 128-157.
13. European Union White Paper on Accession. *Financial Times*, 5 May, 1995. Richard E. Baldwin, Towards an Integrative Europe, London CEPR, pp. 244.
14. Lutz Hoffman, East Germany in Transition, East-Central Europe, JEC, op. cit. page 677. Machowski and Schrettl, op. cit., p. 413.
15. Stanley R. Sloan and Steve Woehrel, NATO Enlargement and Russia: From Cold War to Cold Peace? CRS Report 95-594 S. May 15, 1995. 45 p. John Tedstrom, *Economic Integration in Post-Soviet Space: Russia's Broad Agenda*. Santa Monica, California: RAND Corporation, forthcoming 1995.
16. Ivo Bicanic, *The Economic Causes of New State Formation During Transition, East European Politics and Societies*, Volume 9, No. 1, Winter 1995, pp. 2-14.
17. John P. Hardt, Phillip Kaiser and James Voorhees, *Beyond Chechnya: Some Options for Russia and the West*, CRS-95-338 S, March 3, 1995.
18. Leszek Balcerowicz, Transition to the Market Economy: Poland, 1989-93 in Comparative Perspective in Economic Policy, A European Forum, Lessons for Reform, Cambridge University Press. Paul Marer, Hungary During 1988-1994: An American View, published in French, Economica Press, June 1994, edited by Marie Lavigne, in a book entiteld *Capitalismes a l'Est, un Accouchement Difficile*.
19. Daniel Yergin and Thane Gustafson, Russia 2010 and What It Means for the World. CERA Report, Random House, New York, released 16 November? 1993.

20. Ron Amann, Director of the Center for Russian and East European Studies, Birmingham University first used this reference in the context of regional reform in a discussion of the Russian "identity" crisis.

21. Masahiko Aoki and Hyung-Ki Kim, Corporate Governance in Transitional Economies: Insider Control and the Role of Banks, EDI Development Studies, World Bank, Washington, D.C. 1995.

22. Dani Rodrik, The Dynamics of Political Support for Reform in Transition, London CEPR Discussion Paper No. 1115, January 1995.

23. John P. Hardt and Phillip Kaiser, Investment Environment and Legislative Strategy, A discussion Paper for the Ukrainian Rada, forthcoming 1995.

Selected Bibliography

1. John P. Hardt and Richard F. Kaufman, editors, The Former Soviet Union in Transition, Volumes 1 and 2, February 1993, Washington, Joint Economic Committee [also reprinted by Myron Sharpe].
2. John P. Hardt and Richard F. Kaufman, editors, East-Central European Economies in Transition, released by the Joint Economic Committee: Washington, D.C., GPO, December 1994, (also to be available from Myron Sharpe).
3. PlanEcon, Review and Outlook Analysis and Forecasts to 1999 of Economic Development in Eastern Europe. December 1994.
4. PlanEcon, Review and Outlook for the Former Soviet Republics, Washington, March 1995.
5. WEFA Group, Eurasia Outlook for Foreign Trade and Finance, Washington: January 1995.
6. WEFA Group, Eurasia Economic Outlook, Washington: April 1995.
7. OECD Centre for Co-Operation with Economies in Transition, Short-Term Economic Indicators, Transition Economies, Sources and Definitions, Paris 1995.
8. Jean-Pierre Broclawski et Norbert Holcblat, Repères économiques pour l'Europe centrale et orientale en 1994, le courier des pays de l'Est. Paris: La Documentation Francaise, January-February 1995, pp. 3-10.
9. Jim Nichol, U.S.-Russian Moscow Summit, May 9-11, 1995, A Preview, CRS Report 95-526 F, 25 April, 1995.
10. John P. Hardt, U.S.-Russian Economic Partnership: Benefits and Risks, CRS Report 94-892 S, 30 December, 1994.
11. John P. Hardt, Economic Crisis in Ukraine: Dangers and Opportunities, CRS Report 94-668 S, 18 August, 1994.
12. John P. Hardt, James Voorhees, and Phillip Kaiser, Beyond Chechnya: Some Options for Russia and the West, CRS Report 95 338 S, 3 March, 1995.
13. Patricia A. Wertman, Russia and the IMF: Financing Economic Adjustment, Issue Brief IB92128.
14. Curt Tarnoff, U.S. and International Assistance to the Former Soviet Union, Issue Brief IB91050.
15. William H. Cooper, Russian Foreign Trade: Prospects and Implications for the United States, CRS Report 94-488 E, December 10, 1994.
16. George D. Holliday (coordinator), Trade Policy in the 104th Congress, CRS Report 95-485 E, April 10, 1995.
17. Theodor Galdi, The Nunn-Lugar Cooperative Threat Reduction Program for Soviet Weapons Dismantlement, CRS Report 94-985 updated December 6, 1994.
18. John P. Hardt and Phillip Kaiser, An Agenda for Russian Economic Reform in 1995, edited by John W. Blaney, Congressional Quarterly Inc. (Washington, D.C.) 1995.
19. Anders Aslund, Russia's Success Story, Foreign Affairs, September/October 1994, pp. 58-71.
20. The Economist, A Silent Revolution Russia's Emerging Market, April 8, 1995.
21. PlanEcon, Russian Economic Monitor: With Approval of a 1995 Budget and the IMF Program, There Are Improving Chances for a Russian Economy Recovery in 1996, April 7, 1995, Vol. XI, November 7-8, 1994.
22. Anders Aslund, How Russia Became a Market Economy, Washington, D.C.: Brookings Institution, May 1995.
23. Robert D. Blackwill and Sergei A. Karaganov, (editors), Damage Limitation or Crisis? Russia and the Outside World, CSIA Studies in International Security No. 5. Center for Science and International Affairs John F. Kennedy School of Government, Harvard University. Brassey's Inc., Washington - London, June 23, 1994, p. 327.

CHANCES FOR ACHIEVING STABLE ECONOMIC GROWTH IN LITHUANIA

Eduardas Vilkas

Lithuania, like the other Baltic states, is too small to dream of splendid isolation. She must always look to her neighbours, especially Russia. According to Eduardas Vilkas, the Lithuanian economy is still dependent on Russia to a large extent. All the country's energy, and a substantial amount of her raw materials, come from Russia, who also swallows up most of her exports. Helping democracy and economic reform in Lithuania therefore means doing the same for Russia. The Lithuanian economy, though not in great shape, is on the right track. Double-digit growth is forecast for 1995, and there is great popular enthusiasm for reform. The country's ultimate aim is full membership of the European Union. This, Lithuanians are convinced, is the only way to guarantee economic and political security.

Professor Vilkas is Director of the Institute of Economics, Lithuanian Academy of Sciences, Vilnius.

In Lithuania, as in the other Baltic countries of Estonia and Latvia, liberalisation of economic activity and deregulation of prices took only a couple of years to approach the level enjoyed in Western countries. Since the liberalisation was followed by fast financial stabilisation, the transition to a market economy in these countries seems to be very successful.

At the same time, the problems of industrial restructuring, infrastructure modernisation and institutional changes are so immense that prospects of attaining a stable economic growth can hardly be seen as evident in the current situation of dramatic decline in production output. This paper will seek to address the major factors on which the success of transition policies decisively depends.

One factor must be stressed even at the outset. Lithuania and the other Baltic countries, because of their small size, can only develop as open economies and as such are extremely dependent upon the world economic situation. In particular, economic relations with their closest neighbours have a paramount effect on them. As a consequence of this, the investigation of achieving stable economic growth actually turns out to be guesswork, to the extent that external factors are hardly predictable.

Political Stability

The first two years of independence passed under constant military threat from the USSR and from its fifth column within the country. Therefore the initial conditions for political and economic reform were most unfavourable. However, five years after Lithuania's Declaration of Independence, the political situation can be characterised as reasonably stable.

First, the whole political process is on the track of democratic development. A new Constitution, adopted by referendum on 25 October 1992, recognises human rights in accordance with international standards and adheres to the other principles of Western democracy, including separation of powers. The Parliament has ratified the Human Rights Declaration and most of the protocols to it, as well as many other international conventions.

Second, not only has the country theoretical preconditions for democratic development but also practically, democracy and stability are becoming characteristic of everyday life. Indeed, the very same day the Constitution was adopted, a new Parliament (Seimas) was elected with an absolute majority of one party (Democratic Labour Party) which proclaimed and implemented the continuity of democratic change and transition to a market economy.

Barring any crisis, this government will probably stay in power for its entire four-year term. The President of the Republic elected by universal suffrage in February 1993, came from the same majority party, and until now enjoys support from more than half the population. His term ends in 1998. The country passed its most dangerous period of political confrontation in 1992 before the referendum on the Constitution; the experience of a peaceful solution of the country's problems contributed a lot to the formation of democratic traditions.

Thirdly, speedy integration into European political organisations allows the country to profit from the experience of Western democracies on the one hand, and to be observed by the European Union, on the other.

The preferential demographic situation (81 percent Lithuanians, 8.5 percent Russians and 7 percent Poles) made it possible to adopt a very liberal citizenship law in 1991, allowing every then permanent resident of Lithuania to apply for citizenship and automatically receive it. Thus Russia did not have any complaint on that question. This helped to solve the most sensitive problem of the withdrawal of Russian troops which was carried into effect a year earlier than in Estonia and Latvia. The communist forces tried to play the Polish card just after the declaration of independence and later on. However, it has lost all practical significance after the political treaty with Poland was signed in late 1994. Lithuania does not have a minority problem.

All this supports the conclusion that Lithuanian's interior political stability has been achieved; moreover, it can resist serious attempts to destabilise the situation from outside. This kind of danger cannot be ignored.

Political and Economic Relations with Neighbours

Despite the fears of most Lithuanians arising from the fact that the followers of restoration of the Russian empire enjoy very strong influence on the political processes in Russia, it is understood in Lithuania that helping democratisation and marketisation in Russia is helping ourselves. No iron wall on the Russian side would save Lithuania's independence. However, good neighbours and useful economic and cultural relations may help to reduce the influence of anti-reformers in Russian politics and the possibility of Russian military or economic aggression by the same token. It goes without saying that more reliable security for Lithuania can be achieved only through a system of European security in which Russia is, or could be, a member or at least a partner.

Besides the general impact on Russia's westernisation played by Lithuania as a close and understandable westernising factor, there are two other and perhaps more important circumstances in Lithuanian-Russian relations which can be used for increasing Lithuania's security: the above-mentioned very liberal policies regarding the Russian minority, and Kaliningrad region, to which Lithuania is the shortest transportation route from Russia. Poland and Ukraine can also sometimes improve Lithuania's bargaining position due to Lithuania's historical ties with these countries and common attitudes towards political independence.

As in the case of political security, Russia and only Russia may pose very serious economic problems for Lithuania, since Lithuania imports nearly 100 percent of its primary energy resources from Russia without any alternatives so far. Also, Lithuania imports other raw materials and many kinds of industrial production from Russia. These imports are, in general, cheaper than imports from elsewhere. As important as the supply of raw materials is the possibility to export Lithuanian goods and services to Russia on the same terms the other neighbour exporters have. All this creates possibilities of economic pressure which was actually used by Russia several times in recent years. It is a strategic target for Lithuania to become less vulnerable to threats to cut supplies or close imports. Two projects serve this purpose: Butinge oil terminal for export-import of crude oil and the Klaipeda terminal for export-import of oil products. Implementation of both has started; completion is anticipated in two years.

Other very important factors are the strengthening cooperation with Baltic counterparts and the rapidly improving Polish-Lithuanian relations.

Investment and Economic Restructuring

Lithuania's economy has experienced a dramatic decline in all its sectors. The situation, of course, is much similar to the situation in other post-communist countries trying to adjust to drastic changes in prices of productive inputs, as well as to disintegration of economic area and loss of traditional markets as a consequence of this. In the case of Lithuania, the increase of prices is probably 90 percent responsible for this big drop of output. With the powerful energy sector working entirely on imported cheap primary energy resources and, as a consequence, also with a big part of industry developed as energy-intensive, Lithuania faced the problem of technologies becoming unproductive after manifold increase of energy prices to a greater extent than its neighbours.

Despite all the troubles, the economy is gaining momentum after a successful stabilisation and free market forces at work. Lithuanian official statistics on GDP in 1994 will be available a month from now; unofficial evaluations are around zero. According to World Bank data (Global Economic Prospects and the Developing Countries, 1995. A World Bank publication) Lithuania was the fourth fastest growing country (after Albania, Estonia and Poland) among countries in transition, with about 5 percent GDP growth. One can expect that 1995 will be a year of unquestionable economic growth, even two-digit percentage increase is possible if the oil refinery works not far from full capacity or electricity export increases sufficiently. The Economist Intelligence Unit, a sister organisation of The Economist, published in this journal (25-31 March, 1995) a chart of growth prospects according to its composite index. Lithuania is the fifth after Slovenia, Czech Republic, Slovakia and Hungary. The evaluation supports the opinion that Lithuania has a good chance of fast economic progress.

Progress will depend greatly upon the pace of introducing new technologies which, in its turn, will depend on the availability of credits and direct investment. Up to April 1995 direct foreign investment in Lithuania amounted to $274 million while state borrowing from foreign sources reached $850 million, of which some $450 million have been used. The figures, no doubt, are too small compared with the country's GDP of more than $4 billion in 1994. However, the investment process is accelerating due to financial stabilisation (national currency - the Litasis - was pegged to $ as 1/4 of $1 from April 1994, inflation was 45 percent last year, etc.), signs of economic growth and completed privatisation of all state property, including residential dwellings and most of the land, but excluding the infrastructure of which privatisation is postponed, maybe to 2000.

Environmental Sustainability

The level of pollution in Lithuania was never as great as in Russian industrial centres, and in five years it has decreased significantly with a 70 percent decline in production output. What is currently the main concern is the completion of the wastewater treatment plants in many urban areas, first of all in Vilnius, Kaunas and Klaipeda. Scandinavian countries have made donations for these measures to reduce pollution of the Baltic Sea. There would be no reason to mention environmental sustainability at all if Lithuania did not have the largest nuclear power station in Europe, located in Ignalina. It produces cheap electricity and so is an economic necessity, at least at present, but it frightens the whole region while for Lithuania it poses a deadly danger. Many experts feel the maintenance of the nuclear power plant has been improved considerably in recent years. Nevertheless, improvements continue as the consequences of an accident would be terrible. Not only technical imperfections matter, but actions of terrorists are equally dangerous.

Social Restrictions to Reforms

It is mathematically proved that liberalisation of prices is most efficient if done in a manner of shock therapy, i.e. as rapidly as possible. However, anticipated worsening of the situation of some social groups - or the self-interest of populist opposition, popular movements, etc. - can sometimes make the implementation of sound economic policies impossible. Happily enough, Lithuania did not meet this kind of difficulty; moreover, the first years of transition demonstrated mass enthusiasm. Probability of strikes is negligible as both tradition of strikes and potential organisers are non-existent, also because improvement of the economy has started. Nonetheless, influential groups of agrarians and managers of large enterprises (their behaviour started to change after privatisation), nationalists and populist politicians, constantly try to make the parliament and government diverge from liberal economic policies. These attempts cannot be ignored because state paternalism is the decades-long experience of the population.

Integration into the European Union

Membership in the EU is Lithuania's vision of the future. This factor becomes most important in targeting economic and political reforms. It also is able to neutralise the negative influence of inexperience and other social restrictions mentioned above. Determination to integrate into Western Europe comes from two reasons: security and economics. Of course, the emotional factor of joining the family of democratic European countries has played an even greater role until now.

As mentioned above, Lithuania has no alternative except the European security system to keep its political independence. It would be excellent to know that there will be no Russian aggression in the future. Unfortunately, Russia does not behave in a way which would allow one to make this presumption. Suffice it to say that the situation there is not "aggression-proof". Ironically enough, Russia, most probably, would prevent aggression of any other country.

Economic reasons are obvious. They involve participation in the division of labour of a large and advanced region. Looking at the development programmes for the infrastructure of the Lithuanian economy to become an integral part of the European transportation, energy and communications systems, one can realise how great a stimulus it is for the development and modernisation of all economic sectors - that will follow from the implementation of these programmes. On the other hand, the very development of infrastructure, being a huge investment, may lead to an economic boom.

Conclusion

Transition period problems are numerous and serious. However, bearing in mind what has been achieved, the logic of economic development, and the availability of financial and technical assistance of developed countries, economic growth appears to be guaranteed. Lithuania's security will increase, as economic growth and the country's security reinforce each other.

POLAND'S PARTICIPATION IN ESTABLISHING AN ALL-EUROPEAN SECURITY SYSTEM: THE ECONOMIC CONDITIONS

Janusz Kostecki, Leon Turczynski

The Polish economy is firmly set on the path of growth, and production is on the rise. But it's still not moving fast enough to satisfy the population's economic aspirations. Foreign direct investment is lower than expected. Inflation and unemployment are still big problems. But Janusz Kostecki and Leon Turczynski are confident that their country's 'Big Bang' approach to reform has paid off. Proof of this is that economic policy and performance are moving closer to that of their Western neighbours. Poland has moved out of its crisis and stagnation period, and today it has a lot to offer the West, they say - particularly in those areas of the economy that are associated with security.

Col. Kostecki is a Director, and Lt. Col. Turczynski a Senior researcher, at the Department of Defence, Central Office of Planning, Warsaw.

Introduction

The fundamental transformations in the arena of international politics, especially in Europe, have made substantial changes to the security conditions on our continent. Today, the notion of security (both in its international and national dimension) does not limit itself only to political and military aspects but to a growing extent includes also economic and social aspects (migrations), ecological issues (including the uncontrolled flow of fissile materials) and technological issues. Besides the military challenge, growing importance is attached to non-military aspects, in relation to both individual countries and the entire continent.

We should strive to break the existing barriers and divisions. It is in our mutual interest to have a truly unified Europe, without splitting it into two different parts: one, with accumulated wealth, and a democratic and stable society; and the other, that is underdeveloped and uncivilised, disturbed by one economic and social crisis after another and facing a danger of authoritarian rule. Today it is necessary to recognise that the still-existing economic discrepancies between Western and Eastern Europe give a potential cause for destabilisation of the political situation on our continent in the future.

Poland, to the best of its abilities, makes efforts to manage the heritage of the past. Now we are very much advanced in the process of transformation of our political and economic system. The Polish economy has established itself on a path of growth.

The Character of Polish Economic Transformation in the mid-1990s

Poland assumes a relatively good economic position among other Central and East European countries. The most comprehensive measure of economic abilities of a state is the GDP which in 1994 amounted to about 93.4 billion US dollars. This was a smaller figure as compared to Germany and Russia but bigger as regards the GDP of our other neighbours. In the last three years we achieved relatively fast economic growth. The GDP increase rose from 2.6 percent in 1992 to 5 percent in 1994. The main factor contributing to such a dynamic growth was a rapid increase in industrial production which in 1994 rose almost by 12 percent, as compared to 1993.

The present rate of economic growth in Poland as well as in other Central European countries is insufficient, both from the point of view of a rapid improvement of the standard of living of the population and aspiration to full membership in the European Union.

An important aspect in the attempts to bridge the gap between the Western countries and our own, is the level of foreign investments in Central and Eastern Europe. Despite their rapid growth in volume, they are on a lower level than originally expected and exhibit a strong geographical diversification. A major cause for this diversification is the degree of the investors' trust, which depends on political stabilisation, legal and economic guarantees for foreign capital, an advancement of market reforms and an overall economic development of specific countries. So far, foreign investors have engaged in the form of direct investments, for example: in Hungary 8.5 billion US dollars, in Russia 5 billion, in Poland 5.0 billion and in the Czech Republic 3.7 billion US dollars.

Table I
The Economic Indices of the Central and East European Countries
(by the International Economic Comparisons Institute in Vienna)

	GDP per capita in US $	Growth of the GDP			Budgetary deficit as percent of GDP	Rate of unemploy-ment	Inflation
	1994	1994	1995*	1996*	1994	1995*	1995*
Slovenia	7030	+ 5.5	+ 5.0	+ 5.0	- 1.0	13.5	16.0
Hungary	4083	+ 3.0	+ 1.0	+ 2.0	- 6.6	11.0	25.0
Czech Rep.	3483	+ 2.7	+ 4.0	+ 5.0	+ 1.0	3.5	10.0
Poland	2406	+ 5.1	5.0	+ 5.0	- 3.5	17.0	25.0
Slovakia	2324	+ 4.8	+ 3.0	+ 3.0	- 4.5	16.0	15.0
Russia	19927	- 15.0	- 10.0	- 5.0	- 10.0	3.5	150.0
Romania	1262	+ 3.4	+ 2.0	+ 3.0	- 3.5	14.0	50.0

Projections

An important element in the economies of Poland and other countries is the private sector. Regarding this sector's share in the GDP creation, the best positions are those of Poland (56 percent), the Czech Republic (56 percent), Slovakia (53 percent), Russia (50 percent) and Hungary (50 percent). While transforming their existing systems, these countries carried out retail price reforms, privatised the greater part of small enterprises and liberalised foreign trade. However, the financial sector reform and the restructuring and privatisation of big enterprises were less successful.

The major problems of the transition countries, despite a significant economic revival, are still inflation and unemployment. None of the countries in our region was successful enough to reduce the inflation rate below 10 percent. Bulgaria, Romania and the Commonwealth of Independent States (formerly the Soviet Union), still have a three digit inflation. The basic reason for this situation is that restructuring and privatisation are progressing too slowly, monopolistic structures are maintained; and high customs barriers and price setting by means of administrative decisions have not been changed. The highest unemployment rate is noted in Poland (16.0 percent) and Bulgaria (15.7 percent) and the lowest in the Czech Republic (3.1 percent). At the same time, one should point out that the unemployment rate figures, as presented by individual countries, are much more optimistic than the assessments and forecasts made by various international economic and financial organisations. Hidden unemployment is

255

still high, many employees work part-time or are on compulsory leaves. On the other hand, different countries use different definitions of unemployment and different methods to calculate their unemployment rates.

The budgetary deficit, along with inflation and unemployment, is generally regarded as the major threat to long-term economic growth. Stabilisation policy in many cases restricts itself only to cutting down the budgetary expenses, when the expenses of the state for infrastructure are small. In all the countries in our region, except for the Czech Republic, the state budget expenditures in 1994 exceeded the budgetary revenues, and the ratio of the budgetary deficit to the GDP was differentiated.

The economic indices obtained by Poland and other countries of the region, allow for an assumption that it was possible to overcome the crisis that occurred in the economic transformation. However, there are still many threats which may impede the reforms and structural transformations.

Some of these threats include:

• The gap that still exists between the Western and Central and East European countries.
• A pace of structural transformation that is too slow, including strong inflation pressure, unemployment, budgetary deficit and a growing public debt.
• Alarming uncontrolled migration.

Poland's Interests in Establishing an All-European Security System

Poland's economic potential, including the part associated with security, may constitute an attractive element of the European security system. The economic management system and the functioning mechanisms are more and more close to those in the developed economies. Poland's economy has already left behind the crisis and stagnation period and achieved a significant growth in recent years. Also the forecasts for the oncoming years are positive.

As far as the elements supporting security are concerned, we want to highlight the potential of the defence industry. Although it is now passing through a difficult period, as is also the case of other European countries, nevertheless, it is also going through a process of systematic restructuring and conversion, in order to adjust its capacity to the present and the future projected needs. At the same time, its economic and financial condition is being improved, as well as the level of technology.

Poland has a significant scientific research potential, dealing with the development of technologies associated with security issues. However, working alone, we are unable to launch big and costly research projects and after the Warsaw Pact broke up, formal cooperation between the Central and East European countries faded away. Contracts with the NATO countries are rare and limited only to scientific research cooperation in issues related to storage and liquidation of chemical weapons, of conversion of military industry, environment protection and conversion of military industry scientific employees.

We are particularly interested in entering cooperation in technologies related to the anti-aircraft and anti-tank defence systems. In the transportation sphere defence issues are focused on improving the capacity of communication routes and traffic safety provision.

The programme for construction of motorways (the total length of 2,600 km), express routes (3,800 km) and railway network involves not only the Polish but also the European aspect, since this programme aims at the actual inclusion of Poland into the process of developing a trans-European communication network infrastructure.

In the area of aviation and sea rescue, Poland signed a number of agreements with European countries. We have signed an agreement with Germany on aviation search and rescue and on sea rescue. In transportation we have regulated the legal basis concerning road connections, and negotiations are underway related to cooperation in railway transport of passengers and goods.

In communications, besides a standard international communications system, we recognise a need for defining the scope of international cooperation in communication in case of ecological threats, catastrophes and natural disasters.

We have started to build up a National Communication System which may improve the use of communications systems in defence and security spheres, as well as make it compatible with the NATO communications systems.

As far as strategic raw materials are concerned, Poland has rich deposits of coal, copper and sulphur. In the future these raw materials may provide reserves within the European security system. At the same time, we are much dependent on the delivery of oil and natural gas. The main constraint here is not only a lack of these materials but also insufficiently developed pipelines network.

A much more complex issue is the establishment of a guarantee system for mutual delivery of strategic raw material in case of danger. Besides signing proper legal agreements, there is also a need to provide for transportation of the material.

While presenting these possibilities for international cooperation in the areas of the economy associated with security, we believe that carrying out such cooperation may be a manifestation of mutual trust between the nations. It may also contribute to reducing a burden to our societies, created by the defence and security expenditures. A close neighbourhood of our countries, as well as very good political, military and economic relations, provide favourable conditions for addressing - within the framework of the Partnership for Peace - these economic issues which directly contribute to the security of Poland and of its neighbours, and to building up an all-European security system.

SYSTEMIC CHANGE IN COOPERATION PARTNER COUNTRIES: YARDSTICKS FOR ASSESSMENT, RESULTS, CONCLUSIONS AND PERSPECTIVES

Hans-Hermann Höhmann

Russia and the countries in Central and Eastern Europe are engaged in more than economic reform. They are redefining their statehood, and seeking a new place in the international community. The whole process is fraught with danger, says Hans-Hermann Höhmann. The first requirement is economic stability. Central and Eastern Europe are making good progress, but Russia is lagging behind. All this demands tough monetary policies and a shock therapy approach that threatens the social consensus needed to keep the reform moving forward. The circle can be broken, but the West must invest a lot of political and financial capital, especially in Russia - after all, Western security is also at stake.

Professor Höhmann is Director of Research and Head of the Economic Department of the Bundesinstitut für ostwissenschaftliche und internationale Studien, Köln.

More than five years have passed since the great politico-economic transformation began in Eastern Europe. In some parts of the region, these years have seen an increase in the diverse opportunities that the collapse of communism opened up for the emergence of democratic systems, for social pluralism, and for the transition to market economy. They were linked with the liberation from Soviet domination, with the evolution of a new relationship between East and West, and with intensive efforts to establish a modified cooperation system in Europe.

But in many respects, the years since 1989/90 have also shown that the transformation of communist-style politico-economic systems into democracies and market economies is much more difficult than was assumed in the East or the West in the early days of the transformation process. Successes contrast with failures. Different national courses of development have led to significant distinctions in the re-structuring process.

In some countries, the ongoing changes have bolted away from all state guidance and control and are forging ahead in the form of largely spontaneous turmoil. All this makes it more and more difficult to paint a valid picture of the status of and prospects for economic transformation in Eastern Europe. Consequently, this paper, too, must restrict itself to identifying some specific aspects and discussing some yardsticks which might expediently be applied to assess the status and progress of the transformation processes.

The Complexity of the Transformation Task

If economic transformation in the post-communist countries is to succeed, some extremely complex transformation problems will have to be resolved - under heavy millstones in the form of (in some cases) devastating inherited burdens. This complexity arises first of all from the fact that the transition to new economic conditions, in particular, the changeover to stable, socially-accepted and efficient market economies, must take place in unison with three other major restructuring processes.

This transition will only succeed if a positive interaction can be achieved between economic change and the other principal adaptation processes. These are:
• The redefinition of a national statehood and the development of a national identity, as has become necessary in many countries following the disintegration of long-standing state systems of order.
• The conversion of the political system and society into democratic and pluralist structures.
• The integration of the countries in Eastern Europe into a new international political and economic order.

A close correlation exists in particular between political and economic transformation. On the one hand, the conversion of the political system into a democracy has to be accompanied by economic successes that make themselves felt in the standard of living of the population and thus make the restructuring politically acceptable to a democratic majority. On the other hand, an economic transformation that enhances the well-being of the people can succeed only if the political and legal systems establish propitious background conditions for economic activity.

Thus, any successful economic metamorphosis requires the presence of "political capital" which comprises three principal elements:
1. There must be an adequately broad national consensus at the time the transformation process is launched; this consensus must be characterised by an emphatic condemnation of the old system and by a clear commitment to the change of system, even if this involves some sacrifices.
2. On the basis of this underlying consensus, a viable framework of order must be constructed as soon as possible which establishes the basic institutions of an economic constitution and legal system, defines the instruments of economic policy to be used to influence the economic processes, and ensures by means of a reliable jurisdiction that the rules as established are respected.

3. And finally, political capital includes a government with authority, competence and strength of purpose that is willing and in a position to push through the transformation process actively and speedily.

Economic Restructuring

The restructuring of the economic conditions is an extremely complex procedure involving at least five difficult sub-processes:
• Microeconomic liberalisation of domestic and foreign trade as the "gateway" to market economy, by lifting price controls, abolishing administrative planning of production and distribution, eliminating quotas and licences, and establishing a step-by-step transition to a convertible currency.
• Macroeconomic stabilisation with the cardinal task of combating inflation by practising a stability-orientated, restrictive hard monetary policy and by achieving a well-balanced and soundly funded national budget.
• Institutional interaction comprising the major elements: privatisation as the most important step at the micro level and, at the industry, regional and national levels, the creation of the institutions required for the self-regulatory framework of the market economy and for effective economic policy within a market-economy system (decision-makers, political instruments, institutions of a fiscal and funding system and of a monetary and banking system, legislation on economic affairs).
• The metamorphosis of the real economic structures by promoting economic and technological innovation and the evolution of market-based links between and within the various sectors and branches of the national economy.
• Assurance of adequate social cushioning of the transformation process to preserve the consensus that is essential to the success of the transformation process.
Some of the sub-objectives of economic transformation may, however, be contradictory, and indeed, such clashes regularly occur in practice. In particular, there is a virtually unresolvable conflict between the impact of a resolute macroeconomic stabilisation policy on production and employment on the one hand and the implementation of reforms to the economic system on the other.[1]
In this context there is a danger of a vicious circle forming, which can be described as follows: progress in the change of system requires macroeconomic stabilisation; economic stabilisation imposes more and more severe burdens on the population, especially in the form of rampant unemployment; these hardships in turn jeopardise the societal consensus and incite the population to protest responses such as strikes, swings to the (in most cases post-communist) opposition parties in national and regional elections, or alternatively to political apathy; this civic protest interrupts or at least slows down the change of system and macroeconomic stabilisation.

The likely consequence of this, in turn, is that the social situation of the population again fails to improve and that public approval for economic reforms dwindles still further. Only if the "political capital" is substantial, if the social repercussions of the stabilisation measures are successfully cushioned (for example if assistance is forthcoming from the West to help cope with the adverse impacts of stabilisation), and if the opposition is willing to continue the transformation policy in principle after coming to office, only then is there any hope of being able to break out of the vicious circle.

The complexity and interdependence of the tasks involved in the transformation process have frequently prompted questions as to the proper strategy to be pursued in bringing about the necessary changes: in what order should the reforms be implemented? Should the political or the economic transformation be tackled first? And (taking the restructuring of the economy as a process in itself), what sequence merits priority within the "magic triangle of transformation objectives" - macroeconomic stabilisation, institutional transition, or microeconomic adaptation? And finally, what pace should be set for the transformation, should preference be given to "shock therapy" or to a "gradualist" approach?

One of the major difficulties involved in the search for the most expedient strategy is, of course, that the transformation of a socialist political and economic system into a democratic and market-economy model along Western lines is a unique venture that is without precedent in history. Accordingly, a transformation theory had not been formulated nor paradigms established, nor experience gathered elsewhere. What is more, the countries in transformation have done little to cross-fertilise each other by means of learning processes. As a result, many of their decisions have been and still are based on the "trial and error" principle. In the meantime, numerous theories of transformation have been put forward, dealing with the "sequencing" and pace of restructuring.

However, their practical relevance is severely curtailed by the fact that most of their analytical approaches presuppose a strong state as the central protagonist of transformation. In many countries, especially in the states of the CIS, however, transformation is occurring more as a spontaneous process than as a steered process. With such uncertain terms of reference, success and failure depend less on strategic designs than on the weight of the inherited burdens, on the constellation of the conditions pertaining at the outset, on the response of the outside world, and on the specific nature of the interdependence of politics and the economy in the transition process.

Inherited Burdens and Other Starting Conditions

Any discussion of the burdens hampering the countries in transformation must start off by pointing out that the close correlation between economic and socio-political developments means that not only the economic but also the political and social heritage of the defunct socialist system have a retarding effect on the transformation of the economic conditions in the post-socialist countries. Of special importance in this context are the politically and economically dysfunctional effects of the serious deficits in public power and authority, of the feeble development of democratic forces (and here in particular the tardy emergence of political parties), and the predominance of personal over institutional aspects in politics.

Another factor impeding economic change is that there is little of the effective social self-organisation that is essential for the development of social momentum and the controlling of conflicts in democratic market economies. And finally, the collapse of communism as an ideology has left a more or less pronounced lack of guiding social values and standards of conduct. Although communism had lost the allegiance of the minds and hearts of the people, it was still an important element of social intercourse and "everyday ethics". In many of the post-socialist states, the consequences have been brittle social coherence and an inclination towards anomic and even criminal forms of conduct.

It is thus clear that there is a whole bundle of inherited socio-political burdens that are combining to make the reconstruction of the political system arduous, contradictory and inconsistant — in terms of the constellation of political forces — and to obstruct institutional consolidation and public acceptance of the market economy system.

This problematic political heritage goes hand in hand with complex economic encumbrances. Bureaucratic structures and regional and sectoral interest groups remain intact and are making it even more difficult to restructure the economy and transform the economic system. In particular the socialist system of ownership proved from the very beginning to be a serious obstacle to the transition to a market economy. Other cardinal features of the old system such as paternalism, egalitarianism, and the distorted perception of work performance conditioned by the incentives system under the administrative planned economy had inculcated patterns of economic behaviour that do not exactly promote the change to a market economy. But above all it was the actual structures of the Eastern European economies, dilapidated from decades of neglect, that meant that any attempt to change the system was bound to trigger severe economic and social shock waves that harbour potential for serious political conflicts. The following, especially, fall under the heading of the "structural heritage":

• The partly hypertrophic, partly underdeveloped state sector.
• The over-dimensioned heavy and arms industries.
• Obsolescence of the capital stock as a result of shortage of funds or misguided investment policies.
• The inadequately extensive, outdated and partly derelict infrastructure.
• Massive environmental problems culminating in ecological disasters.
• High levels of hidden unemployment in the labour structures inherited from the planned labour market era.

• The outdated and disproportionate structures of foreign trade (due partly to priorities under the administrative planned economy and partly to the division of labour under Soviet hegemony).

A comparison of the behavioural and structural heritage of the various economies in transformation in Eastern Europe shows that, despite many similarities, there are also some considerable differences from country to country. In this context, the starting conditions in Poland, Hungary and Czechoslovakia already appeared much more propitious from the very beginning than they were in Russia and the other states of the CIS, and the results of their transition to date fully corroborate that initial appraisal.

However, the different relative weights of the burdens inherited from socialism are compounded by other, specifically local, conditions at the onset of transformation in the various countries:

• The extent of the economic disruption already taking place before the inception of the transformation process, for example the scale of stagnation in growth and drops in production, pent-up inflation, and debt in hard currency.

• The availability of natural resources (this is one of the few instances in which Russia is at an advantage).

• The intensity of prior contacts with market-economy systems in the West and (last but not least).

• The specific character of the local "economic culture", defined as the totality of the knowledge, experience, perceptions, assessments and patterns of conduct, with respect to the economic sector, present within the respective nations or within certain function elite and population groups of a given society.

It is generally true that the weaker the economic situation, the less the "political capital". Equally, the more resistant the old administrative structures are to change, the more distorted and obsolete the capital, production and employment structures will be with respect to the opportunities opened up by a market economy, the more remote the foreign trade organisation will be from the world markets, and the more hostile the local economic culture will be to a market environment; the more difficult it is to resolve the tasks involved in transformation. This applies virtually irrespective of whatever transformation strategy is actually attempted.

If a gradual approach is taken, poorer conditions heighten the danger of the transformation process running aground before it has really got under way, as in the case of Ukraine. And if a radical approach is taken, the concussion triggered by the initial "direction shock"[2] is felt all the more strongly, making it all the more probable that the measures introduced will have to be stretched, diluted or even retracted.

The Central European Countries as the Pioneers of Transformation

The divergence that has already become apparent between the various countries in transformation holds true for all sectors of the reconfiguration, in particular for the degree of macroeconomic stabilisation achieved (measured above all in terms of the reduction in inflation rates), the progress made in privatisation, the pace with which market-economy institutions are set up, and the headway made in adapting the economy proper (structural change). It is consistently evident that the countries which have made the greatest progress in their transformation process are also the ones which have been most successful in overcoming the transformation-induced recession.[3]

Measured in terms of the degree of politico-economic restructuring achieved and the economic recovery to date, a number of zones distinguished by the intensity of the transformation process can by now be discerned, albeit with fuzzy boundaries and with considerable differentiation still necessary within each zone. Clearly in the top zone of the declining intensity scale are the five states of East Central Europe: the Czech Republic, Poland, Hungary, the Slovak Republic and Slovenia (ECE/5 states).

Here, despite all the difficulties, transformation has made significant progress, and the general economic situation has also improved considerably in the meantime. The other end of the scale is also quite clearly defined: all countries affected by wars or civil wars and which are beset by chaos and rampant decline (the former Yugoslav and Transcaucasian Republics, Tajikistan).

The leading ECE/5 states also have many impediments from the past to overcome, but they also benefit from a number of more favourable conditions:
• The inherited burdens are relatively light.
• The transformation process was able to carry on from earlier reforms.
• A broad national consensus made it possible to agree quickly on the course to be followed in economic policy and to embark on transformation without delay.
• The political conditions were and still are relatively stable.
• There was a favourable response from the West, in particular in the form of the opening up of the European Union towards Eastern Europe initiated since late 1991 with the "European Cooperation Treaties".[4]

Since 1994, all ECE/5 states have been experiencing positive growth, and Poland is now in its third successive year. The transformation-induced recession has also been considerably less severe in these countries, the drop in gross domestic product (GDP) since 1990 totalling only about 15 percent. Considering that in terms of per capita gross national product the Czech Republic and Slovenia are now not too far behind Greece and Portugal, this indicates that the ECE/5 states are on their way to catching up economically with the weakest members of the EU and thus to becoming, in economic policy terms, "normal European problem children".

Further to the growth achieved in GDP, other factors meriting a favourable assessment are the return to growth in investment and the moderate trends in annual inflation rates, which were reduced to levels between 10 percent (Czech Republic) and (32 percent) Slovak Republic in 1994 and which can now be described as by all means "in keeping with transformation".[5]

On the other hand, there are a number of adverse macroeconomic trends in evidence in the ECE/5 states:

• Unemployment rates are still relatively high (1994 figures) at levels between 16 percent in Poland and 11 percent in Hungary (the Czech Republic's very low figure of 3.5 percent is an outstanding exception).

• Real wages have dropped since 1990, and social inequality is on the increase.

• Domestic and foreign debt is mounting up on a large scale, and public budget deficits are considerable (again, with the exception of the Czech Republic).

• And finally, despite noteworthy successes in regional restructuring, there is a danger of chronic deficits in the balance of trade with the West.

Favoured by the benign starting conditions outlined earlier, the ECE/5 states were able to introduce a whole bundle of transformation-policy measures and even to implement some of them relatively quickly: abolition of price controls, a harder financial and monetary policy, mutual convertibility of currencies, and liberalisation of foreign trade. Important steps were also taken in the transition towards a market economy system: phase-out of central planning institutions and methods, development of instruments for indirect steering of the economy, establishment and/or extension of a two-tier banking system (central bank/commercial banks).

Also of special importance was the rapid commencement of privatisation (especially "small business privatisation"), even if there are numerous problems still to be overcome in this context.[6] For instance, "large-scale business privatisation" is still progressing only very slowly, is riddled with interventionist measures, is being distorted by subsidies, and is not inducing enough structural change. Where privatisation has already started to take effect, the efficiency of business activity is frequently stifled by inadequate capitalisation, limited entrepreneurial know-how, insufficient controls ("corporate governance"), and restrictions on competition. These deficits in privatisation entail the danger of future insolvencies and at the same time imply that the ECE states' prospects of sustained economic growth are dependent upon a real consolidation of the private sector. The changes of government in Poland and Hungary that brought post-communist (*de facto* social democratic) parties into power were not without their repercussions on the content and pace of reform policy in those countries. Shifts in emphasis and some deceleration effects were inevitable. However, there has been no change of course back to administrative forms of economic control. As long as such changes in economic policy do not involve too much interventionism, changes in government as a result of general elections may even have a stabilising effect on the transformation process, because they head off public discontent and channel it in a way that is normal in any democracy.

The three Baltic states - Estonia, Latvia and Lithuania - are attempting to catch up with the top five, with some major successes in stabilisation and systemic change, even if they still have to climb out of much deeper transformation-induced recessions.[7]

Despite numerous short-term adaptation problems - and contrary to many prognoses (even by Western observers) - the process of extricating the three states from the old Soviet economic conglomerate has had a beneficial effect on the Baltic region, not least thanks to the considerable "political capital" bonus associated with independence and to the smooth and rapid reorientation of external economic relations to the north and west. In Bulgaria and Romania, by contrast, the transition has been slow and not very effective, though not without some encouraging prospects for stabilisation and systemic change.

Russia and the Other States of the CIS as Stragglers in the Transformation Steeplechase

Because of geographical dimensions and its geopolitical weight, Russia is a special case in itself. Certainly the most advanced country undergoing transformation among the states of the CIS, its evolution towards democracy and market economy is being hampered by a multitude of adverse factors. These include:

• The persistently poor economic situation (in 1994 the GNP, industrial production, and investment again declined by between 15 and 25 percent, inflation remained high, and the rouble exchange rate ran into speculation-induced turbulence).

• The particularly oppressive inherited burdens, not least in terms of the sectoral and regional structure of the economy.

• The unresolved question of national identity.

• Contradictory political designs in connection with unclear power constellations.

• The weakness of the central state in the face of the regional dimension of transformation.

• The adverse repercussions at home and abroad of the war in Chechnya.

At any rate, the prospects for Russian economic policy being tightened up and given a clearer conceptual profile, or for progress being made in the institutional reorganisation of the Russian economic system have hardly improved since the December 1993 elections. Admittedly, the acute confrontation between the old Supreme Soviet and President Yeltsin has been remedied, and the new constitution also gives the Russian President extensive powers in the field of economic policy.

However, left-wing and right-wing opponents of reform command considerable influence in the new State Duma, while the reform front performed unexpectedly badly in the elections and, what is more, is disunited in itself. And as regards the significance of the new constitution for economic policy, the plethora of powers it grants to the President are looking more and more like pseudo-competencies in the shadow of the immense weight wielded by sectoral and regional interest groups. It is thus no wonder that Yeltsin is attempting to side-step the constitution and the government with the aim of extending the dimensions and the functions of the presidential apparatus in economic affairs.

On various occasions in 1994/95, Yeltsin and Chernomyrdin have again spoken out in favour of continuing with market-economy reforms, and privatisation has made some significant progress by now. However, it is frequently associated with practices that are legally unfounded or even criminal. But what most makes privatisation to date appear more formal than factual is that monetary and fiscal policy as practised at present is geared towards satisfying the enterprises' demand for subsidies, relegating banks to the role of distribution points for state-ordained loans, and that there are no functioning financial markets that could put pressure on the production units to improve efficiency. The same financial markets would, however, also have to be capable of mobilising the capital required for modernising the obsolete capital stock and for the urgent restructuring of the economy.[8]

Thus, privatisation can help improve systems policy only if it is complemented by an attempt to make a new start in monetary and fiscal policy. Such a new beginning has been proclaimed on various occasions and was most recently made a part of the agreement reached with the IMF in mid-March 1995 on a loan to the tune of $6.25 billion. Chernomyrdin, too, has repeatedly advocated a stricter monetary and fiscal policy, but implementation has always failed to follow the proclaimed intentions.

What is more, many concrete actions taken, from the ongoing practice of subsidising enterprises and sectors that would otherwise be threatened with collapse (to the co-option of reactionary politicians into the government), would tend to indicate that economic policy is more likely to continue in the future, too, to pursue a lobby-dictated and socially-compatible gradualist approach rather than to attempt any stability-orientated and institutional breakthroughs.

The hopes which for some time now have been placed on industrial-policy intervention are likewise to be seen in this context. Their aim is to cushion the rapid structural upheaval that is currently going on in Russia in the form of drastic drops in production in the arms industry and in broad sectors of civilian machine manufacturing and light industry and which in some regions is threatening to take on the proportions of a full-scale deindustrialization with serious social consequences (unemployment, impoverishment).

In most of the other states of the CIS, transformation is even further behind than in Russia. Here, too, comprehensive transformation projects have been devised for individual sectors but great difficulties are being experienced in implementing them, threatening in some extreme cases to paralyse the entire project. On the other hand, these countries also share with Russia the crucial drawback to any deliberate rejection of a reform course: there is simply no promising alternative to a more or less resolutely pursued policy of systemic change.

For one thing, it is quite obvious that intensified interventionist measures - for instance across-the-board price controls, wide-ranging subsidies for unprofitable production units or selective administrative intrusions - tend to generate "functionally weak hybrid systems" (Egon Tuchtfeldt) that are at best not particularly efficient, at times even counter-productive. But a complete return to the old regime of planned-economy socialism would be even less of a valid option. The shortcomings of the "administrative command system" have become too evident, the political pre-requisites for a planned economy could not be restored, and opposing vested interests have by now grown too strong.

The economic pre-conditions for a planned economy - the availability of reserves for the pursuit of political priorities and to compensate for the inefficiency that is typical of the system - have likewise ceased to apply. But of course, the lack of any fundamental alternative to a policy of reforms does not rule out administrative intervention in the transformation process nor changes of course or zigzags in economic policy, be they born of economic necessity or in response to persistent political barrage from reactionary forces.

Conclusions and Security Implications

The different statuses attained in transformation to a market-economy system and in economic consolidation in the countries in Eastern Europe influence and are themselves reflected in the domestic and foreign policies of the states concerned. Thus, different stages of progress are evident in political transformation, in particular differences in the extent to which democratic systems have been established and political stability achieved.

Significant differences are also apparent in the degree to which new national identities have evolved, in foreign-policy interest constellations, and, related to the latter, in the extent to which convergence with Western Europe has been achieved or is intended, whether in the form of closer relations with individual Western European states or with alliance systems and politico-economic communities such as NATO and the European Union. Altogether, four groups of countries can be distinguished, and though each group exhibits further differences within itself each can be characterised by many similarities across all aspects of economic, social and political life: Russia, Russia's "near abroad", Central and Eastern, and Southeastern Europe, and ex-Yugoslavia.

Especially problematic from the security aspect is Russia's inclination to re-define itself if not as a competitive great power, then at least as a regional leading power. However, it would be mistaken to construe for Russia too close a correlation of interdependence between progress made in the transformation of its politico-economic systems, i.e. the evolution of democracy and a market economy, and its performance on foreign-policy issues. The question as to the potential for and the dimensions of a new great power role for Russia is relatively independent of any progress made in transformation and is just as significant and cogent to reactionary, national-conservative politicians as it is to reformers.

The implications that the ongoing changes in Eastern Europe entail for the Western alliance systems ensue from the fact that the loss of a clearly defined adversary and the associated loss of a clearly defined defence mission have also brought a loss of function on the part of NATO. At the same time, the interests of the Western countries are diverging, in particular there is a growing discrepancy between European and US interests, for example with respect to the proper approach to be adopted in Bosnia and Herzegovina, relations with Iran, the question of Russian membership of NATO, and developments in world trade.

To be sure: the situation in the East of Europe is generally agreed to be insecure. But opinions and perceptions differ as to the nature and dimensions of this insecurity. Some see the political conditions in the region as a whole as unstable - not least in the light of the return of leftist governments to power (Lithuania, Poland, Hungary, Bulgaria). Others stress possible economic setbacks as insecurity factors. But many are united in fearing the future course of development in Russia, some focusing more on the destructive potential of a country beset by disintegration, crime and environmental risks, others worrying more about perceived trends towards authoritarian, militaristic and expansive forms of conduct.

These new insecurities in the east and the quest especially by the countries of Eastern Europe for membership of NATO have given rise to a heated debate about the expansion of NATO towards the east. Three defence experts of the Rand corporation - R. Asmus, R. Kugler and S. Larrabee - have attempted to structure this debate.

They distinguish three ways in which the Western defence alliance could expand:[9]

• The expansion of NATO as an evolutionary process to take place over a period of ten years, because the economic and political problems are seen as being more urgent than the security problems and accordingly the countries of Eastern Europe should not be admitted to NATO until after they have joined the European Union.

• The expansion of NATO as a stability transfer, to be assured by the countries of Central and Estern Europe joining NATO in three to five years, because the political situation in East Central Europe is precarious, the security vacuum between NATO's eastern boundary and Russia constitutes a threat to the democratic development of the "intermediate region" and so it is not possible to wait for economic consolidation followed by membership of the EU.

• The expansion of NATO as a strategic response on the part of the Western alliance in which the countries of East Central Europe are not admitted until Russian policy makes this step necessary by building up its forces in the vicinity of its neighbours, violating the sovereignty of Ukraine and/or the Baltic states, or prematurely terminating nuclear disarmament.

To conclude: Unfortunately, an assessment of the status of transformation and of the economic situation in the East of Europe is of little help to the decision-makers in the Western world in their review of these options. The future functions of NATO and in particular the question as to an expansion to the East are primarily political decisions.

Today, as the Finnish diplomat M. Jakobsen sees it, NATO is attempting to pursue two incompatible objectives at the same time:[10] "It is treating Russia as a reliable partner and it is promising the Central and Eastern Europeans that it will protect them against Russian aggression". Here, indeed, a political dilemma is evident: the economic and political situation in Eastern Europe and the status of systemic transformation give grounds for concern about consolidation of democracy and the market economy, but by isolating Russia the extension of NATO could exacerbate precisely that insecurity that the expansion of the Western alliance is intended to allay.

Footnotes

1. Cf. on this and the following A. Brüstle/R. Döhrn, Systemtransformation in Ostmitteleuropa - eine Zwischenbilanz, in: RWI-Mitteilungen, 2, 1994, p. 179.
2. Cf. W. Schrettl, Konjunktur und Transformation: Probleme der russischen Schocktherapie, Arbeiten aus dem Osteuropa-Institut, München, No. 156, December 1992, p. 5.
3. Cf. J. Kornai, Transformational Recession: The Main Causes, in: Journal of Comparative Economics, 19, 1994, pp. 39 et seq.
4. Cf. C. Meier, Der politisch-ökonomische Transformationsprozeß in Ostmitteleuropa - eine Zwischenbilanz im Herbst 1993, in: Forum Institut für Management (Ed.), Produktionsmöglichkeiten in Polen, Ungarn und der Tschechischen Republik, Heidelberg 1993, pp. 1-7.
5. Cf. A. Asland, Lessons of the First Four Years of Systemic Change in Eastern Europe, in: Journal of Comparative Economics, 19, 1994, pp. 24 et seq.
6. Cf. Bertelsmann-Stiftung (Ed.), Mittel- und Osteuropa auf dem Weg in die Europäische Union, reprint, Gütersloh 1995, p. 21.
7. On developments in the Baltic cf. S. Lainela/P. Sutela, The Baltic Economies in Transition, Helsinki 1994.
8. Cf. Die wirtschaftliche Lage Russlands, Wochenbericht des DIW, 47-48, 1994.
9. R.D. Asmus, R.L. Kugler, F. Larrabee, NATO Expansion: The Next Steps, in: Survival, vol. 37, No. 1, Spring 1995, pp. 7-33.
10. Quoted after T. Sommer, Erst denken, dann dehnen, in: Die Zeit, 2.6.1995, p. 3.

OPPORTUNITIES, CONSTRAINTS AND SECURITY IMPLICATIONS

Márton Tardos

Economic ideologies and textbook cases that are transplanted into the economies in transition will not show these countries the way to effective reform, says Márton Tardos. While some observers say that they 'know the right reform formula', he argues that there are no set rules - primarily because this type of economic situation has never existed before. But he does highlight two practical pieces of advice that hold true for every European economy in transition. Firstly - it is strong investment and trade links with the West, not aid, that will drive reform. And secondly - that each economy in transition must find its own way - and use a 'trial and error' policy to adapt global economic principles to its specific situation.

Dr. Tardos is Chairman of the Economic Committee of the Hungarian National Assembly.

I see two central themes to the discussion of economic transformation in the countries of Central and Eastern Europe:

• NATO was established many decades ago to neutralise the military risk connected with the existence of the USSR. Today, no world superpower - let alone the USSR - exists.

• The topic of our discussion is to stabilise the economies of Central and Eastern Europe - of those independent countries formerly of the zone dominated by the USSR that are starting a new history after the collapse of the past political system. However the fall of the USSR has brought with it new risk factors and obligations, both for the region's citizens and for NATO countries.

What is the New Risk Factor?

Those who have been liberated from the dictatorial reign of the USSR have a strong desire to join in the efficiency of the developing free world of parliamentary democracies and market economies. However recent history has demonstrated that - having already reached a certain level of freedom (which is defined as having a parliamentary democracy and a market economy based on free trade) - the promise of transformation must follow a very painful course even if the region's citizens are willing to bear the burdens of the transition which has proved to be more difficult than expected.

Those involved knew that the reconstruction of existing capacities - the development of new economic structure and learning how to adapt a country's production to the new rules of unknown and rapidly-changing market demand - would not be easy. On the contrary, it was assumed that the ability and education of the people in the region, and their recollection of the inconvenience of oppression would accelerate the process and the positive results, and that reconstruction would quickly push aside the unavoidable sacrifices.

As discussion at the NATO Economics Colloquium has shown, the practical results of this transformation are too ambiguous. On one hand, there are positive indicators, on the other, there are signs of widespread disappointment and discontent.

Individual countries' results and errors concerning the transition are divergent. There is a group of countries that - according to some experts - have already stabilised their economies and are moving toward sustainable growth. Or they are hoping to stabilise their economy and soon begin sustainable growth. During the Colloquium, positive 1995 results for the Czech Republic, Poland, Estonia, Slovenia and Albania were strongly emphasised because of their outstanding statistical indicators for this year. This group could be completed or even amended by adding those countries that have completed the process of installing a parliamentary democracy, and a legal framework for a market economy. In this regard, the remaining countries of the Visegrad agreement and those countries of the Baltic which were not mentioned in the previous group should be considered.

Economic Growth
(Annual change of GDP, percent)

	1990	1991	1992	1993	1994	1995
Albania	-10.0	-27.1	-9.7	11.0	8.0	-
Bulgaria	-9.1	-11.7	-5.6	-4.2	-5.1	0.0
Czech Republic	-0.4	-14.2	-7.1	-0.3	3.5	4.0
Poland	-11.6	-7.6	1.5	3.8	4.5	4.5
Hungary	-3.5	-11.9	-4.3	-2.3	2.0	1.0
Slovakia	0.4	-14.5	-7.0	-4.1	4.0	2.0
Romania	-5.0	-12.9	-13.6	1.0	0.0	0.0
Belarus	-3.0	-1.2	-9.6	-11.6	-30.0	-
Estonia	-8.1	-11.0	-25.8	-7.8	5.0	5.0
Kazakhstan	-0.4	-12.0	-13.0	-13.0	-11.0	-
Kirgizia	3.2	-5.0	-25.0	-16.0	-10.0	-
Lithuania	-5.0	-13.1	-37.7	-16.2	4.0	-
Latvia	2.9	-8.3	-33.8	-11.7	5.0	5.0
Russia	-	-9.0	19.0	-12.0	-15.0	-7.0
Ukraine	-3.4	-12.0	-17.0	14.0	-20.0	-5.0
Slovenia	-4.7	-8.1	-5.4	1.3	4.5	5.0

At the other extreme, there are countries in which civil war has broken out and continues today. In some countries, governments are not able to stop triple-digit inflation and neutralise the consequences of widespread economic uncertainty. It is worth mentioning that such extreme experiences were not addressed during the Colloquium.

It is my impression that after five years of transformation we are still not able to see the final outcome. Are the changes in some countries real indications that the end of the transformation tunnel is in sight? Moreover, can we really be certain - as was mentioned on many occasions by participants in this meeting

- that the partial success of some countries fully justifies the conservative and drastic policies recommended by the international financial institutions (IMF, World Bank, etc.).

I base my doubts in this regard on two factors:

• Firstly, the story of many Latin American countries has shown that long-lasting periods of economic slump and stagnation can be interrupted by shorter growth periods. I wonder whether the growth of some Central and East European countries in 1994-95 is not a similar process.

• Secondly, it certainly is not clear to me whether the temporary success of some countries are merely the consequence of postponed market-oriented changes, the delay of central wage control, subsidisation of enterprises, delay of the introduction of bankruptcy laws, delayed restructuring of large firms or the consequence of the well-set conditions for market prosperity.

I hope that time will refute my doubts, and that my early statements will instead become a reality.

Nevertheless it is clear to me that conflicts will continue to take place in this region, even as political freedom and consumer sovereignty develop, and even if the freedom of job selection and business activity have been achieved. The question remains: after decades of job security, comparatively equal living standards and a relatively well-functioning welfare system - under what conditions do the citizens of the region consider that these achievements are full compensation for the high level of unemployment, a decrease in living standards and increased income differences?

My general conclusion is that citizens of the region will continue to pay a high price for the transition. We must realise that the current and future situation is leading to one that will continue to have long-lasting and painful consequences. On the one hand, positive consequences require changes in the production structure; but on the other, transformation measures also have ambiguous results.

Profit produced under conditions of market insulation no longer appears, with the result that the state budget is much less able to finance the health care system, schools and universities than it was under the "real socialist" system. The second negative consequence is that the collateral on which banking credits were based in the previous period have shrunk substantially. Because of this, the reorganised banking system remains in a deep crisis.

Under these conditions, several open questions remain: how can the region or any individual country overcome this transitional crisis? Are the citizens of the region ready to consciously accept a low consumption level and strongly-reduced social expenditures for a long period of time? What is required to overcome this crisis of transformation?

The Colloquium has shown that the long-lasting and unsatisfactory performance levels of the economies in transition have brought with them not only dangerous ethnic conflicts in some regions, but other worrying phenomena such as increasing ecological risks and a rising death rate and health situation - which are a danger to the entire world.

What do we Know About the Therapy?

It is clear to everyone, including the citizens of the region, that the final end to this crisis of transition will only come with sustainable growth. The citizens of the region are also keenly aware that only sustainable growth will decrease and finally close the gap between the developed world and the "former socialist" countries. This is everyone's basic hope.

What Details do we Know about the Therapy for a Transformation Crisis?

Based on the economic success of West Germany, Japan and some Far Eastern countries, we are aware that the transition should be primarily achieved through the individual efforts of each country involved. Economic assistance and debt reform reduction from Western companies might only be of secondary importance in the development of a country's economy. Additionally, these countries may even ask a price for the assistance - in the form of health and economic development, to minimise the risk of this development.

Moreover, it is also clear that a country which displays the following characteristics can produce such an economic miracle:

1. One where domestic consumption is lower then the revenue produced. In other words, a high savings rate is needed.

2. One where the domestic currency is undervalued. In other words, where strong export and import substitution drives are built in.

3. One where state budget expenditures are in harmony with the performance level of the country and where the tax system is transparent and stable.

4. One where the Central Bank is independent and therefore able to keep the value of domestic currency under control.

5. One where private interests dominate the economy, and where strong practical programme "agent" relationships are set.

But these five leading requirements are not enough to design a practical programme. Quite a few questions still remain open, such as:

• What are the right requirements for monetary policy, and how can restriction measures be combined with the right credit launching to produce profitable firms?

• What is the right way to manage inherited debt?

• How can fiscal expenditure be cut and a transparent and stable economy be created that is acceptable to the citizens and business agents?

• How can state-owned assets be privatised while constraining corruption, and setting good conditions for profitable structural change?

It is clear that there are no ready-made solutions to these questions and that there is no standard recipe available from any of the world's international institutions. Nor is there a conservative, liberal or social democratic solution that can be offered.

Country-specific programmes should be a trial and error procedure in which the politicians should consider two important constraining factors:

Firstly, there is no possible way for any country to keep its creditworthiness unless it has strong, secure and reliable connections with the world capital markets.

And finally, no country will be able to secure economic growth and success without strong cooperation from its citizens to fulfil the programme.

SUMMARY OF DISCUSSIONS*

Panel I - Balance Sheet of Economic Reforms in Cooperation Partner Countries

The debate expanded on some of the presentations, but it also brought up some new ideas and fields of discussion not mentioned by the experts. Difficult as it is to discuss such a vast and complex question in hardly one hour, many points remained unanswered. Still, the participants laid the ground for further detailed discussion of more specific problems during the following four panels.

Agriculture

One participant highlighted the interesting contrasts in the sector of agriculture - a sector that was rather left aside by the speakers - from one transition country to the other. Some states, such as Poland, had a considerable share of privately owned farms already before the collapse of communism, in others there was only state production. The importance of agriculture also varies as to size and overall share of the economies. Another participant asked the audience to bear in mind, that privatisation is no 'cure-all medicine'. Some countries, such as Hungary, he argued further, had experienced an overdeveloped agriculture, and cutbacks might cause serious problems. It would also depend on what form of private property replaces the former publicly-owned collectives.

Concerning the role of the European Union (EU) and the negative impacts of EU restrictions on agricultural imports on the performance in Central and Eastern Europe (CEE), a member of the panel pointed out that there is considerable pressure from inside the EU to abolish these restrictions. Especially the tax payer, faced with ever-rising costs for subsidised and protected goods, would oppose limitations on agricultural imports from CEE. On the other hand, production and export expansion would only in the short term appear to be appropriate solutions. In the long term, bearing in mind the situation on the current food market, the economic crisis will not be solved through increasing output, but through strategic decisions, which have to be taken, either by the government or by the market.

* Prepared by Ulrich Gerza during his internship with the NATO Economics Directorate.

Ukraine

In the context of the presentation on the state of economic reform in Ukraine, the question of this country's relations with Russia was raised, also taking into consideration Belarus' recent efforts to tie its economy more closely into the Russian system. It was argued that the development of foreign trade - Ukraine in 1994 had a negative balance of payments of about $1 billion, in 1995 estimates amount to $5.5 billion - and the solution of the energy dependence on Russian supply will play the decisive role, as to whether Ukraine will have to integrate into the CIS or not.

The difficulties are increased by Ukraine's enormous energy production costs, which are twice those of Russia. Despite abolishment of all export limitations this factor would hinder Ukraine's products from being competitive in terms of price and quality on the world market. The participant added that unless the International Finance Institutions (IFIs), the EU, as well as bilateral agreements provide Ukraine with substantial help, they will not succeed in balancing their trade balance and might, as a consequence, be forced to accept further economic integration into the CIS. In this view 1995 will be the decisive year for Ukraine's reform process.

Social Instability and Regional Policy

Concerning potential social instabilities in Ukraine, due to tough stabilisation policies, the general attitude was rather positive, as unemployment is not too high, despite potentially high hidden unemployment. Still, it was emphasised, that increased pressure for change in resources-poor regions and ethnic areas, which, especially in the CIS, enjoy more independence from the centre, might cause turnarounds towards authoritarian regimes. This would not only be the case for republics in the Russian Federation but also for former USSR republics, such as Belarus, which might look to Moscow for a more authoritarian policy.

Differentiation was made between rural and urban populations. On the one hand, the situation in heavily populated city areas is often worse than in less populated, resources-rich regions, assuming a higher potential for social upheaval. On the other hand, education is much better in city areas than in the country side, explaining why most democratic driving forces can be found in urban areas, whereas communism is still quite popular in rural areas.

It was also argued that, contrary to what was said in the presentation, factor endowment will play a decisive role for regions in their relations to the central government. As they do not have direct access to Central Bank money and capital markets, this is the only way to the important valuta. Limited means of power also lie in the possibility to refuse payment of taxes.

Currency Reform

The discussion further focused on a declaration by Ukraine's President Kuchma, that the upcoming currency reform would not have confiscatory character. It was argued that this question has not yet been solved and that the situation is expected to be extremely difficult this autumn. The low income group (monthly income of $30-40) would even support confiscatory reform, as they do not have any important deposits. Economists would still be in favour of a simple denomination of the currency as confiscation would not affect those it is attended to.

Stabilisation of the new currency would require funding of approximately $1.5 billion. Agreements on this sum have been reached with IFIs, which also agree on the most urgent tasks of containing and neutralising inflation, which is likely to rise in the summer due to seasonal factors, as well as diminishing the budget deficit.

Privatisation

The question was raised whether privatisation programmes were merely politically motivated or whether they could indeed be considered an economic act. Some participants underlined the different situations, and therefore different motivation, of the various transition countries. In some cases, such as Slovakia and the Czech Republic, privatisation can be seen as a political act, in others social dimensions would dominate the reasoning. The multiplication of objectives could cause the loss of the principal objective of privatisation, that is improving efficiency and productivity.

The lack of a competent and capable banking system acting as intermediary between investors, companies and governments was also mentioned.

Comparison to Other Transition Economies

A comparison was drawn by one speaker with the Chinese example, where transition to market economy was achieved with more creation, less destruction, less social tensions and less unemployment. The difference though, pointed out by another participant, was that the Chinese authorities managed to keep political control over the reform process, whereas the societies in CEE just exploded and gradual progress was made impossible. It was also questioned whether purely economic criteria would be sufficient to judge efficiency of the reform progress, let alone cultural differences and expatriate investment by the large Chinese world community.

Panel II - Living Standards and Social Welfare

The discussion mainly focused on the interdependencies of monetary and economic policies, therefore of financial and economic indicators, and social welfare and living standards. Many arguments were about the different interpretation of certain indicators, such as money supply, consumption, unemployment or inflation. The debate was generally very difficult and based on assumptions because of the uncertainty of almost all numbers and statistics.

Being now in a position to gain from experience of the first years of reform, it was made clear that the collapse of the administrative command economy had to result in declining output (~20-50 percent) and increasing inflation (~1000 percent) in most transition countries. The question is how quickly those countries will succeed in recovering. It was argued that the collapse and its consequences would have happened anyway, even when keeping the old system.

Commenting on a rating proposed by one of the panelists, other speakers pointed out the differences in political systems and attitudes, in tradition and cultures and in the starting situation as well as the time lag since the beginning of reform activities of the five 'top group' countries. Albania, for example, only just started reform, whereas Poland started in 1991.

Central Bank Monetary Policies

Some participants agreed upon the responsibility of central bankers for socially bearable policies. Tight policies could lead to enormous decline of the economy. Most central banks, though, are more interested in controlling real inflation than looking at figures of money supply growth. IMF policies are very tough in that respect and therefore some problems are also political issues.

People's Expectations

Doubts were expressed whether the population of transition countries will believe that, by applying the right policies and accepting the consequent decline in social welfare, living standards and the overall economic situation, the situation will improve within a certain time frame. This argument was countered by reference to the actual experience of some countries applying those strict policies. Those that have not followed orthodox policies yet, can therefore expect to experience the same.

GDP Growth

Participants highlighted the importance of investment for substantial growth, especially where sustained over a number of years. Despite a lack of this investment, some countries on the fringe of the EU (Czech Republic, Slovakia, Slovenia...) might experience what other less wealthy European states, such as Spain, Portugal or Greece have experienced. They benefited from the increasing demand from other EU countries resulting in rising exports and capital flows towards low cost countries.

Disagreement also became obvious when sustainability of high growth rates, such as the proposed 5 percent annual growth, was discussed. Whereas this was considered too high by some, others emphasised that this was indispensable for potential accession to the EU.

Consumption and Demand

Consumption was seen as an important indicator for social welfare and living standards. Where, as in Russia, no real welfare programmes exist, the problem of poverty and poor consumption, especially in the food sector, is all the bigger. Poor demand is closely connected to this problem, therefore the key question to the solution of the agriculture crisis will be how to push the demand side.

Savings

A considerable rise in Russian savings was noted, up from 5-8 percent in 1980 to about 30 percent in 1994, maybe thus showing first signs of improving real income. For other participants this only proved the high inequality in income and illustrated the problem of capital flight, as much of the savings are in hard currency.

Unemployment

Agreement was expressed on the issue of unemployment, where expectations a couple of years ago largely surpassed real figures. Social crisis and unrest have been avoided, so far. In countries, though, where reform is lagging, such as Belarus, one can also note a complete absence of strategy on social welfare and unemployment. This might in the medium and long term lead to social problems and confrontation.

It also became obvious that any interpretation of unemployment figures is highly speculative, as nobody really has correct and reliable data.

Shadow Economy

As mentioned before, agreement was also reached on the unreliability of statistics. When talking about living standards, one has to include grey economy activities, sometimes amounting to one third of economic activity. In the case of Poland, consumption is growing disproportionally faster than income, suggesting that living standards might be significantly higher than shown in official statistics. Other paradoxes, carrying on the example of Poland, include foreign trade statistics, not accounting for about $3-4 billion unregistered border trade. This, argued one speaker, was partly due to under-reporting of private companies or individuals for tax reasons.

Panel III - Privatisation and Industrial Restructuring

During this discussion the main focus was on the identification of the major problems facing Cooperation Partner countries during their privatisation and restructuring process. The numerous points raised by the participants highlighted the complexity and diversity of problems occurring during this important step of economic reform. All problems seem to be, in one way or the other, linked to each other, which made it even harder to concentrate on the most important issues.

Inherited Burdens

Many speakers mentioned this problem. In some extremely severe cases, such as Albania, inherited obsolete structures and technologies date back to the Stalin period. Whereas technology progressed in other CEE countries from 1960 to 1990, no development could be noticed in Albania. Inherited foreign debts also constitute a huge burden for privatised companies. In some countries, the governments and commercial banks just do not have the means to provide necessary financial means needed for efficient restructuring. Institutional changes also prove to be problematic, as inherited structures, strengthened through almost 50 years of communism, are not easy to dismantle.

Speakers made clear that the current process is unprecedented, and therefore no unified rules exist on the modalities of privatisation. Different situations in the various countries make it even difficult to draw comparisons between one state and the other. Successful policies implemented by one government might be inadequate for others.

It was also pointed out that authorities have major difficulties finding a just and efficient way to deal with restitution of property, with claims that sometimes date back to before the Second World War.

Investment

All participants agreed that lack of investment, foreign and national, and financial resources was one of, if not the major obstacles to successful privatisation. In some cases, such as Albania, this was due to overall instability and the fear of a spill-over of the conflict in the neighbouring region.

In many countries the stock exchange markets, as well as transaction facilities and capital markets, are still in a poor state. Though slowly developing this still makes it very difficult and uncertain for foreign investors to invest in portfolios in the emerging markets.

Despite this sceptical overall impression, successful examples of privatised companies were given, where comparatively fewer debts and innovative products attracted considerable investment. Positive results were also seen in joint ventures with foreign corporations.

In Russia strategic investor activity did not change much or even deteriorated with the beginning of the second phase of privatisation. The recent proposal of some Russian commercial banks to give loans to the government in exchange for public company shares, in case the government cannot pay back these loans, was viewed as unlikely to have any positive impact, as most banks involved are owned by industrial companies, which invest their operational profits through the banks instead of paying the salaries of their employees.

Crime, Fraud and Corruption

Due to the lack of a centralised registration agency for property in the CIS and other CEE states, crime, fraud and corruption often interfere or even dominate in the privatisation process. Consensus between the major interest groups, that is the federal and local authorities, labour, foreign investors and organised crime was therefore believed to be indispensable. Only strict regulation would enable state authorities to effectively deal with this problem.

Quality of Management

The quality of management was widely thought to be more important than any other factor for successful privatisation. This argument was underlined by the results of a study of Russian middle and large size privatised firms from different regions. Despite negative examples, foreign advisors and investors were reported to often be surprised by the abilities and skills of the new managers. The problem was rather lack of interest in change than the incapacity to adapt to the changes.

Privatisation being often not much more than a symbolic act without real changes in leadership, the more decisive process of restructuring - in terms of efficiency, competitiveness and profitability - totally depends on the ability of the new management. As we can also observe in the West success greatly depends on the skill of the managers. In Russia, for example only 10 percent of the managers were replaced in the first phase of privatisation.

Underestimation of Company Values

Underevaluation of many former state companies is due to different reasons. Without elaborating on that question, participants cited not only the inherited lack of accounting measures, but also the sharp Rouble depreciation in relation to the dollar. In the example of Russia, this and other reasons led to a total value of all Russian enterprises of $50 billion. In comparison to the New Stock Exchange with a total market value of company shares of $3 trillion, this appears rather small and underestimated.

Budgetary Interests

The question was raised whether privatisation was just abused as a tool to equalise budget deficits. Speakers, though, denied these allegations for most of the states, saying that, as in the case of Slovakia, most direct sales were financed through loans. It is correct that some privatisation money is used to finance subsidies, but only in very few cases for the budget deficit.

Panel IV - External Economic Relations and Integration into the World Economy

The debate very much turned around the question of which measures and policies might permit transition countries to service and reduce foreign debts, to attract foreign and national investment and to balance the current account deficits. The very fruitful and constructive discussion developed some interesting recommendations for CEE policy makers, although some disagreement about which approach might be the most promising was registered. The participants also discussed potential security risks in external trade relations, such as possible trade wars, interest conflicts, etc, and how best to minimise those risks.

External Debt

A solution for the heavy external debt burden was seen as one of the most urgent problems by many speakers. Different situations in the size and nature of debt in the various countries were pointed out. Therefore, no common, unified solution seemed appropriate. Russia, for example, faces other problems than Hungary, which never decided to reschedule any of its $20 billion inherited debts, despite recommendations by IFIs to do so.

Hungary was rewarded, though, by considerable capital inflows, which otherwise might have ceased. Through servicing their debts, countries sustain their credit worthiness. If, on the other hand, the inherited debt burden is unbearable for the national economy, as is the case for Russia, the authorities have to seek a solution with their creditors, mostly through the two Paris- and London-based clubs, representing respectively governments and commercial banks. A proposal has been worked out and most speakers were optimistic about its outcome. As was the case in Poland last year this could also have positive effects on Russia's credit worthiness. Export potentials in Russia are very promising. Therefore it might be possible in the future to repay the debts.

Other participants underlined the importance of the efficient use of credits, considering the appropriate utilisation of foreign loans more important than the question of servicing these debts.

Exchange Rates

As mentioned before in the case of foreign debts, exchange rate problems also vary from country to country. Estonia, for example, decided to choose the so-called currency board system, which was judged as appropriate by one panelist. The Hungarian system consists of a crawling peg, where the national currency is automatically devalued daily by 0.06 percent against a basket of the ECU and the American dollar. Still, as was emphasised by the speakers, neither system is necessarily applicable to other countries.

In general all transition economies have problems with revaluation of their currencies, thus negatively influencing their exports. They should, therefore, aim for mechanisms of deliberate devaluation, as in the example of Hungary.

Investment

Most speakers mentioned the lack of investment, foreign and national, as a major shortcoming of the economic reform process. The example of Russia shows that most joint ventures have not received sufficient financial transfers from the West. Instead, one participant argued, Western companies only transfer technological equipment, marketing experience and management capacity, which they then count as capital transfers. On the other hand, less than 15 percent of investments in Russia actually work and only 5 percent have proven to be profitable. Another participant underlined that, in most cases, experience has shown that transfer of technology and intellectual capacity are indispensable for the success of a project.

Credit ratings by powerful neutral agencies often determine not only the amount of foreign investment a country receives, but also the access possibilities to financial and capital markets. In fact, the influence of the five biggest credit ranking agencies on foreign investor behaviour, nowadays, is probably much higher than that of IMF and World Bank together. A few speakers complained about the lack of transparency in these ratings, which do not show clearly whether short-term indicators, such as inflation or budget deficit, are decisive or long-term factors, such as the progress of restructuring. A comparison was also drawn to criteria for accession to the EU laid out during the Copenhagen summit last year.

Comparative Advantages

It was said that Western industries would probably have enough capacity to produce most industrial goods needed in CEE countries. Lower labour and production costs, however, constitute a non-negligible advantage for CEE industries, thus allowing optimistic expectations for the export sector of these economies. Low productivity and export restrictions, though, limit the foreign trade activity. CEE entrepreneurs are often not well enough informed about their opportunities and clearly lack experience in trade with Western economies.

The division of labour might also play a decisive role on the way to accession to the EU. In this respect, some countries are already more advanced than others. Poland, for example, for a long time had strong external economic relations with non-CEE countries. Others will in the future have to compete with South-East Asian countries for lower production costs.

Legal, Fiscal and Institutional Reform

Another major obstacle to effective foreign trade, that came up during the discussion, was the lack of a sufficient legal, fiscal and institutional framework. As long as this framework is not provided for by transition countries, investment and capital flows will be very restricted. Especially urgent is the establishment of a functioning capital market, capable of attracting portfolio investment.

Access to financial markets becomes crucial when current account deficits need to be balanced. Apart from the Czech Republic and Bulgaria all CEE states show a deficit in their current accounts, whereas only the Czech Republic and Poland have credit rankings that would enable them to finance those deficits on foreign capital markets.

Special Lecture - Ecological Challenges to Economic Reforms in CIS Countries

The short discussion after the excellent but shocking presentation by Dr. Feshbach on the state of ecology in the former Soviet Union only reinforced the overall impression of a potential future disaster, which would affect not only the CIS states but also the whole of Europe.

Some participants wondered whether the West has been doing anything at all in order to slow down this destructive process. Some timid answers, referring to single and still inefficient projects on the behalf of the EU or other international organisations only confirmed the general opinion that not much has been done. Only when public attention is drawn towards a specific situation, as in the case of the recent Komi accident, Western governments tend to react. More than 600 Komi-like accidents occur in Russia every year that nobody ever hears about. If the West really wanted to improve the situation, one speaker argued, it should strengthen the few NGOs that exist in the CIS and put diplomatic pressure, combined with financial incentives, on the Russian government to tackle this very urgent problem.

Wondering about the statistical reliability of the presented data, participants were told that reality is probably even worse, as some statistical methods still try to conceal the real situation.

The attitude of Russian society and politicians was also discussed. Unfortunately, it had to be noted that widespread frustration and lack of motivation, especially among hospital personnel, shows that there are very few driving forces within the Russian population that might force a change. Unless the Russian population recognises the fatal situation, considerable changes are unlikely.

Closing Remarks

OBSERVATIONS FINALES DU PRESIDENT
Daniel George
Directeur des Affaires économiques de l'OTAN

Pour conclure le Président a souligné les points marquants du Colloque 1995.

La question de départ - le pire est-il déjà derrière nous? le processus de réforme a-t-il dépassé la phase de dégradation, ouvrant la route vers la croissance? - reste, à son avis, ouverte. C'est aussi et surtout un problème de perception. L'évaluation est rendue plus difficile par le manque de statistiques valables, problème souvent mentionné par les participants. L'économie grise pourrait éventuellement améliorer de manière significative la situation d'un pays. Dans l'ensemble, une tonalité optimiste a été perceptible.

Le point d'irréversibilité des réformes, si l'on en croit la majorité des participants, est dépassé, dans la mesure où la société civile émergente est déjà trop forte, trop établie, pour que des forces subversives puissent renverser le processus de démocratisation et d'ouverture.

La forte dégradation du niveau de vie et de sécurité doit être vue dans le contexte général de l'effondrement d'un système économique et exige une réponse efficace de la part des gouvernements des Etats en transition. Le coût de la réforme, en matière sociale, financière et politique, pèse souvent lourdement sur les populations.

Malgré certains doutes sur ses modalités, la privatisation a généralement bien évolué. En revanche la deuxième phase, la restructuration, commence seulement bien qu'elle soit indispensable pour une intégration future dans les structures économiques européennes. Elle est également nécessaire pour attirer les investissements étrangers et convaincre les marchés financiers internationaux. Dans ce contexte on ne peut que souligner l'importance d'une approche raisonnable du problème de la dette extérieure, hérité en grande partie du communisme. L'ouverture des marchés au commerce international constitue un autre objectif fondamental, même si dans certains cas un protectionnisme limité et temporaire peut être légitime afin de permettre la restructuration et l'adaptation au niveau de l'économie mondiale dans une période transitoire.

A l'issue du Colloque le Président tire des conclusions plutôt positives ou au moins optimistes sur l'avenir des réformes, malgré des tâches nombreuses